MORE

HTML

FOR

DUMMIES®

2ND EDITION

MORE HTML FOR DUMMIES®
2ND EDITION

by Ed Tittel and Stephen Nelson James

IDG Books Worldwide, Inc.
An International Data Group Company

Foster City, CA ◆ Chicago, IL ◆ Indianapolis, IN ◆ Southlake, TX

MORE HTML For Dummies,® **2nd Edition**

Published by
IDG Books Worldwide, Inc.
An International Data Group Company
919 E. Hillsdale Blvd.
Suite 400
Foster City, CA 94404
http://www.idgbooks.com (IDG Books Worldwide Web site)
http://www.dummies.com (Dummies Press Web site)

Library of Congress Catalog Card No.: 97-72408

ISBN: 0-7645-0233-6

Printed in the United States of America

10 9 8 7 6 5 4 3 2 1

2E/SW/QW/ZX/IN

Distributed in the United States by IDG Books Worldwide, Inc.

Distributed by Macmillan Canada for Canada; by Transworld Publishers Limited in the United Kingdom; by IDG Norge Books for Norway; by IDG Sweden Books for Sweden; by Woodslane Pty. Ltd. for Australia; by Woodslane Enterprises Ltd. for New Zealand; by Longman Singapore Publishers Ltd. for Singapore, Malaysia, Thailand, and Indonesia; by Simron Pty. Ltd. for South Africa; by Toppan Company Ltd. for Japan; by Distribuidora Cuspide for Argentina; by Livraria Cultura for Brazil; by Ediciencia S.A. for Ecuador; by Addison-Wesley Publishing Company for Korea; by Ediciones ZETA S.C.R. Ltda. for Peru; by WS Computer Publishing Corporation, Inc., for the Philippines; by Unalis Corporation for Taiwan; by Contemporanea de Ediciones for Venezuela; by Computer Book & Magazine Store for Puerto Rico; by Express Computer Distributors for the Caribbean and West Indies. Authorized Sales Agent: Anthony Rudkin Associates for the Middle East and North Africa.

For general information on IDG Books Worldwide's books in the U.S., please call our Consumer Customer Service department at 800-762-2974. For reseller information, including discounts and premium sales, please call our Reseller Customer Service department at 800-434-3422.

For information on where to purchase IDG Books Worldwide's books outside the U.S., please contact our International Sales department at 415-655-3200 or fax 415-655-3295.

For information on foreign language translations, please contact our Foreign & Subsidiary Rights department at 415-655-3021 or fax 415-655-3281.

For sales inquiries and special prices for bulk quantities, please contact our Sales department at 415-655-3200 or write to the address above.

For information on using IDG Books Worldwide's books in the classroom or for ordering examination copies, please contact our Educational Sales department at 800-434-2086 or fax 817-251-8174.

For press review copies, author interviews, or other publicity information, please contact our Public Relations department at 415-655-3000 or fax 415-655-3299.

For authorization to photocopy items for corporate, personal, or educational use, please contact Copyright Clearance Center, 222 Rosewood Drive, Danvers, MA 01923, or fax 508-750-4470.

About the Authors

Ed Tittel is the co-author of numerous books about computing and the World Wide Web, including *The Foundations of World Wide Web Programming, with HTML and CGI,* and *The Hip Pocket Guide to HTML* (the first book's authors include Mark Gaither, Mike Erwin, and Sebastian Hassinger; the second book's co-author is James Michael Stewart, who also contributed substantially to this book, even though his name does not appear on the cover). These days, Ed is aiming his efforts at Internet programming-related topics, both as a writer and as a member of the NetWorld + Interop program committee.

Ed has been a regular contributor to the trade press since 1987 and has written over 200 articles for a variety of publications, including *Computerworld, Infoworld, Maximize, Iway,* and *NetGuide.* He's a regular contributor to *Windows NT* magazine and works for several online 'zines, including *Interop Online.*

These days, Ed enjoys working at home, where his real job is keeping Dusty, his large and rambunctious yellow labrador retriever, company. When he's not pounding the keyboard, he's either out walking Dusty, playing pool, or cooking up something in his kitchen for friends and family.

Contact Ed at etittel@zilker.net or visit his Web site at http://www.lanw.com.

Stephen Nelson James is the co-author (with Ed Tittel) of the best-selling *HTML For Dummies* and also of *ISDN Clearly Explained* and *PC Telephony for Home and Small Office.* He has also authored numerous computer-related magazine articles, software user's manuals, and WWW pages. Steve is a former environmental biologist and ex-president/CEO of FYI, Inc., a software development company. When he's not writing or surfing the Net, you can find him out on the roads in the hills around Austin doing what he really loves to do best: riding his bicycle!

Contact Steve at snjames@wetlands.com.

ABOUT IDG BOOKS WORLDWIDE

Welcome to the world of IDG Books Worldwide.

IDG Books Worldwide, Inc., is a subsidiary of International Data Group, the world's largest publisher of computer-related information and the leading global provider of information services on information technology. IDG was founded more than 25 years ago and now employs more than 8,500 people worldwide. IDG publishes more than 275 computer publications in over 75 countries (see listing below). More than 60 million people read one or more IDG publications each month.

Launched in 1990, IDG Books Worldwide is today the #1 publisher of best-selling computer books in the United States. We are proud to have received eight awards from the Computer Press Association in recognition of editorial excellence and three from *Computer Currents'* First Annual Readers' Choice Awards. Our best-selling *...For Dummies®* series has more than 30 million copies in print with translations in 30 languages. IDG Books Worldwide, through a joint venture with IDG's Hi-Tech Beijing, became the first U.S. publisher to publish a computer book in the People's Republic of China. In record time, IDG Books Worldwide has become the first choice for millions of readers around the world who want to learn how to better manage their businesses.

Our mission is simple: Every one of our books is designed to bring extra value and skill-building instructions to the reader. Our books are written by experts who understand and care about our readers. The knowledge base of our editorial staff comes from years of experience in publishing, education, and journalism — experience we use to produce books for the '90s. In short, we care about books, so we attract the best people. We devote special attention to details such as audience, interior design, use of icons, and illustrations. And because we use an efficient process of authoring, editing, and desktop publishing our books electronically, we can spend more time ensuring superior content and spend less time on the technicalities of making books.

You can count on our commitment to deliver high-quality books at competitive prices on topics you want to read about. At IDG Books Worldwide, we continue in the IDG tradition of delivering quality for more than 25 years. You'll find no better book on a subject than one from IDG Books Worldwide.

John Kilcullen
CEO
IDG Books Worldwide, Inc.

Steven Berkowitz
President and Publisher
IDG Books Worldwide, Inc.

Eighth Annual Computer Press Awards 1992

Ninth Annual Computer Press Awards 1993

Tenth Annual Computer Press Awards 1994

Eleventh Annual Computer Press Awards 1995

IDG Books Worldwide, Inc., is a subsidiary of International Data Group, the world's largest publisher of computer-related information and the leading global provider of information services on information technology. International Data Group publishes over 275 computer publications in over 75 countries. Sixty million people read one or more International Data Group publications each month. International Data Group's publications include: **ARGENTINA:** Buyer's Guide, Computerworld Argentina, PC World Argentina; **AUSTRALIA:** Australian Macworld, Australian PC World, Australian Reseller News, Computerworld, IT Casebook, Network World, Publish, Webmaster; **AUSTRIA:** Computerwelt Osterreich, Networks Austria, PC Tip Austria; **BANGLADESH:** PC World Bangladesh; **BELARUS:** PC World Belarus; **BELGIUM:** Data News; **BRAZIL:** Annuario de Informática, Computerworld, Connections, Macworld, PC Player, PC World, Publish, Reseller News, Supergamepower; **BULGARIA:** Computerworld Bulgaria, Network World Bulgaria, PC & MacWorld Bulgaria; **CANADA:** CIO Canada, Client/Server World, Computerworld Canada, InfoWorld Canada, NetworkWorld Canada, WebWorld; **CHILE:** Computerworld Chile, PC World Chile; **COLOMBIA:** Computerworld Colombia, PC World Colombia; **COSTA RICA:** PC World Centro America; **THE CZECH AND SLOVAK REPUBLICS:** Computerworld Czechoslovakia, Macworld Czech Republic, PC World Czechoslovakia; **DENMARK:** Communications World Danmark, Computerworld Danmark, Macworld Danmark, PC World Danmark, Techworld Denmark; **DOMINICAN REPUBLIC:** PC World Republica Dominicana; **ECUADOR:** PC World Ecuador; **EGYPT:** Computerworld Middle East, PC World Middle East; **EL SALVADOR:** PC World Centro America; **FINLAND:** MikroPC, Tietoverkko, Tietoviikko; **FRANCE:** Distributique, Hebdo, Info PC, Le Monde Informatique, Macworld, Reseaux & Telecoms, WebMaster France; **GERMANY:** Computer Partner, Computerwoche, Computerwoche Extra, Computerwoche FOCUS, Global Online, Macwelt, PC Welt; **GREECE:** Amiga Computing, GamePro Greece, Multimedia World; **GUATEMALA:** PC World Centro America; **HONDURAS:** PC World Centro America; **HONG KONG:** Computerworld Hong Kong, PC World Hong Kong, Publish in Asia; **HUNGARY:** ABCD CD-ROM, Computerworld Szamitastechnika, Internetto online Magazine, PC World Hungary, PC-X Magazin Hungary; **ICELAND:** Tolvuheimur PC World Island; **INDIA:** Information Communications World, Information Systems Computerworld, PC World India, Publish in Asia; **INDONESIA:** InfoKomputer PC World, Komputek Computerworld, Publish in Asia; **IRELAND:** ComputerScope, PC Live!; **ISRAEL:** Macworld Israel, People & Computers/Computerworld; **ITALY:** Computerworld Italia, Macworld Italia, Networking Italia, PC World Italia; **JAPAN:** DTP World, Macworld Japan, Nikkei Personal Computing, OS/2 World Japan, SunWorld Japan, Windows NT World, Windows World Japan; **KENYA:** PC World East African; **KOREA:** Hi-Tech Information, Macworld Korea, PC World Korea; **MACEDONIA:** PC World Macedonia; **MALAYSIA:** Computerworld Malaysia, PC World Malaysia, Publish in Asia; **MALTA:** PC World Malta; **MEXICO:** Computerworld Mexico, PC World Mexico; **MYANMAR:** PC World Myanmar; **NETHERLANDS:** Computer! Totaal, LAN Internetworking Magazine, LAN World Buyers Guide, Macworld Netherlands, Net, WebWereld; **NEW ZEALAND:** Absolute Beginners Guide and Plain & Simple Series, Computer Buyer, Computer Industry Directory, Computerworld New Zealand, MTB, Network World, PC World New Zealand; **NICARAGUA:** PC World Centro America; **NORWAY:** Computerworld Norge, CW Rapport, Datamagasinet, Financial Rapport, Kursguide Norge, Macworld Norge, Multimediaworld Norge, PC World Ekspress Norge, PC World Nettverk, PC World Norge, PC World ProduktGuide Norge; **PAKISTAN:** Computerworld Pakistan; **PANAMA:** PC World Panama; **PEOPLE'S REPUBLIC OF CHINA:** China Computer Users, China Computerworld, China InfoWorld, China Telecom World Weekly, Computer & Communication, Electronic Design China, Electronics Today, Electronics Weekly, Game Software, PC World China, Popular Computer Week, Software Weekly, Software World, Telecom World; **PERU:** Computerworld Peru, PC World Profesional Peru, PC World SoHo Peru; **PHILIPPINES:** Click!, Computerworld Philippines, PC World Philippines, Publish in Asia; **POLAND:** Computerworld Poland, Computerworld Special Report Poland, Cyber, Macworld Poland, Networld Poland, PC World Komputer; **PORTUGAL:** Cerebro/PC World, Computerworld/Correio Informático, Dealer World Portugal, Mac*In/PC*In Portugal, Multimedia World; **PUERTO RICO:** PC World Puerto Rico; **ROMANIA:** Computerworld Romania, PC World Romania, Telecom Romania; **RUSSIA:** Computerworld Russia, Mir PK, Publish, Seti; **SINGAPORE:** Computerworld Singapore, PC World Singapore, Publish in Asia; **SLOVENIA:** Monitor; **SOUTH AFRICA:** Computing SA, Network World SA, Software World SA; **SPAIN:** Communicaciones World España, Computerworld España, Dealer World España, Macworld España, PC World España; **SRI LANKA:** Infolink PC World; **SWEDEN:** CAP&Design, Computer Sweden, Corporate Computing Sweden, Internetworld Sweden, it.branschen, Macworld Sweden, MaxiData Sweden, MikroDatorn, Nätverk & Kommunikation, PC World Sweden, PCaktiv, Windows World Sweden; **SWITZERLAND:** Computerworld Schweiz, Macworld Schweiz, PCtip; **TAIWAN:** Computerworld Taiwan, Macworld Taiwan, NEW VISION/Publish, PC World Taiwan, Windows World Taiwan; **THAILAND:** Publish in Asia, Thai Computerworld; **TURKEY:** Computerworld Turkiye, Macworld Turkiye, Network World Turkiye, PC World Turkiye; **UKRAINE:** Computerworld Kiev, Multimedia World Ukraine, PC World Ukraine; **UNITED KINGDOM:** Acorn User UK, Amiga Action UK, Amiga Computing UK, Apple Talk UK, Computing, Macworld, Parents and Computers UK, PC Advisor, PC Home, PSX Pro, The WEB; **UNITED STATES:** Cable in the Classroom, CIO Magazine, Computerworld, DOS World, Federal Computer Week, GamePro Magazine, InfoWorld, I-Way, Macworld, Network World, PC Games, PC World, Publish, Video Event, THE WEB Magazine, and WebMaster; online webzines: JavaWorld, NetscapeWorld, and SunWorld Online; **URUGUAY:** InfoWorld Uruguay; **VENEZUELA:** Computerworld Venezuela, PC World Venezuela; and **VIETNAM:** PC World Vietnam. 3/24/97

Acknowledgments

Our biggest thanks go to our readers, who made the first edition such a great success. Their feedback should continue to improve this second edition as well! We have way too many folks to thank, so we'd like to begin by thanking everybody who helped us whom we don't mention by name. Actually, we couldn't have done it without you, even if we don't name you here! Thanks for your help, information, and encouragement.

Ed Tittel

I want to share my thanks with a large crew. First off, to my family — you were there for me when it counted. Thanks! Second, a talented crew of technical people helped me over a variety of humps, large and small. I would like to specifically mention Mark Gaither, Michael Stewart, Dawn Rader, and Natanya Pitts. You guys are the greatest! Third, there's a whole crowd of other folks whose information has helped me over the years, especially the originators of the Web — most notably, Tim Berners-Lee, Dan Connolly, and the rest of the W3C team. I'd also like to thank the geniuses, sung and unsung, at NCSA, Netscape, Microsoft, and at all the other Web sites we visited, for helping provide so much of the impetus for this book. I'd also like to thank Steve James for sticking with me from the first edition to the second!

Steven Nelson James

First and foremost, a heartfelt thank you to Ed Tittel for his inspiration and enthusiasm during the sometimes tedious revisions necessary to create this second edition of *MORE HTML For Dummies*. As always, my eternal gratitude to my family, Trisha, Kelly, and Chris for their understanding and support of my writing habit. And finally, a very sincere thank you to all of you who purchased *MORE HTML For Dummies*, first edition, and made this edition possible. Please continue to keep our e-mail filled with your great comments and suggestions.

Together, we want to thank the editorial staff at IDG books, especially Diane Smith, our copy editor; Heather Stith, one of the best project editors we've ever had the chance to work with; Mike Kelly, the guy who made it all happen; Diane Steele, who let us keep this "strange torpedo" moving; and the other editorial folks, including Dennis W. Cox, Joe Jansen, and Jen Davies.

Please feel free to contact either of us, care of IDG books, IDG Books World-wide, 919 E. Hillsdale Blvd, Suite 400, Foster City, CA 94404. Ed's e-mail address is etittel@zilker.net; Steve's is snjames@wetlands.com. The publisher would like to give special thanks to Patrick J. McGovern, without whom this book would not have been possible.

Publisher's Acknowledgments

We're proud of this book; please send us your comments about it by using the IDG Books Worldwide Registration Card at the back of the book or by e-mailing us at feedback/dummies@idgbooks.com. Some of the people who helped bring this book to market include the following:

Acquisitions, Development, and Editorial

Project Editor: Heather Stith

Acquisitions Editor: Michael Kelly

Associate Permissions Editor:
Heather H. Dismore

Copy Editors: Diane Smith, Joe Jansen, Jen Davies

Technical Editor: Dennis W. Cox

Editorial Manager: Mary C. Corder

Editorial Assistant: Chris H. Collins

Production

Project Coordinator: Valery Bourke

Layout and Graphics: Lou Boudreau, Linda M. Boyer, Dominique DeFelice, Pamela Emanoi, Maridee V. Ennis, Todd Klemme, Tom Missler, Mark C. Owens, Heather Pearson, Brent Savage, Michael A. Sullivan

Proofreaders: Arielle Carole Mennelle, Christine Saboni, Nancy Price, Robert Springer

Indexer: Liz Cunningham

General and Administrative

IDG Books Worldwide, Inc.: John Kilcullen, CEO; Steven Berkowitz, President and Publisher

IDG Books Technology Publishing: Brenda McLaughlin, Senior Vice President and Group Publisher

Dummies Technology Press and Dummies Editorial: Diane Graves Steele, Vice President and Associate Publisher; Judith A. Taylor, Product Marketing Manager; Kristin A. Cocks, Editorial Director

Dummies Trade Press: Kathleen A. Welton, Vice President and Publisher

IDG Books Production for Dummies Press: Beth Jenkins, Production Director; Cindy L. Phipps, Supervisor of Project Coordination, Production Proofreading, and Indexing; Kathie S. Schutte, Supervisor of Page Layout; Shelley Lea, Supervisor of Graphics and Design; Debbie J. Gates, Production Systems Specialist; Tony Augsburger, Supervisor of Reprints and Bluelines; Leslie Popplewell, Media Archive Coordinator

Dummies Packaging and Book Design: Patti Sandez, Packaging Specialist; Lance Kayser, Packaging Assistant; Kavish + Kavish, Cover Design

♦

The publisher would like to give special thanks to Patrick J. McGovern, without whom this book would not have been possible.

♦

Contents at a Glance

Table of Contents

Introduction

*W*elcome to the wild, wacky, and wonderful possibilities inherent in the World Wide Web. In this book, we'll continue our exploration of the mysteries of the HyperText Markup Language (HTML) used to build Web pages, explore some weird and wonderful Web extensions technologies, and continue your initiation into the wildly burgeoning community of Web authors.

This book expands on the basic coverage of HTML that you'll find in the *HTML For Dummies*, 3rd Edition, also from IDG Books Worldwide, Inc. In this book, we assume that you've explored the basics of HTML and are reasonably familiar with HTML 2.0, the current official standard version, and with HTML 3.2, the World Wide Web Consortium's (W3C's) current "recommended" standard for HTML. In this book, we extend your knowledge base beyond the basics to include some important emerging HTML standards and proprietary extensions, a plethora of Web-based applications, and some sound principles of Web site management. We also cover a number of cool Web extension technologies that you can use to add considerable spice to your current Web sites and documents.

When we wrote this book, we took a straightforward approach to telling you about authoring documents for the World Wide Web. We've tried to keep the amount of technobabble to a minimum and stuck with plain English as much as possible. Besides plain talk about hypertext, HTML, and the Web, we've included sample programs and tag-by-tag instructions for building your very own Web pages. If you see unfamiliar terms, check the Glossary at the back of this book; we've tried to define any and all terms that don't fall into everyday speech.

About This Book

Think of this book as a friendly, approachable guide to advanced HTML, Web site management, Web-based applications, and incorporating extension technologies into your Web. Although HTML isn't hard to learn, nor the associated technologies hard to use, it can be hard to remember all the details involved in creating interesting Web pages and in keeping track of your Web site.

Some sample topics you'll find in this book include the following:

✔ Using advanced HTML markup on your pages

✔ Employing cool Web extensions like Shockwave for Director, VRML, VBScript, Java, and more

✔ Working with Web-based applications to extend your site's capabilities

✔ Mastering the many aspects of Web publication and management

Although you might think that building Web pages requires years of training and advanced aesthetic capabilities, this just ain't so. If you can tell somebody how to drive from their house to yours, you can certainly build a Web document that does what you want it to. The purpose of this book isn't to turn you into a rocket scientist. This book will show you all the design and technical elements you need to build a good-looking, readable Web page. It should also give you the know-how and confidence to extend your Web beyond basic HTML, while explaining the tools necessary to manage and maintain the results!

How to Use This Book

This book starts with what's involved in designing and building effective Web documents that exploit a bumper crop of new and emerging advanced markup and Web extensions, if that's what you want to do. Then it tells how to manage and maintain your Web site easily and effectively.

All HTML code appears in monospaced type like this:

```
<HEAD><TITLE>What's in a Title?</TITLE></HEAD>...
```

When you type HTML tags or other related information, be sure to copy the information exactly as you see it between the angle brackets (< and >) because that's part of the magic that makes HTML work. Other than that, you'll learn how to marshal and manage the content that makes your pages special, and we'll tell you exactly what you need to do to mix the elements of HTML with your own work.

Due to the margins in this book, some long lines of HTML markup or designations for World Wide Web sites (called URLs, for Uniform Resource Locators) may wrap to the next line. On your computer though, these wrapped lines should appear as a single line of HTML or as a single URL, so don't insert a hard return when you see one of these wrapped lines. Each instance of wrapped code will have a code continuation arrow to indicate that the line continues, as shown in the following example:

```
http://www.infomagic.austin.com/nexus/plexus/lexus/sexus⟹
        /this_is_a_deliberately_long.html
```

HTML doesn't care if you type tag text in uppercase, lowercase, or both (except for character entities, which must be typed exactly as indicated in Chapter 6 of *HTML For Dummies,* 2nd Edition). For your own work to look like ours as much as possible, you should enter all HTML tag text in uppercase only.

A Few Assumptions

They say that making assumptions makes a fool out of the person who's making them and the person who's the subject of those assumptions. Nevertheless, we're going to make a few assumptions about you, our gentle reader:

- ✔ You can turn your computer on and off.
- ✔ You know how to use a mouse and a keyboard.
- ✔ You want to build your own Web pages for fun, profit, or because it's part of your job.
- ✔ You understand the basics of HTML markup in general and are reasonably familiar with HTML 2.0 and 3.2 markup in particular. (If this ain't so, don't fret — just rush right out and buy our companion volume *HTML For Dummies*, 3rd Edition, where you'll find everything you need to come up to speed.)

In addition, we assume you already have a working connection to the Internet and one of the many fine Web browsers available by hook, by crook, or by download from that selfsame Internet. You don't need to be a master logician or a wizard in the arcane arts of programming, nor do you need a Ph.D. in computer science. You don't even need a detailed sense of what's going on in the innards of your computer to deal with the material in this book.

If you understand the basic components of an HTML document and can tell a <BODY> from a <HEAD>, you will be able to build and deploy your own documents on the World Wide Web. If you have an imagination and the ability to communicate what's important to you, you've already mastered the key ingredients necessary to build useful, attractive Web pages. The rest is details, and we'll help you with those!

How This Book Is Organized

This book contains six major parts. Each part contains three or more chapters, and each chapter contains several modular sections. Any time you need help or information, just pick up the book and start anywhere you feel like it, or use the table of contents and index to look up specific topics or key words.

Here is a breakdown of the six parts and what you'll find in each one:

Part I: Advanced HTML Markup

HTML mixes ordinary text with special strings of characters, called markup, that instruct browsers how to display HTML documents. In this part of the book, you'll learn about some new and advanced HTML capabilities under development within the standards organizations and within browsers like Netscape's Navigator and Microsoft's Internet Explorer. We cover HTML tables, frames, style sheets, applets, objects, and more. By the time you've finished Part I, you should at least be able to appreciate what's going on behind some of the most interesting pages on the Web, if not build some of these pages for yourself!

Part II: Beyond HTML: Extending Your Web

Part II examines a number of new technologies available to extend your Web's capabilities well beyond those delivered by vanilla HTML. Starting with a discussion of what extensions are, how they work, and how best to use them, we cover Macromedia's fascinating Shockwave for Director technology, the Virtual Reality Modeling Language (VRML) that's used to create three-dimensional virtual worlds on the Web, Sun Microsystems' incredible Java programming language, and finally, a quick look at several of the many scripting languages available to add interactivity, forms support, and layout control over Web pages of all kinds.

Part III: Cool Web Applications

In Part III, we examine several of the many categories of Web-based applications that you can add to your Web site to give it special capabilities and to foster more involvement with your user community. First, we cover the ins and outs of using a search engine to help users find stuff on your site (and elsewhere on the Internet, if need be). Next, we cover a number of Web-based threaded message forum packages that let your users maintain and review running "conversations" across the Web.

Part IV: Serving Up Your Web

In this group of chapters, we talk about what's involved in bringing the world of users on the Web together with the contents of your newly published (or recently revised) Web site. Beginning with a discussion of how to test your site and perform some necessary quality control checks, we describe how to make sure your site is ready for prime time and how to get the word out that your pages are ready for perusal. Part IV concludes with a discussion of the all-important Web maintenance routine so necessary to keeping things fresh and interesting on your site, rather than allowing them to grow old and moldy.

Part V: Running a Successful Web Site

This part covers the ins and outs of understanding and managing a coherent collection of Web documents and materials that we call a Web site. We start off with a tour of a typical site and its components and discuss the virtues of planning and organization. In the chapters that follow, we cover the basics of administering a Web site, cover a plethora of tools to manage your site and its materials, and document what's involved in managing information via the Web (what we call "the Web publication process"). By the time you're finished with Part V, you should have a good appreciation of the routine elements in managing a Web site and a keen understanding of the tools and techniques you can use to maximize your labors in that area.

Part VI: Shortcuts and Tips Galore

In the concluding part of the book, we sum up and distill the very essence of what you've learned. Here, you'll have a chance to review the top do's and don'ts for Web site maintenance, to rethink your views on advanced HTML markup, and to review what you've learned about Web extension technologies herein. Our goal is to revisit the most important ideas covered throughout the book in order to give you a condensed and epitomized version to use as a reference at any time.

Icons Used in This Book

This icon signals technical details that are informative and interesting, but not critical to writing HTML. Skip these if you want (but please, come back and read them later).

This icon flags useful information that makes HTML markup, Web page design, or other important stuff even less complicated that you feared it may be.

This icon points out information you shouldn't pass by — don't overlook these gentle reminders (the life you save could be your own).

Be cautious when you see this icon. It warns you of things you shouldn't do; the bomb is meant to emphasize that the consequences of ignoring these bits of wisdom can be severe.

This spider web symbol flags the presence of Web-based resources that you can go out and investigate further.

This icon points to another area of the book that covers similar ground. If you're looking for more information on a particular subject, this icon can help lead the way.

Where to Go from Here

This is the part where you pick a direction and hit the road! *More HTML For Dummies* is a lot like the parable of the seven blind men and the elephant: it almost doesn't matter where you start out; you'll be looking at lots of different stuff as you prepare yourself to extend your Web pages and get a better grip on your Web site. Who cares if everybody else wonders what you're up to — we know you're following your bliss onto the Web.

Enjoy!

Part I
Advanced HTML

The 5th Wave   By Rich Tennant

KYLE AND TODDS SOFTWare Co.

"THAT'S RIGHT, DADDY WILL DOUBLE YOUR SALARY IF YOU MAKE HIM MORE APPLETS."

In this part . . .

This part covers a whole slew of standard HTML information, plus a number of interesting proprietary tags and extended attributes. In Chapter 1 we begin with a general description of how HTML markup is developed and standardized and the forces in the marketplace that keep things moving. In the following chapters, we cover families of tags for building tables (Chapter 2), constructing subwindows, called frames, within the browser display (Chapter 3), followed by coverage of recent advances in defining style sheets for HTML documents (Chapter 4). In Chapter 5 we discuss the various tags used to invoke applets, plugins, and other kinds of Web extensions and conclude with a detailed discussion of HTML forms tags and controls and how best to deploy them in your own Web pages.

Chapter 1

Understanding How HTML Happens

· ·

In This Chapter

▶ Making standards, officially speaking

▶ Tracking down and using the prevailing HTML Document Type Definitions

▶ HTML worth watching

▶ Examining applets, scripts, and forms

· ·

*H*ave you ever wondered who's responsible for deciding which HTML features become official and standard? Would you like to know who can be thanked (or blamed) for creating renegade extensions such as `<BLINK>`? Or perhaps you would like to know who determines what exciting tags an up-and-coming HTML standard should contain? If so, read on and be enlightened.

The "Official" Channel: IETF

For an Internet protocol to become a standard, it must pass a hard-core series of development stages specified by the Internet Engineering Task Force (IETF), the Internet's protocol engineering and development arm. The IETF's mission is to coordinate the technical developments of new protocols, and it possesses the power to decide what becomes standard within the Internet protocol suite. Although anyone can join the IETF, most of its members are network designers, network operators, marketplace representatives, and researchers.

The IETF's history is heavily connected to the government, as is the Internet's. Created in 1986, the IETF was intended to coordinate technical developments for contractors working on U.S. defense projects (so it's obvious why they control the standards for today's blisteringly paced Web developments, right?).

The IETF sees its mission like this:

- ✔ To identify operational and technical problems in the Internet and propose corresponding solutions
- ✔ To specify the usage and development of protocols and the near-term architecture
- ✔ To facilitate technology transfer from the Internet Research Task Force to the Internet community at large
- ✔ To provide a forum for the exchange of information between Internet researchers, users, vendors, network managers, and agency contractors

Nine topical areas exist in which working groups address technical activity on specific Internet topics. Each group has a director (or two) who assumes responsibility for the group's area of activity, and together these directors form the Internet Engineering Steering Group. These nine areas include:

- ✔ Applications
- ✔ Internet
- ✔ IP, Next Generation (IPnG)
- ✔ Network Management
- ✔ Operational Requirements
- ✔ Routing
- ✔ Security
- ✔ Transport
- ✔ User Services

These groups aren't permanent; after their mission is accomplished, they can disband (many persist, but others come and go).

Although these groups hold meetings three times a year, most debate and decision making occurs through electronic mailing lists. No formal votes are taken; instead, a group's members discuss and demonstrate most ideas until the group reaches a rough consensus. If you're interested in more information about these groups, sign on to the IETF announcement list by sending a request to:

```
ietf-announce-request@cnri.reston.va.us
```

Before you descend on an IETF meeting, it's a good idea to read *The Tao of the IETF*, written specifically for the hordes of IETF newcomers. Here's where you can find it:

```
http://www.ietf.cnri.reston.va.us/tao.html
```

The "Unofficial" Channel: W3C

The World Wide Web Consortium has always had a hand in new HTML developments. This organization includes CERN, MIT, and other organizations that are interested in the growth of HTML. Check out the W3C's various list archives at:

```
http://lists.w3.org/archives/public
```

How a Proposal Becomes a Standard

The Internet has many proposed protocols but few of them make it through the long, arduous process of becoming an Internet standard. The IETF puts all protocols through a series of rigorous development stages, beginning with an informal experimental stage. If a protocol passes this stage, it must have the prescribed characteristics to continue rising through the standards hierarchy. This hierarchy consists of three stages: proposed standard, draft standard, and standard.

Proposed standard

When a standard is proposed, the following information must be provided:

- Demonstrated utility
- Credible and complete specification

The proposed standard stage lasts for a minimum of six months and a maximum of two years. After this period, the protocol is either elevated, depreciated, or recycled. (A protocol is permitted to re-enter the standards track at a later date if appropriate.)

Draft standard

Drafts also have requirements, such as:

- Must work well in limited operational experience
- Must have independent, multiple, interoperable implementations

The draft standard stage lasts a minimum of four months and a maximum of two years. The protocol can then be elevated, depreciated, recycled, or sent back to the proposed stage.

Standard

To become official, the standard must meet the following requirements:

- ✔ Must have a demonstrated operational stability
- ✔ Must have been successfully implemented at least twice during the draft period

After a protocol becomes standard, it can be classified in any of these categories:

- ✔ **Required:** The protocol must be included in any TCP/IP implementation.
- ✔ **Elective:** This standard is optional, and the developer can use the protocol as he or she desires.
- ✔ **Recommended:** This status is used for standards that aren't required but are highly recommended, usually because they are widely used or demanded.
- ✔ **Information or historic:** These categories are used only occasionally. *Information* is used to describe a part of the standards process, whereas *historic* is employed for standards that are no longer in use.

Finally, Internet standards take the form of documents called *Requests for Comment*, usually abbreviated as RFCs. Although the name sounds kind of tentative, these documents have all the force that's necessary to dictate a full-blown, official Internet standard.

A Brief Review of HTML Standards to the Present

HTML standards are currently numbered zero through three, which is something of a misnomer, as you find out a little later on. A series of code names have also been introduced more recently, including names such as Wilbur and Cougar. You will encounter this naming convention frequently, so read on for the details.

HTML 0.0

HTML 0.0, the original HTML language, was a text-only markup language developed at the European Laboratory for Particle Physics (called CERN, the acronym for its French name) by Tim Berners-Lee. It was used at CERN as a prototypical language while CERN was developing the first generation of Web browsers. HTML 0.0's capability to handle text, although ground-breaking at the time, is rudimentary by current standards.

HTML 1.0

Dan Connolly began developing HTML 1.0 in March 1992 and released it to the Web community in July of that year. Tim Berners-Lee wrote an Internet draft RFC (Requests for Comment) for HTML 1.0 in 1993, which resulted in its release to the general public. In addition to the text control that HTML 0.0 offers, HTML 1.0 can also reference graphical elements. Browsers still exist (such as Cello and Lynx) that use HTML 1.0.

HTML 2.0

HTML 2.0 is HTML's second major implementation, and it defines the first real standard HTML document type. Dan Connolly and Tim Berners-Lee began working on 2.0 as soon as HTML 1.0 was released. HTML 2.0 can handle text better than its predecessors; it provides tags for interactive forms and image maps, which both contributed to the Web's increase in popularity.

Although it incorporates all of HTML 1.0's beneficial markup elements, HTML 2.0 ameliorates many of HTML 1.0's elements and eliminates several elements that had become obsolete (such as `<XMP>` and `<LISTING>`). HTML 2.0 also introduces a fill-in form interface. The IETF finally accepted HTML 2.0 as an official standard in 1996. As we're writing this book, HTML 2.0 is still the official HTML standard, but most implementers are now following the World Wide Web Consortium (W3C) recommendations for HTML 3.2 (which we discuss later in this chapter). HTML 2.0 remains a very safe "lowest common denominator" for Web site implementations.

HTML+

HTML+ never made it to the standard level, and it never will. That's a factual statement rather than a pessimistic one — HTML+ was recast as HTML 3.0. Because Dave Raggett, the creator of HTML+, was involved in the development of HTML 3.0, the two were smoothly integrated. Many of the same ideas were proposed in HTML+ as in HTML 3.0, such as math equations and table definitions.

If you're curious about HTML+, you can read its proposal at:

```
http://www.mcis.duke.edu/duke/html3.0/htmlPlus.html#2
```

HTML 3.0

Even though the collection of standards once known as HTML 3.0 has been scrapped, you still see many references to this term, even at the W3C's own Web site. Dan Connolly, Dave Raggett, and Tim Berners-Lee of the World Wide Web Consortium originally led this effort. Even though its components are important, are still under development, and are making their way through the standards process, HTML 3.0 has been killed as a standards designation.

The HTML 3.0 collection was defined as an application of the International Standard ISO ISO8879:1986 Standard Generalized Markup Language (SGML). This specification has been proposed as an Internet Media Type (RFC 1590) as well as MIME Content Type (RFC 1521) and is still called `text/html; version=3.0` despite the formal demise of HTML 3.0 in November, 1995.

HTML 3.2 (aka Wilbur)

HTML 3.2 is a W3C recommendation for HTML, which was developed together with vendors such as IBM, Microsoft, Netscape Communications Corporation, Novell, SoftQuad, Spyglass, and Sun Microsystems. You can find copies of all the relevant documents and information about HTML 3.2 at the W3C Web site at:

```
http://www.w3.org/pub/WWW/MarkUp/Wilbur/
```

Note that the URL contains the string Wilbur; this was the code name for the collection of HTML standards candidates before the 3.2 appellation was applied. HTML 3.2 improves on HTML 2.0 by adding popular features such as tables, applets, text flow around images, and superscripts and subscripts. Even though HTML 3.2 has yet to become a set of IETF standards, it's still regarded as the reigning HTML specification and is the one most worth following for current Web-site implementations.

Cougar

Cougar is the code name for the up-and-coming version of HTML. It represents the leading edge of this technology, which means that Cougar includes the newest and most exciting HTML capabilities, but that these capabilities are still in the process of being defined. Experimenting with the capabilities of Cougar is okay, but don't invest too heavily in implementations based on Cougar at this point, simply because the existing Cougar definitions are bound to change en route to standardization. If you have the time and energy to keep up with its shifting definitions, Cougar's the place to be; but unless your organization implements HTML technology as its main business objective, Cougar is probably too close to the forefront of the industry for most companies. For more information about Cougar, check out this URL:

```
http://www.w3.org/pub/WWW/MarkUp/Cougar/
```

The never-ending HTML standards story . . .

The process of HTML standards development is ongoing and is open to suggestions from Netizens. If you want to participate in the discussion, visit the archives of the `www-html` discussion list at:

```
http://www.eit.com/goodies/lists/www.lists/
```

You can also investigate AMAYA, the World Wide Web Consortium's HTML 3.0 browser at this site:

```
http://www.w3.org/pub/www/amaya/
```

Pressure from the Marketplace

The amount of time a protocol requires to pass through the labyrinthine process of becoming an IETF standard is often too leisurely for the speed of 20th-century capitalism. By the time the IETF accepts an HTML standard, its elements are often old hat (or, simply, already accepted by users as standards) because they have been available through commercial Internet implementations for many months. This situation is currently the case with HTML 2.0 (the current official standard) and HTML 3.2 (the W3C's currently recommended HTML implementation).

Cognizant of the fact that the hottest technology often attracts the most customers, companies such as Netscape and Microsoft have jumped at the opportunity to profit by creating new HTML tags and extensions. The Web's user base also influences the development of new HTML standards. Netscape may have pioneered frames and tables, but the company did so because the Web community demanded them — and because, clearly, the lethargic IETF process wouldn't produce the necessary technology quickly enough.

When the IETF was founded in 1986, its founders clearly had no idea how forcefully market forces would challenge their standards-making process. Although the IETF would like to think that its standards are the most influential, the fact is that the extensions and tags created by private industry incite a great deal more excitement among the Web community.

The IETF's standards are still considered important — after all, they are "The Standard," which means that those standards are always safe to use and have at least a modicum of enduring value. But because the Web's free-for-all nature enables companies, such as Netscape and Microsoft, to ignore the standards-making process and extend HTML as they see fit, these companies frequently exercise the "proprietary option."

By taking a nonstandard route, vendors can push functionality into users' hands quickly. This strategy gives them an ephemeral competitive edge, builds a stronger customer base, and diminishes the control of the standards bodies. But, unfortunately, this approach also diminishes the truly global reach of the Internet (and the Web) and may ultimately lead to its balkanization, fragmenting a single community into ever more mutually incompatible communities of interest (or of users of particular software, as the case appears to be).

Netscape extensions

Netscape isn't trying only to create exclusive extensions but is hoping that, by proving that its extensions have value, these technologies may appear in one HTML standard or another. When such inclusion occurs, it's a powerful example of collaboration between commercial interests and standards bodies. But when these groups diverge, the result for Webmasters and content creators is often an exercise in frustration.

 Numerous Netscape extensions exist, and their number and capabilities change regularly. You can find them fully outlined and explained in the companion volume, *HTML For Dummies*, 2nd Edition (on the CD-ROM), or you can discover them for yourself at:

```
http://home.netscape.com/assist/net_sites
           /html_extensions.html
```

Internet Explorer extensions

In case you are speculating about how long it will be before Microsoft seeks to dominate Web development, wonder no more: Microsoft has endowed its Internet Explorer with unique extensions that create online video, marquee effects, and background sounds. Internet Explorer also features support for

Internet shopping applications and delivers Secure Socket Library (SSL) support. The extensions to the HTTP protocol keep the channels open between the server and the client to speed up communications.

FONT FACE and FONT COLOR are two of Explorer's new extensions. They let you specify what color and typeface you want to use for text and give you more control over your document without requiring cumbersome bitmap files.

MARQUEE is another new Explorer extension. It lets you select a portion of text to use as a moving marquee on a page. Used in moderation, this tag can be an effective way to convey information. Used too freely, it has the potential to be even more irritating than the <BLINK> tag!

Microsoft has taken steps to ensure that Explorer will be able to handle future HTML standards. Like Netscape Navigator, Explorer already supports popular emerging HTML standards, such as frames, tables, scripting, and style sheets. For the latest information about Internet Explorer and its HTML capabilities, please visit the excellent online course at:

```
http://www.microsoft.com/train_cert/ffie3/new_feat.htm
```

Finding, Understanding, and Using HTML DTDs

Understanding HTML Document Type Definitions is easier if you understand a little about Standard Generalized Markup Language (SGML). SGML is a metalanguage that defines structured document types and the markup languages that represent a formal description of a document's type and representational capabilities. HTML is built on SGML, so whenever a conflict occurs, SGML overrules HTML.

The nature of an SGML document

Every SGML document is divided into three parts, whose descriptions follow:

✔ **SGML declaration:** The SGML declaration attaches SGML syntax token names and processing quantities to specific values. In the HTML DTD, the SGML declaration specifies that </ opens an end tag and no name can be more than 72 characters.

✔ **Prologue:** The prologue includes one or more DTDs, which are responsible for specifying the element relationships, element types, and attributes. The HTML 3.0 DTD tells you specifically what syntax is allowed in HTML documents that incorporate its current markup tags and capabilities.

✔ **References:** References can be represented by markup. They contain a document's data and markup of the document. To represent instances of that data type, HTML refers to the document type as well as the markup language.

For more information about SGML, check out the Official TEI site at the University of Illinois-Chicago:

```
http://www.uic.edu/orgs/tei/sgml/teip3sg/index.html#TOC
```

Or take a look at A little bit of SGML at this site:

```
http://www.ozemail.com.au/~dkgsoft/html/sgml.html
```

About DTDs . . .

DTD stands for Document Type Definition. A DTD is a formal description of how a particular class of documents is structured in SGML. The DTD is the file that's responsible for specifying how the various parts of an SGML document relate to each other. The DTD declares what all the document's elements are, specifying the name and data content model of each element. DTDs are generally used to:

✔ Formalize the document's markup conventions so that other applications can parse (or interpret) conforming documents

✔ Let parsing tools perform document validation and deviation reports

✔ Define what a document's "official" structure is

✔ Declare names for a document's external data (such as sound or graphics files) and their notations

What does a DTD contain?

Any HTML DTD tells you the specifics of what's legal for every element. Most elements in a DTD are specified so that they contain other elements, although elements can also contain parsable character data (#PCDATA).

You can tell how frequently an element occurs by the symbol that's attached to the element name. Here are the three occurrence indicators in an SGML DTD:

 ✔ ? means zero or one occurrence.

 ✔ * means zero or more occurrences.

 ✔ + means one or more occurrences.

If you don't see an occurrence indicator in a content data model, the element occurs only once. This single occurrence means that the element's presence is mandatory and can't be repeated.

Within a DTD, you can use three "connectors" between elements:

 ✔ | indicates that one of the elements in the list must occur.

 ✔ , indicates that both elements have to occur in a specific order.

 ✔ & indicates that both elements must occur, but in any order.

A DTD also includes an element's *declared* content data model, which may be one or more of the following:

 ✔ RCDATA means that the entity references are recognized but no content is permitted.

 ✔ CDATA means that any markup except </ within a tag is ignored.

 ✔ EMPTY means that the element can't ever have content or an end tag.

A DTD's elements are allowed to have mixed content models, so you can create a combination of subelements with character data. However, be cautious when you're mixing content data models, because their ambiguous language may be confusing.

Where the DTDs live

The DTD for HTML 2.0 is at:

```
http://www.ics.uci.edu/pub/ietf/html/rfc1866.txt
```

You can view the HTML 3.2 DTD at:

```
http://www.webtechs.com/sgml/Wilbur/DTD-HOME.html
http://www.w3.org/pub/WWW/MarkUp/Wilbur/HTML32.dtd
```

Although it's tempting to follow the HTML 3.2 DTD to the letter, remember that it's just a matter of time before it, too, becomes obsolete. Locate and read the DTDs for the individual markup elements (frames, tables, math notation, style sheets, and so on) to get the ultimate level of detail. A bit of judicious investigation at the WebTechs (`http://www.webtechs.com`) or W3C's (`http://www.w3.org`) Web sites helps you find these in a hurry.

Deciding Which Flavor of HTML to Use

As the IETF's approval of new HTML standards draws nearer, many developers are choosing to create content using those standards. Netscape Navigator and Microsoft Internet Explorer offer their own types of HTML as well, and some of their proprietary extensions have a seductive appeal.

The safest choice is always the "official" standard (currently HTML 2.0) because it's guaranteed to work with just about any browser. Or you can follow the industry and use the less official but highly prevalent 3.2 recommendation. Ponder these points if you have difficulty choosing an HTML specification:

- ✔ **Who will be viewing the document that you create?** If you write a document using extensions that are viewable only with Internet Explorer and the majority of your viewing audience doesn't use Explorer, your hard work goes to waste. Some World Wide Web tools, such as HotMetaL, load only valid HTML 2.0 documents. By using an unapproved HTML DTD, you run the risk of alienating your users, because even if they want to see what you're doing with your fancy extensions, they can't. They may consequently seek out a site that's more easily read.

- ✔ **How long will your content be around?** If you think that your creation's life is only a few months, worrying about standards is not crucial. However, if your content must endure, use an established standard.

- ✔ **Are you concerned about automatic Web document construction?** If so, having a stable DTD to work with is preferable. May I recommend the HTML 2.0 DTD for now?

- ✔ **How much work can creating content in a new or unstable DTD create in the long run?** If your DTD won't be around in a few months, you'll have to sink time into retyping and restructuring. Depending on how long you take to finish your project, you may want to adopt an emerging DTD rather than a diminishing (or soon-to-be-depreciated) one.

The advantages of using valid HTML

Any number of HTML checking and validation services are available on the Internet today. These tools check your documents and flag deviations from the DTDs that you choose to govern them. Using these services is definitely the best way to make sure that your pages are "legal," and this approach offers a range of other benefits as well:

- ✔ The increased portability means that your valid HTML document can move to another WWW server with only minor adjustments.

- ✔ The compliance with a known DTD legitimizes a document's content and structure.

- ✔ A valid HTML document's information has greater fidelity, which improves its capability to communicate.

- ✔ A valid HTML document can be parsed successfully by an SGML parser (such as sgmls), so you don't have to rely on a human to inspect your site.

- ✔ It's easier for a software robot to index your site if it follows standard HTML style, which translates into greater exposure for your site.

The disadvantages of using valid HTML

Although it's hard to believe that "crimes against the standard" may be beneficial, you'd be surprised how many authors proceed along this course. Just for the record, here are some reasons why authors choose to violate standards in the face of opprobrium:

- ✔ By the time an HTML level becomes a standard, it's no longer on the cutting edge.

- ✔ Creating valid HTML requires you to have the necessary tools and a rigid, well-documented publication process. Although you can find HTML validation checks to run, some human involvement is still necessary.

- ✔ Valid standards are very rigid, and you don't have the option of playing around with their structure.

New HTML Worth Watching

With all the efforts to extend HTML underway, both standard and propri-etary, you can easily get lost in the number of options and capabilities. To help steer you through this swamp, the following sections describe our choices for the main contenders to future HTML immortality.

A major trend is that HTML's representational capabilities are getting better and better and will only continue to improve. The <FRAMESET> tag and the <TABLE> tag contribute significantly to this process because their strides in formatting let you showcase your page's data in a whole new way.

Tables

The <TABLE> tag extends HTML to support tables. The <TABLE> formatting options unleash an entirely new realm of formatting possibilities, because you can place almost any other HTML tag into a table cell. HTML 3.2 provides a great reference point for table implementations, and defines most of Netscape Navigator's and Internet Explorer's capabilities in this area, including:

✔ Alignment on designated characters such as "." and ":" (for example, aligning a column of numbers on the decimal point)

✔ Greater flexibility for specifying table frames and rules

✔ Support for scrolling tables with fixed headers, as well as improved support to break tables across page boundaries for printing

✔ Incremental display for large tables as data is received

✔ Optional column-based defaults for alignment properties

Netscape Navigator, NCSA Mosaic, and Microsoft Internet Explorer have all incorporated the <TABLE> tag into their browsers. For more information about these implementations, head to Chapter 2.

Frames

Why would you use the <FRAMESET> tag? Because it brings powerful flexibility to the surfing experience. Frames let you display important but static information, such as copyright, title bars, and control graphics, in an individual frame. This information holds its form even while surrounding content is being redrawn. Frames also allow interesting new formats, such as side-by-side question-and-answer frames. Although tables may let you format information onto the browser screen, they don't have the dynamic capabilities that frames offer: You can't scroll within frames when you're using tables, but you can when you're using frames.

<FRAMESET> lets you create HTML documents that allow information to move within and between frames. You can keep information on display in one frame, while you're simultaneously scrolling through dynamic content or large amounts of text in another. Chapter 3 covers frames in all their flexible and complex glory.

Style sheets

Style sheets let Web authors exert much greater control over their documents, including font selection, spacing, kerning, and much more. Whereas earlier HTML implementations left a document's appearance up to the browser that renders the final page on a user's screen, style sheets give the document's author much greater control over a browser's behavior. This extension promises to add a new level of sophisticated control over page appearance, not just on a per-document basis, but also for entire sites where particular style sheets apply.

The advent of style sheets takes HTML into a whole new arena. Content creators and Web users alike have been champing at the bit for the arrival of the kind of fabulous control offered by these babies. When your Web site is armed with a style sheet, your creative control increases dramatically because you can specify how you want the design elements and layout to appear in terms of fonts, colors, and indentation depths.

With the constantly growing variety of Web browsers, style sheets are a welcome addition — no longer is a document's appearance completely at the mercy of the browser! Check out Chapter 4 for an in-depth discussion of style sheets.

Mathematics notation

The <MATH> element is used to include math expressions in the current line. HTML math has the capacity to describe whatever range of math expressions you create in common word-processing packages. In addition, it's suitable for rendering to speech equations and other mathematical forms of expression.

Applets, scripts, forms, and more

The final chapters in Part I cover some other important emerging HTML capabilities. In Chapter 5, you find out about embedding Java applets, along with scripts of varying kinds and capabilities, to increase the interactivity and capabilities of your Web pages (primarily by expending some elbow grease on programming various kinds of widgets to include on your Web pages). In Chapter 6, we close out this part of the book with a look at using the standard HTML forms tags to solicit input directly through HTML itself. Between the two different approaches to interactivity that direct programming and forms support, you get a great overview of what you can do to reach out and communicate with your users through your Web pages!

When it's all said and done, the proliferation of new tags and extensions, of both the standard and proprietary variety, brings exciting new possibilities to HTML markup. The battle between proprietary extensions and standard ones is one that merits watching, so keep an eye out. Even the best-informed industry insiders have a difficult time predicting accurately what the Web will look like in a few years — but it's sure to have a different, more powerful look than it does now. The material we cover in this chapter helps explain why that's true. The next chapter begins an investigation of the details and tackles tables on their own home ground.

A parting word of wisdom: If your Web page absolutely, positively must endure through the ages, use a standard DTD for creation.

Chapter 2

HTML Tables in Depth

Chapter 9 of the companion book *HTML For Dummies* introduces you to the concept and construction of HTML tables. If you are new to tables, you need to read that chapter and get yourself up to speed. If you basically understand tables, then this chapter introduces you to more interesting aspects of tables.

Tables are probably the most popular layout and design element on the Web. Early on in the life of HTML and the Web, the capability to control the placement and display of text and images was limited and restrictive. You could either have the image before the paragraph, or you could have the image after the paragraph. Needless to say, the artistic flair of many an HTML author was stifled. However, with the use of tables, HTML masters have near-perfect control of the layout and display of their Web creations.

Table Hindsight

Before you jump right into the thick of things, here's a quick review of the important aspects of HTML table markup.

A table is constructed from three (sometimes four) basic markup tags:

✔ <TABLE> is the main table tag. This tag pair surrounds all markup within a single table.

✔ <TR> is the table row tag. This tag pair surrounds all markup within a single row.

✔ <TD> is the table data cell tag. This tag pair surrounds all markup within a single table cell.

✔ <TH> is the table header tag. You can use this tag pair in place of the <TR> set to define a header row that usually displays in italics or bold.

But just knowing these tags won't get you anywhere without a few more conventions:

✔ All table tags must open and close in proper nesting order, FILO (first in, last out) or LIFO (last in, first out).

✔ Every row must contain the same number of data cells (but, when using ROWSPAN, the spanned data cell does not need to appear in each row).

✔ A data cell must be closed before opening a new data cell.

✔ A row must be closed before opening a new row.

✔ A data cell can contain the markup for another table (nesting tables is a common design strategy).

Now, with all that out of the way, here is what a no-nonsense (and basically useless) table looks like:

```
<TABLE>
  <TR>
    <TH> Header: row 1, column 1</TH>
    <TH> Header: row 1, column 2</TH>
  </TR>
  <TR>
    <TD> Cell: row 2, column 1</TD>
    <TD> Cell: row 2, column 2</TD>
  </TR>
</TABLE>
```

Notice a few important construction elements:

✔ Spaces offset the various levels of the table.

✔ Each element of the table is on a separate line.

✔ Each markup tag is matched with its closing tag either on the same line or the same indention level.

If you create your tables in an organized fashion, you'll find troubleshooting and alteration are much simpler. Before we get to the really good new stuff, we want to highlight a few other issues.

Laying out tabular data for easy display

First of all, make a sketch of how you want your table to look. Then make a small HTML table with only a few rows of data to test your methodology and to see whether the table looks the way you want. If you're using multicolumn and multirow spanning heads, you may need to make some adjustments to get them properly spaced to fit your data. Finally, you may want to test your tables with several browsers to see how they look.

Multirow and multicolumn

Remember, you must build your tables by rows. If you use ROWSPAN="3" in one table row (<TR>), you must account for the extra two rows in the next two <TR>. The general concept is to leave out the cell in each row or column that will be assumed or spanned into by the ROWSPAN or COLSPAN cell. A ROWSPAN example follows:

```
<TABLE BORDER>
    <TR><TD ROWSPAN=3>Letters</TD><TD>A</TD></TR>
    <TR>                          <TD>B</TD></TR>
    <TR>                          <TD>C</TD></TR>
</TABLE>
```

Here's a COLSPAN example:

```
<TABLE BORDER>
    <TR><TD COLSPAN=2>ID</TD>              <TD>#</TD></TR>
    <TR><TD>b</TD>          <TD>B</TD><TD>1</TD></TR>
    <TR><TD>c</TD>          <TD>C</TD><TD>2</TD></TR>
</TABLE>
```

Nesting

Nesting is an important concept of building tables. The method of creating a table is nesting one set of tags within another set that is itself nested within yet another set of tags. Getting lost and confused is easy when you are building nested tables. So, to keep the confusion to a minimum, always type both the opening and closing tags of a tag pair before adding attributes or content. This effort ensures that you always close your tags.

Tremendous Table Tags

You are already familiar with the top four table tags: `<TABLE>`, `<TR>`, `<TD>`, and `<TH>`; and Chapter 9 of *HTML For Dummies* discusses the `<CAPTION>` tag. Here's a quick look at the `<CAPTION>` tag and the other tags we didn't mention:

- `<CAPTION>`: The `<CAPTION>` tag pair defines a caption for the table. The caption can appear just after the `<TABLE>` opening tag so the text appears above the resultant table, or the caption can appear just before the `</TABLE>` closing tag so the text appears just below the resultant table. Usually the caption text displays centered and in bold.

- `<COL>` (Internet Explorer): The `<COL>` elements let you group columns within the table and globally apply properties, such as alignment, to the columns without having to specify these properties in each `<TD>` element.

- `<COLGROUP>` (Internet Explorer): The `<COLGROUP>` elements let you group columns within the table and globally apply properties, such as alignment, to the columns without having to specify these properties in each `<TD>` element.

- `<TBODY>` (Internet Explorer): The `<TBODY>` tag pair defines the table body similar to the way the `<BODY>` tag defines the body of an HTML document. The table body separates the table rows of the main body from the rows of the header or footer of the table.

- `<TFOOT>` (Internet Explorer): The `<TFOOT>` tag pair defines the table footer.

- `<THEAD>` (Internet Explorer): The `<THEAD>` tag pair defines the table header.

Like all good tags, these and the original four have lots and lots of attributes. In the next section, we list all the attributes we could find for each tag and tell you what they do.

The Awesome Attributes

This list of attributes is long and ugly. So, to help ease the suffering involved in reading this list, we use a new convention for discussing these items. First, we list each tag and all the possible attributes associated with that tag. Some attributes are browser-specific, and these are identified by a code in parentheses: N for Netscape Navigator or IE for Microsoft Internet Explorer. Notice that in some cases, the same attribute has different values depending on the browser. After all tags are listed, we list all of the attributes and what they do. We label each attribute with the N and IE designations (in parentheses), as well as the tag it corresponds to. Enjoy!

<CAPTION> ... </CAPTION> Caption

```
<CAPTION
ALIGN="BOTTOM"|"TOP"
ALIGN="CENTER"|"LEFT"|"RIGHT" (IE)
STYLE="string" (IE)
TITLE="string" (IE)
VALIGN="BOTTOM"|"TOP" (IE)
>
```

<COL> ... </COL> Column (IE)

```
<COL
ALIGN="CENTER"|"LEFT"|"RIGHT"
SPAN="integer"
STYLE="string"
TITLE="string"
VALIGN="BASELINE"|"BOTTOM"|"CENTER"|"TOP"
WIDTH="string"
>
```

<COLGROUP> ... </COLGROUP>
Column Group (IE)

```
<COLGROUP
ALIGN="CENTER"|"LEFT"|"RIGHT"
SPAN="integer"
STYLE="string"
TITLE="string"
VALIGN="BASELINE"|"BOTTOM"|"CENTER"|"TOP"
WIDTH="string"
>
```

<TABLE> ... </TABLE> Table

```
<TABLE
ALIGN="LEFT"|"RIGHT"
ALIGN="CENTER" (IE)
BACKGROUND="URL" (IE)
BGCOLOR="color"
BORDER="value"
```

(continued)

(continued)

```
BORDERCOLOR="color" (IE)
BORDERCOLORDARK="color" (IE)
BORDERCOLORLIGHT="color" (IE)
CELLPADDING="value"
CELLSPACING="value"
COLS="string" (IE)
FRAME="ABOVE"|"BELOW"|"BORDER"|"BOX"|"HSIDES"|"LHS"|"RHS"|"VOID"|"VSIDES"
         (IE)
HEIGHT="height"
HSPACE="pixHoriz"(N)
RULES="ALL"|"COLS"|"GROUPS"|"NONE"|"ROWS" (IE)
STYLE="string" (IE)
TITLE="string" (IE)
VSPACE="pixVert" (N)
WIDTH="pixels"|"value%"
>
```

<TBODY> ... </TBODY> Table Body (IE)

```
<TBODY
ALIGN="CENTER"|"LEFT"|"RIGHT"
BGCOLOR="color"
STYLE="string"
TITLE="string"
VALIGN="BASELINE"|"BOTTOM"|"CENTER"|"TOP"
>
```

<TD> ... </TD> Data Cell

```
<TD
ALIGN="CENTER"|"LEFT"|"RIGHT"
BACKGROUND="URL" (IE)
BGCOLOR="color"
BORDERCOLOR="color" (IE)
BORDERCOLORDARK="color" (IE)
BORDERCOLORLIGHT="color" (IE)
COLSPAN="value"
HEIGHT="string" (IE)
NOWRAP
ROWSPAN="value"
STYLE="string" (IE)
TITLE="string" (IE)
VALIGN="BASELINE"|"BOTTOM"|"MIDDLE"|"TOP"
```

```
WIDTH="string" (IE)
>
```

<TFOOT> ... </TFOOT> *Table Footer (IE)*

```
<TFOOT
ALIGN="CENTER"|"LEFT"|"RIGHT"
BGCOLOR="color"
STYLE="string"
TITLE="string"
VALIGN="BASELINE"|"BOTTOM"|"CENTER"|"TOP"
>
```

<TH> ... </TH> *Table Head*

```
<TH
ALIGN="CENTER"|"LEFT"|"RIGHT"
BACKGROUND="URL" (IE)
BGCOLOR="color"
BORDERCOLOR="color" (IE)
BORDERCOLORDARK="color" (IE)
BORDERCOLORLIGHT="color" (IE)
COLSPAN="value"
HEIGHT="string" (IE)
NOWRAP
ROWSPAN="value"
STYLE="string" (IE)
TITLE="string" (IE)
VALIGN="BASELINE"|"BOTTOM"|"MIDDLE"|"TOP"
WIDTH="string" (IE)
>
```

<THEAD> ... </THEAD> *Table Header (IE)*

```
<THEAD
ALIGN="CENTER"|"LEFT"|"RIGHT"
BGCOLOR="color"
STYLE="string"
TITLE="string"
VALIGN="BASELINE"|"BOTTOM"|"CENTER"|"TOP"
>
```

Silly Syntax

Here's a brief explanation of the syntax used in the tags and attributes sections in this chapter. First, when you see an item in quotes, such as `"value"`, know that you must always use double quotes around this item. A vertical bar (I) separates two or more possible values for an attribute; you only have to choose one such value.

Pay close attention to the information enclosed in the curly brackets and the parentheses. An N or an IE in parentheses identifies elements that are supported or added by either Netscape Navigator (N) or Microsoft Internet Explorer (IE), respectively. In the attributes section, curly brackets indicate those tags that the corresponding attributes may be used within (and also which browsers support such specific attributes or values, where applicable).

<TR> ... </TR> Table Row

```
<TR
ALIGN= "CENTER"|"LEFT"|"RIGHT"
BGCOLOR="color"
BORDERCOLOR="color" (IE)
BORDERCOLORDARK="color" (IE)
BORDERCOLORLIGHT="color" (IE)
HEIGHT="string" (IE)
STYLE="string" (IE)
TITLE="string" (IE)
VALIGN="BASELINE"|"BOTTOM"|"MIDDLE"|"TOP"
>
```

Attribute definitions

You can find more attributes here than you can shake a stick at (so don't try it — you'll strain yourself). Be sure to pay attention to the associated tags and browsers in the curly brackets for each attribute and/or each value; these define what's legal for that attribute and where such attributes may appear (see the sidebar entitled "Silly Syntax" for more discussion of this subject).

- ✔ `ALIGN=` defines an element's alignment.
  - `"BOTTOM"` forces bottom alignment {`<CAPTION>`}.
  - `"TOP"` forces top alignment {`<CAPTION>`}.

- "CENTER" forces center alignment {<CAPTION> (IE), <COL>, <COLGROUP>, <TABLE> (IE), <TBODY>, <TD>, <TFOOT>, <TH>, <THEAD>, <TR>}.

- "LEFT" forces left alignment {<CAPTION > (IE), <COL>, <COLGROUP>, <TABLE>, <TBODY>, <TD>, <TFOOT>, <TH>, <THEAD>, <TR>}.

- "RIGHT" forces right alignment {<CAPTION > (IE), <COL>, <COLGROUP>, <TABLE>, <TBODY>, <TD>, <TFOOT>, <TH>, <THEAD>, <TR>}.

✔ BACKGROUND="URL" defines the graphic to be displayed in the background {<TD> (IE), <TH> (IE), <TABLE> (IE)}.

✔ BGCOLOR="color" defines the background color; this value can be a color name or an #RRGGBB hex value {<TH>, <TR>, <TABLE>, <TBODY>, <TD>, <TFOOT>, <THEAD>}.

✔ BORDER="value" defines the size of the table border in pixels; the default is zero {<TABLE>}.

✔ BORDERCOLOR="color" defines the color of the border; it must be used with the BORDER attribute. This value can be a color name or an #RRGGBB hex value {<TABLE> (IE), <TD> (IE), <TH> (IE), <TR> (IE)}.

✔ BORDERCOLORDARK="color" defines the color of the shadow edge used in the 3D border; this attribute must be used with the BORDER attribute. This value can be a color name or an #RRGGBB hex value {<TABLE> (IE), <TD> (IE), <TH> (IE), <TR> (IE)}.

✔ BORDERCOLORLIGHT="color" defines the color of the highlight edge used in the 3D border and must be used with the BORDER attribute. This value can be a color name or an #RRGGBB hex value {<TABLE> (IE), <TD> (IE), <TH> (IE), <TR> (IE)}.

✔ CELLPADDING="value" defines the amount of space in pixels between the sides of a cell and its contents {<TABLE>}.

✔ CELLSPACING="value" defines the amount of space in pixels between the exterior of the table and the cells, as well as the space between the individual cells {<TABLE>}.

✔ COLS="string" defines the number of columns within a table {<TABLE> (IE)}.

✔ COLSPAN="value" defines the number of columns the data cell spans or overlaps {<TH>, <TD>}.

✔ FRAME= defines which sides or portions of a table's borders are displayed {<TABLE> (IE)}.

- "ABOVE" puts borders on the top side of the table frame.

- "BELOW" puts borders on the bottom side of the table frame.

- "BORDER" puts borders on all sides of the table frame.

A Hex Upon that Color!

When color definitions use hexadecimal values to set a specific color, these values take the form #01F803. In this case, the 01 sets the value for red, the F8 sets the value for green, and 03 sets the value for blue. Together, this combination of three values can establish unambiguous definitions for over four million color combinations and strains the limits of all but the most capable Super VGA computer displays (or their equivalents). For more information about RGB colors, and a great chart of well-known color values, please consult this URL:

```
http://developer.netscape.com/
    library/ documentation/
    htmlguid/colortab.htm
```

- "BOX" puts borders on all sides of the table frame.

- "HSIDES" puts borders on the top and bottom sides of the table frame.

- "LHS" puts borders on the left side of the table frame.

- "RHS" puts borders on the right side of the table frame.

- "VOID" means that no borders are on the table frame.

- "VSIDES" puts borders on the left and right sides of the table frame.

✔ HEIGHT="height" defines the height in pixels {<TABLE>, <TD> (IE), <TH> (IE), <TR> (IE)}.

✔ HSPACE="pixHoriz" defines the horizontal space in pixels into which a table must fit {<TABLE> (N)}; for example, HSPACE="100" means that the table must fit into a space that is no more than 100 pixels wide, on any display.

✔ NOWRAP defines that the contents of the cell should not be wrapped {<TH>, <TD>}.

✔ ROWSPAN="value" defines the number of rows the data cell spans or overlaps {<TH>, <TD>}.

✔ RULES= defines the rules or lines to be displayed within the table {<TABLE> (IE)}.

- "ALL" puts rules around all rows and columns.

- "COLS" puts rules between columns.

- "GROUPS" puts rules between groups as defined by <THEAD>, <TBODY>, <TFOOT>, and <COLGROUP>.

- "NONE" indicates that no interior borders are present.

- "ROWS" puts rules between rows.

✔ SPAN="integer" defines the number of columns in a group {<COL>, <COLGROUP>}.

✔ STYLE="string" specifies the inline style sheet to be used {<CAPTION> (IE), <TABLE> (IE), <TD> (IE), <TH> (IE), <TR> (IE), <COL>, <COLGROUP>, <TBODY>, <TFOOT>, <THEAD>}.

✔ TITLE="string" defines a title that often appears as a tool tip {<CAPTION> (IE), <TABLE> (IE), <TD> (IE), <TH> (IE), <TR> (IE), <COL>, <COLGROUP>, <TBODY>, <TFOOT>, <THEAD>}.

✔ VALIGN= defines the vertical alignment of specified table elements {<COL>, <COLGROUP>, <TBODY>, <TFOOT>, <THEAD>, <TH>, <TR>, <TD>}.

- "BASELINE" aligns elements on the baseline.

- "BOTTOM" bottom-aligns elements {can also specify the location of the caption for <CAPTION> (IE)}.

- "CENTER" aligns elements in the center.

- "TOP" top-aligns elements {can also specify the location of the caption for <CAPTION> (IE)}.

✔ VSPACE="pixVert" defines the vertical space in pixels into which the table must fit {<TABLE> (N)}; for example, VSPACE="100" means that the table must fit into a vertical space that is no more than 100 pixels high, on any display.

✔ WIDTH="height" defines the width in pixels or as a percentage {<TABLE>, <TD> (IE), <TH> (IE), <COL>, <COLGROUP>}.

Some of the Good Stuff

For a few tips from the pros (yeah, that's right; we rub elbows with the best), take a look at these little gems.

Run for the borderline

When you construct your tables, use the BORDER attribute in the <TABLE> tag to easily picture what is going on. By setting BORDER=1, you can see the edges of the table and every cell. This view lets you investigate your markup visually. After you finish prodding and poking, you can remove the BORDER attribute to hide your tables. Then all that is left is a perfectly controlled layout of your content.

Force the issue

You may often find yourself attempting to create an empty table cell that always seems to collapse instead of remaining open. Even if you use the HEIGHT and WIDTH attributes in the <TD> tag, the cell still closes. Often, tables rearrange themselves to fit the display area or to accommodate cell content. This rearrangement can be very frustrating. For a cell to display as an empty cell instead of as a cell "blank," you need to enter something in the cell. (As shown in Figure 2-1, a blank is a table cell that is displayed without the sunken-in area. See the upper-left cell of the table in the graphic from the next section.) But placing just a single space or even a   (nonbreaking space) inside a cell can cause it to collapse around the small character.

A great trick to force the cell to exactly the size you want is to use a spacer graphic. A spacer graphic is a 1 x 1 pixel GIF file that is transparent. Using the spacer graphic, the WIDTH and HEIGHT attributes "expand" the table cell, for example:

```
<IMG SRC="graphics/space.gif" WIDTH=100 HEIGHT=50>
```

This markup within a table cell forces it to be 100 pixels wide and 50 pixels high. Isn't that simple!

If you want to make your own spacer graphic, go ahead. Just create a 1 x 1 pixel canvas with your favorite paint program, turn it transparent, and then save it. If you bought the 3rd Edition of *HTML For Dummies*, you can grab it out of the \H4D3E\GRAPHICS subdirectory on the CD-ROM; it's called SPACE.GIF.

A slick trick for the upper-left problem

Using empty cells with COLSPAN and ROWSPAN is a nifty formatting trick to help you with the pesky upper-left corner problem that can sometimes plague your tables. This problem occurs when the first column of left-hand cells is used to label rows and the first row of upper cells is used to label columns (in that case, the upper left cell must be left blank because it labels neither a row nor a column). Check out Listing 2-1 and the display in Figure 2-1.

Listing 2-1	Solving the Upper-Left Corner Problem

```
<TABLE BORDER>
<CAPTION>Blank Upper Left Corner</CAPTION>
 <TR>
   <TH ROWSPAN="2"></TH>
   <TH COLSPAN="2">COLUMN HEADING</TH>
   <!-- empty data cell for colspan -->
 </TR>
 <TR>
   <!-- empty data cell for previous rowspan -->
   <TH>Subhead 1</TH>
   <TH>Subhead 2</TH>
 </TR>
 <TR>
   <TH ROWSPAN="3">ROW<BR>HEADING</TH>
   <TD>Element 1</TD>
   <TD>Element 2</TD>
 </TR>
 <TR>
   <!-- empty data cell for rowspan -->
   <TD>Element 3</TD>
   <TD>Element 4</TD>
 </TR>
 <TR>
   <!-- empty data cell for rowspan -->
   <TD>Element 5</TD>
   <TD>Element 6</TD>
 </TR>
</TABLE>
```

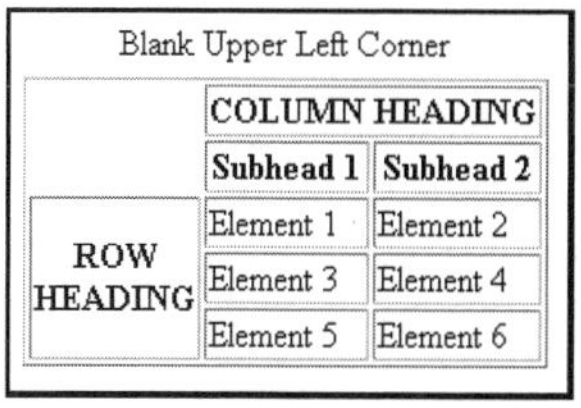

Figure 2-1:
A table with a blank upper-left corner is a common layout.

Blank Upper Left Corner		
	COLUMN HEADING	
	Subhead 1	**Subhead 2**
ROW HEADING	Element 1	Element 2
	Element 3	Element 4
	Element 5	Element 6

In English and many other languages, people read from left to right and top to bottom. So, isn't it strange that the upper-left corner of so many tables is blank? I guess people leave the corner blank because they don't know what to do with it. Anyway, now you know how! You can also start building your own tables by using these tags. All you need to do is mix and match the elements to get the table you want. You may need to experiment a bit, but you'll have fun finding out how various combinations of table tags and attributes result in interesting presentations.

Just remember that you must build your tables by rows. If you use ROWSPAN="3" in one table row (<TR>), you must account for the extra two rows in the next <TR> (as shown in the preceding example).

Comment schmomment!

After you get the hang of creating complex tables, make it a habit to include comments within your markup to give yourself a clue when you try to edit that file again in six months. Commenting your HTML is a great habit for any markup, but especially for tables. Just throw in a "<!--", followed by some witty information, followed by a "-->", and you've got yourself a comment.

Good things to comment on include:

- ✔ Color schemes used
- ✔ The contents of each cell or the purpose of the cell
- ✔ Cascading tables (tables within cells within tables within cells)
- ✔ Work-arounds or compromises
- ✔ Tasks for future sessions

If the table was strange, difficult, or hard to code the first time, it will be just as difficult to decipher and edit later unless you include comments. So, get into gear and start writing!

SPANning the gap

You can use the data cell attributes of ROWSPAN and COLSPAN to create some very interesting tables. We suggest that you get to know how these attributes really work so you can exploit them. Even after you master the art of SPANning, always lay out your code to highlight the spanned areas.

In the earlier section, "A slick trick for the upper-left problem," we include comments in the table markup to identify the missing or empty data cells that are required to accommodate the SPAN activities. Believe us, by adding in these missing or overlapping cells in your code with comments, you'll make troubleshooting and future editing of your complex tables easier.

On Your Own

There is really only one way to master tables, and it's not reading about it in a book. You need to take the time to experiment and build your own tables. Go wild. You'll be amazed at what you can do with tables if you only try. You can include just about other markup within a table cell, including other tables. Try nesting a table within a table within a table just to see if you can do it. Try adding graphics and hyperlinks. The time you spend finding out about tables will pay off the next time you create a Web site; you'll already know everything and will be able to concentrate on the content.

Another great way to find out about tables is to look at other people's examples. The following list of Web pages is a repeat of the excellent examples we mention in *HTML For Dummies*. These pages are *the* place to start when you want to understand tables by viewing other people's efforts. After you load these documents into your Web browser, take a look at their source (probably View, Source from your menu bar). You can see how complex their markup is (and often how poorly they arrange that markup — but then again, they didn't ask us).

Well, what are you waiting for? Pull up one of these pages:

- ✔ C|Net: This entire site uses tables for all the complex layout. Notice that they often use tables within tables within tables:

  ```
  http://www.cnet.com/
  ```

- ✔ Yahoo!: The most popular search engine on the Net uses tables to display the front page and all of the navigation items on all results pages:

  ```
  http://www.yahoo.com/
  ```

- ✔ Holodeck 3: The quintessential, unofficial *Star Trek* site uses tables to present a fantastic futuristic display of its offerings:

  ```
  http://www.holodeck3.com/
  ```

- ✔ Dilbert Zone: The only engineer on the planet to publicly disparage his boss and still keep his job, this daily dose of Dilbert is completely presented using tables:

  ```
  http://www.unitedmedia.com/comics/dilbert/
  ```

So now you know all about the latest and greatest feature of HTML: the <TABLE>. (Just pretend that Java, VRML, and other more outrageous extensions don't exist for now, okay?) Hey, you're smart. You bought this book, didn't you? Now you know how to use table tags and attributes to make your Web site all the more inviting to potential users. In the next chapter, we tackle the topic of frames, which allow you to break your user's browser window into separate, scrolling display areas.

Chapter 3

HTML Frames in Full

- -

In This Chapter

▶ Reviewing the basics

▶ Understanding all the frame tags and attributes

▶ Discovering the tips and tricks of frame construction

▶ Experimenting on your own

- -

In Chapter 10 of *HTML For Dummies* (3rd Edition), we introduce the concepts and construction of HTML frames. If you're new to frames, please visit that chapter and get yourself up to speed. If you already understand frames in a general way, this chapter introduces some of their more interesting aspects.

Frames offer a flexible way to create and manipulate Web sites. What are frames you may ask? Frames are independent regions on a Web page displayed in a single browser window, where each area is independently controlled and presents a separate HTML document. But even with such a great definition, picturing the concept may be difficult; therefore, please check out one of these Web sites:

```
http://home.netscape.com/assist/net_sites/frames.html
http://www.microsoft.com/workshop/author/default.asp
```

Both sites are constructed using frames, and both present content about frames (could that be why they are such good examples?).

Frames are not part of any of the current, official HTML standards; in other words, frames are proprietary constructions that major browser vendors maintain without present support from the standards commissions. However, the Cougar specification includes a complete definition of frame-related markup and syntax, and both of the major Web browsers (that is, Netscape Navigator and Internet Explorer) already support them. All your visitors may not be properly equipped to view them with their browsers, though, so introduce any framed content through an unframed warning page that gives users notice that strange views may lie ahead.

On the bright side, frames can be quite useful. With frames you can:

- ✔ Create a static area in your page layout that always displays navigation controls, a company logo, or other important information.

- ✔ Create hyperlinked tables of contents, menus, or outlines that will always be on hand.

- ✔ Use one frame to collect data from users and another to display results.

One of the coolest things about frames is that the framed areas you create can contain any HTML markup, including other frames! We could go on and on about the uses of frames, but we won't. Instead, we get right into the thick of things!

Frame Hindsight

Just in case you don't have *HTML For Dummies*, 3rd Edition, or just don't remember Chapter 10 from that book, here's a quick refresher course. You can create frames using three basic tags:

- ✔ <FRAME> is the frame definition tag. This singleton tag defines the attributes of a single frame.

- ✔ <FRAMESET> is the frame group tag. This tag pair surrounds all other frame markup.

- ✔ <NOFRAMES> is the frame alternative tag. This tag pair surrounds markup to be displayed or used if a browser does not support frames.

But, just knowing these tags won't get you anywhere without a bit more explanation about their proper usage:

- ✔ The <FRAMESET> tag pair is used instead of the <BODY> tags in the frame setup document.

- ✔ Always close <FRAMESET> tags.

- ✔ The <FRAMESET> attribute that defines the number of frames can be either ROWS or COLS, but never both in the same tag.

- ✔ <FRAMESET> tags can be nested or used in a series to combine row and column-oriented frame areas.

- ✔ Always name every individual frame, using the NAME attribute of the <FRAME> tag.

Now, with all that out of the way, here is an example of what a two-paneled frame construction (as shown in Figure 3-1) looks like using the ROWS attribute:

```
<HTML>
<HEAD>
<TITLE>Two Frame ROWS Example</TITLE>
</HEAD>
<FRAMESET ROWS="150, *">
  <FRAME SRC="top.htm" NAME="Top Frame">
  <FRAME SRC="bottom.htm" NAME="Bottom Frame">
   <NOFRAMES>
    <BODY>
     Sorry, your browser is not able to display frames.
     Therefore you cannot access this site.<P>
    </BODY>
   </NOFRAMES>
</FRAMESET>
</HTML>
```

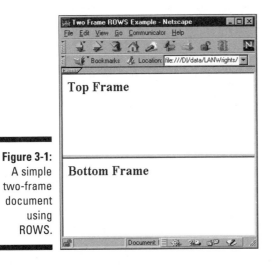

Figure 3-1:
A simple
two-frame
document
using
ROWS.

Here is an example of what a two-paneled frame construction (shown in Figure 3-2) looks like using the COLS attribute:

```
<HTML>
<HEAD>
<TITLE>Two Frame COLS Example</TITLE>
</HEAD>
```

(continued)

(continued)

```
<FRAMESET COLS="150, *">
  <FRAME SRC="left.htm" NAME="Left Frame">
  <FRAME SRC="right.htm" NAME="Right Frame">
   <NOFRAMES>
    <BODY>
     Sorry, your browser is not able to display frames.
     Therefore you cannot access this site.<P>
    </BODY>
   </NOFRAMES>
</FRAMESET>
</HTML>
```

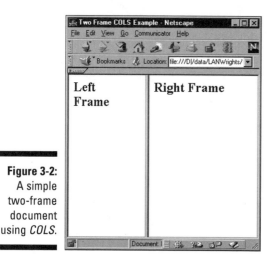

Figure 3-2:
A simple
two-frame
document
using *COLS*.

The `top.htm`, `bottom.htm`, `left.htm`, and `right.htm` documents, plus the others we use in this chapter, are all simple documents, such as:

```
<HTML>
<HEAD>
<TITLE>Two Frame ROWS Example</TITLE>
</HEAD>
<BODY>
<H2>Top Frame</H2><P>
</BODY>
</HTML>
```

Notice a few important construction elements:

✔ Spaces are used to offset the various levels of markup.

✔ Each element appears on a separate line.

✔ Each markup tag is matched with its closing tag either on the same line or at the same indention level.

✔ Every frame panel created must have a corresponding ⟨FRAME⟩ tag which points to a document or object to load into that frame.

✔ The ⟨FRAMESET⟩ tag set is used in place of the standard ⟨BODY⟩ tag set.

✔ A ⟨NOFRAMES⟩ tag set is included for browsers that lack frame support.

If you follow our lead and create your frames in an organized fashion, you'll find troubleshooting and alteration to be much easier. Before we get to the advanced stuff, we take a closer look at all the frame markup.

When you link to a page that is not on your site, be sure to target the blank or top page, just in case the outside page is formatted into frames. If you don't, then you get the frames in frames in frames look, which can be very confusing.

Fabulous Frame Tags

You are already familiar with the three common frame tags: ⟨FRAME⟩, ⟨FRAMESET⟩, and ⟨NOFRAMES⟩. But you may not know about the ⟨IFRAME⟩ tag from Microsoft. ⟨IFRAME⟩ stands for inline floating frame. This markup is used with Microsoft Internet Explorer to create frames that are not attached to the edges of the browser or any other frames. Like all good tags, all four have lots of attributes. In the next section, we list all the attributes we could find for each tag, and we tell you what each attribute does.

Introducing the attributes

This list of attributes is long and intricate. To make reading this list a little easier, we use a convention to discuss these items. First, we list each tag and all its possible attributes. In parentheses, we also specify which browser understands these tags and attributes. We use N for Netscape Navigator and an IE for Microsoft Internet Explorer. In some cases, the same attribute takes different values, depending on the browser involved.

<FRAME> Frame Definition

```
<FRAME
BORDERCOLOR="color" (IE, N)
FRAMEBORDER="1"|"0" (IE)
FRAMEBORDER="YES"|"NO" (N)
HEIGHT="value" (IE)
MARGINHEIGHT="value" (IE, N)
MARGINWIDTH="value" (IE, N)
NAME="name"|"_blank"|"_parent"|"_self"|"_top" (IE, N)
NORESIZE (N)
NORESIZE="NORESIZE"|"RESIZE" (IE)
SCROLLING="YES"|"NO"|"AUTO" (IE, N)
SRC="URL" (IE, N)
TITLE="string" (IE)
WIDTH="string" (IE)
>
```

<FRAMESET> ... </FRAMESET> Frame Group

```
<FRAMESET
BORDER="value" (IE, N)
BORDERCOLOR="color" (IE, N)
COLS="ColumnWidthList" (IE, N)
FRAMEBORDER="1"|"0" (IE)
FRAMEBORDER="YES"|"NO" (N)
FRAMESPACING="value" (IE)
ROWS="RowHeightList" (IE, N)
TITLE="string" (IE)
>
```

<NOFRAMES> ... </NOFRAMES> No Frames

```
<NOFRAMES
STYLE="string" (IE)
TITLE="string" (IE)
>
```

<IFRAME> Inline Frame (IE)

```
<IFRAME
ALIGN="ABSBOTTOM"|"ABSMIDDLE"|"BASELINE"|"BOTTOM"|"LEFT"|"MIDDLE"
|"RIGHT"|"TEXTTOP"|"TOP"
BORDER="integer"
BORDERCOLOR="color"
FRAMEBORDER="1"|"0"
```

```
FRAMESPACING="value"
HEIGHT="value"
HSPACE=variant
MARGINHEIGHT="value"
MARGINWIDTH="value"
NAME="name"|"_blank"|"_parent"|"_self"|"_top"
NORESIZE="NORESIZE"|"RESIZE"
SCROLLING="AUTO"|"NO"|"YES"
SRC="URL"
STYLE="string"
TITLE="string"
VSPACE="value"
WIDTH="string"
>
```

Explaining frame attributes

You can find more attributes here than you can shake a stick at (so don't try — you'll strain your back). Be sure to pay attention to the associated tags and browsers in the curly brackets for each attribute and each value; these bracketed items define what's legal for that attribute and where such attributes may appear (see the sidebar entitled "Silly Syntax" in Chapter 2 for more discussion of this subject).

- ✔ ALIGN= defines an element's alignment {<IFRAME> (IE)}.
    - • "ABSBOTTOM" forces absolute bottom alignment.
    - • "ABSMIDDLE" forces absolute middle alignment.
    - • "BASELINE" forces baseline alignment.
    - • "BOTTOM" forces bottom alignment.
    - • "LEFT" aligns left.
    - • "MIDDLE" forces middle alignment.
    - • "RIGHT" aligns right.
    - • "TEXTTOP" forces top of text alignment.
    - • "TOP" forces top alignment.
- ✔ BORDER="value" defines the space between frames in pixels {<IFRAME> (IE), <FRAMESET> (IE, N)}.
- ✔ BORDERCOLOR="color" defines the color of the frame border; the color can be a color name or an #RRGGBB hex value {<FRAME> (IE, N), <FRAMESET> (IE, N), <IFRAME> (IE)}.

✔ COLS="ColumnWidthList" defines the number of frame columns and their widths. Widths are specified by pixels, percentage (%), or relative size (*) separated by commas {<FRAMESET> (IE, N)}.

✔ FRAMEBORDER= renders a 3-D edge border around the frame.

- "1"|"0" sets frame border display on ("1") or off ("0") {<FRAME> (IE), <FRAMESET> (IE), <IFRAME> (IE)}.

- "YES"|"NO" sets frame border display on ("YES") or off ("NO") {<FRAME> (N), <FRAMESET> (N)}.

✔ FRAMESPACING="value" defines additional space between frames in pixels {<IFRAME> (IE), <FRAMESET> (IE)}.

✔ HEIGHT="value" defines the height of a frame in pixels {<IFRAME> (IE), <FRAME> (IE)}.

✔ HSPACE="value" defines the horizontal margin space between a frame border and its contents {<IFRAME> (IE)}.

✔ MARGINHEIGHT="value" defines the height of the frame margin between the border and its contents {<FRAME> (IE, N), <IFRAME> (IE)}.

✔ MARGINWIDTH="value" defines the width of the frame margin between the border and its contents {<FRAME> (IE, N), <IFRAME> (IE)}.

✔ NAME= defines the name of the frame {<FRAME> (IE, N), <IFRAME> (IE)}.

- "name" is a custom name.

- "_blank" loads the link into a new unnamed window.

- "_parent" loads the link over the parent — if no parent exists, this value refers to _self.

- "_self" replaces the current page with the link.

- "_top" loads the link at the topmost frame level.

✔ NORESIZE defines the frame as static; the viewer cannot resize the area {<FRAME> (N)}.

- ="NORESIZE" defines the frame as static {<IFRAME> (IE), <FRAME> (IE)}.

- ="RESIZE" defines the frame as resizable {<IFRAME> (IE), <FRAME> (IE)}.

✔ ROWS="RowHeightList" defines the number of frame rows and their heights. Heights are specified by pixels, percentage (%), or relative size (*) separated by commas {<FRAMESET> (IE, N)}.

✔ SCROLLING= defines the scrolling ability of the frame area {<IFRAME> (IE), <FRAME> (IE, N)}.

- • "AUTO" means that scrolling ability is determined by size of content.

- • "NO" means that the frame area is never scrollable.

- • "YES" means that the frame area is always scrollable.

✔ SRC="URL" defines the resource to be loaded in the target frame {<FRAME> (IE, N), <IFRAME> (IE)}.

✔ STYLE="string" specifies the inline style sheet to be used {<IFRAME> (IE), <NOFRAMES> (IE)}.

✔ TITLE="string" defines a title that often appears as a tool tip {<IFRAME> (IE), <NOFRAMES> (IE), <FRAMESET> (IE), <FRAME> (IE)}.

✔ VSPACE="value" defines the vertical margin space between a frame border and its contents {<IFRAME> (IE)}.

✔ WIDTH="string" defines the width of a frame in pixels {<IFRAME> (IE), <FRAME> (IE)}.

<A>dditional Frame Markup

When you use frames, you have to use more than just the four frame-specific markup tags to make things work. You must also use the anchor tag (<A>) with a special attribute named TARGET. Here's an example:

```
<A TARGET="Right Frame" HREF="sometext.htm">Click Here</A>
```

This type of hyperlink using the TARGET attribute allows you to create buttons or navigation controls in one frame and squirt the results of that link into a differently named framed area. (The technical term "squirt" is derived from the Latin *esquirtoe*, meaning "to inject, to redirect, to change destination.") By using this fabulous method to direct the destination of hyperlinks to other framed areas, you can establish standard navigation controls that remain visible at all times.

Complex Frame Creations

At first glance, creating and using frames seems simple, and, on a basic level, it is. But as the number of frames and the complexity of the layout of those frames increases, the effort involved in managing multiple HTML frames becomes mind-numbing. Now that you know the basics of frame creation, here's some of the hard stuff.

Creating a two- or even three-paneled framed page set is easy, as we demonstrate in the following code and in Figure 3-3 (***Note:*** we left out the `<NOFRAMES>` section to save space):

```
<HTML>
<HEAD>
<TITLE>Three Frame ROWS Example</TITLE>
</HEAD>
<FRAMESET ROWS="100, 100, *">
  <FRAME SRC="top.htm" NAME="top">
  <FRAME SRC="middle.htm" NAME="middle">
  <FRAME SRC="bottom.htm" NAME="bottom">
</FRAMESET>
</HTML>
```

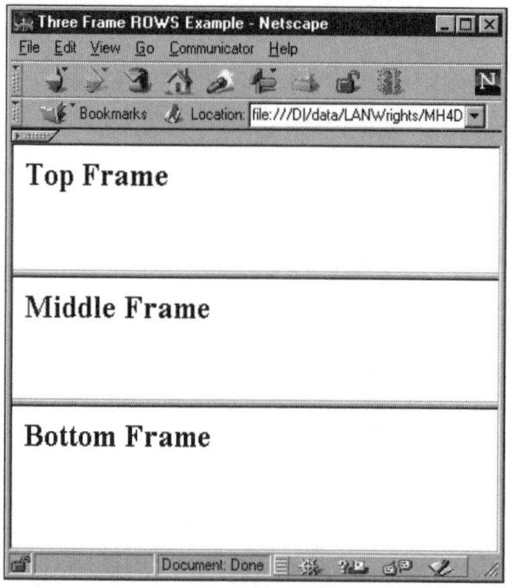

Figure 3-3: A three-frame document using ROWS.

But the same effect can be created using a different method. Pay attention to the double `<FRAMESET>` tags:

```
<HTML>
<HEAD>
<TITLE>Three Frame ROWS Example</TITLE>
</HEAD>
<FRAMESET ROWS="200, *">
  <FRAMESET ROWS="100,*">
    <FRAME SRC="top.htm" NAME="top">
    <FRAME SRC="middle.htm" NAME="middle">
  </FRAMESET>
```

```
    <FRAME SRC="bottom.htm" NAME="bottom">
</FRAMESET>
</HTML>
```

In this last example, the resulting image, shown in Figure 3-4, looks no different from the one shown in Figure 3-3. But it does show one important feature of HTML frames — you can substitute a complete <FRAMESET> tag pair for a single row or column frame area.

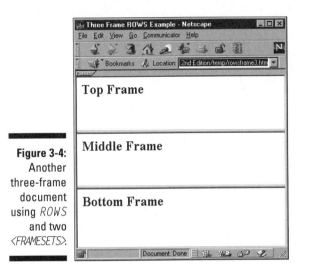

Figure 3-4:
Another three-frame document using *ROWS* and two *<FRAMESETS>*.

In the last example, <FRAMESET ROWS="200, *"> defines two frame rows. The definition of the first row (the 200 pixel row) is another <FRAMESET>, namely <FRAMESET ROWS="100,*">, which in turn creates two more frame rows, where each one is defined by a <FRAME> tag, first the top row, and then the middle row. After closing the <FRAMESET> that defines the frame row area for the first <FRAMESET>, the second row created by the first <FRAMESET> is defined by its own <FRAME> tag. If you didn't understand this paragraph the first time through, please read it again.

This simple approach lets HTML authors like you create multiple levels of ROWS- and COLS-defined frames within the same document, instead of requiring a separate file for each new frame designation. Here's another example (shown in Figure 3-5):

```
<HTML>
<HEAD>
<TITLE>Another Three Frame Example</TITLE>
</HEAD>
```

(continued)

(continued)

```
<FRAMESET ROWS="200, *">
  <FRAMESET COLS="*,*">
    <FRAME SRC="left.htm" NAME="left">
    <FRAME SRC="right.htm" NAME="right">
  </FRAMESET>
  <FRAME SRC="bottom.htm" NAME="bottom">
</FRAMESET>
</HTML>
```

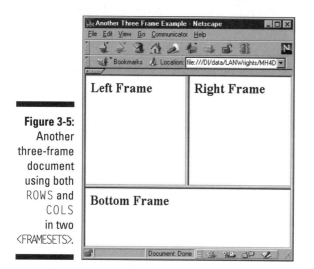

Figure 3-5:
Another
three-frame
document
using both
ROWS and
COLS
in two
<FRAMESETS>.

As you can see, this design is more compact and elegant than the following, equally legal, alternative:

```
<HTML>
<HEAD>
<TITLE>A Two Frame Example</TITLE>
</HEAD>
<FRAMESET ROWS="200, *">
  <FRAME SRC="lnr.htm" NAME="top">
  <FRAME SRC="bottom.htm" NAME="bottom">
</FRAMESET>
</HTML>
```

To make this code work, write the following HTML code to a separate file named lnr.htm (it provides the definition of the first frame element from the preceding block of HTML code):

```
<HTML>
<HEAD>
<TITLE>A sub-two Frame Example</TITLE>
</HEAD>
<FRAMESET COLS="*,*">
  <FRAME SRC="left.htm" NAME="left">
  <FRAME SRC="right.htm" NAME="right">
</FRAMESET>
</HTML>
```

If you use these files in conjunction, you get the results shown in Figure 3-5. Because both methods work, use whichever one you like best. To alternate between subframed sections and non-framed sections, the second method lets you target the top portion to replace left and right documents with a single document. But if your divisions are static, the first method may work better. Suit yourself!

By now, the idea should be clear that if you use a multifile method to establish framed areas within framed areas, you can create an infinitely recursive frame construct by linking a file back to itself. If you can stomach this idea, put it out of your head immediately. The concept may be a great theoretical or philosophical notion, but will eventually cause any browser that views it to crash. If you don't believe us, visit the Crash Site, where this recursive frame idea is put to use just to show its darker side:

```
http://www.newdream.net/crash/index.html
```

Another idea that you may find more useful is to combine the effects of ROWS defined framed areas and COLS defined framed areas, you must use multiple <FRAMESET> tag sets. You can either build a single master frame definition document, or multiple subframe definition documents to realize this concept. We recommend using whatever method makes the most sense to you. Because you are responsible for keeping things working, you must be comfortable with your design approach.

Some of the Good Stuff

For a few tips from the pros (that's right, we rub elbows with the best), take a look at these little gems:

Borderline, feels like I'm gonna lose my mind . . .

A standard take on frames (as shown in Figures 3-1 and 3-2) displays an ugly 3-D border between the framed areas. This display looks horrid. Instead, we prefer to hide our frame edges so the display is smoother, better integrated, and less segmented in appearance. When we create framed Web pages, we tend to turn off their borders (as shown in Figure 3-6). Here's an example that shows how:

```
<HTML>
<HEAD>
<TITLE>No Border Frame Example</TITLE>
</HEAD>
<FRAMESET ROWS="60,*,60" BORDER="0"
   FRAMEBORDER="0" FRAMESPACING="0">
  <FRAME SRC="header.htm" NAME="header">
  <FRAMESET COLS="114,*">
    <FRAME SRC="nav.htm" NAME="nav">
    <FRAME SRC="body.htm" NAME="body">
  </FRAMESET>
  <FRAME SRC="message.htm" NAME="message">
</FRAMESET>
</HTML>
```

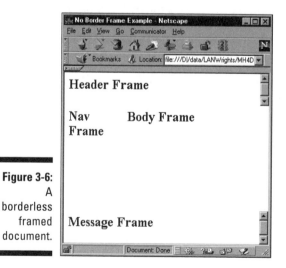

Figure 3-6:
A borderless framed document.

As you can see, we used `BORDER="0"`, `FRAMEBORDER="0"`, and `FRAMESPACING="0"` in the `<FRAMESET>` tag to force no borders for Netscape Navigator and Internet Explorer viewers. If you like the look of borderless frames, feel free to use this approach.

Request for comments!

After you get the hang of creating complex framed sites, be sure to include comments within your markup to document your design. Should you return to edit that site again in six months, you will be able to understand and appreciate your own work. Commenting HTML is a good idea for any complex or intricate markup, but frames need comments in particular.

Good things to document in comments include:

- Color schemes
- The contents of each framed area or each area's purpose
- Cascading frames (frames within frames)
- Work-arounds or compromises you made to realize your design
- Tasks for future sessions to help you (or your successor, should you move on to greener pastures) determine what remains to be implemented

Anything strange, difficult, or hard-to-code the first time around will be just as difficult to decipher and edit later — unless you include comments. So, get into gear and comment away!

Frame Scorn

Not everyone views frames benignly. Many netizens strive to remove frames from the Internet and attempt to erase their past from the history books (not unlike the Columbus reformists). We think that these radical revisionists may have a valid point, but we still use frames anyway. Just be aware that not everybody loves frames (just like not everybody loves broccoli).

A long and distinguished list of frame haters is available at Yahoo! if you use `"humor frames"` as your search string. Visit them all if you like, but here are the three sites that seem to be the best nonpareils of antiframe bigotry on the Web:

- The Frame Haters Union
    `http://www.concentric.net/~Vburton/fhu.sht`

✔ Why Frames Suck

```
http://www.ummed.edu/pub/i/ijosh/frames/
```

✔ Frames Free Campaign

```
http://www2.ucsc.edu/~dego/framesfree.html
```

Frame It Yourself

The only way to master frames is to create them, not simply read about them. You must take enough time to experiment with frame markup and build several of your own framed sites. As long as your audience can appreciate your work — by using the right browser — frames offer terrific capability to control site behavior and layout.

Another good way to learn more about frames is to look at other people's work. Here's a repeat of the Web sites with good frame examples from *HTML for Dummies*. These sites are *the* place to start when you want to find out about frames by following other peoples' examples:

✔ Netscape's Devedge Online HTML Specification:

```
http://developer.netscape.com/library/↩
          documentation/htmlguid/index.htm
```

✔ Wired News:

```
http://www.wired.com/
```

✔ THE Netscape Frames Tutorial by NewbieNET International

```
http://www.newbie.net/frames/
```

✔ Dylan Green's Windows 95 Starting Pages:

```
http://www.dylan95.com/StartMenu.html
```

Now that you know something about the `<FRAME>` tag, you must master it so you can flaunt your knowledge and newfound skills. The eternal question "To frame, or not to frame" may never get a real answer, but until the World Wide Web Consortium makes frames standard, you may want to steer clear of them anyway. But that's not our opinion — we think they're great, especially for tutorials and other educational materials. But for now, let's move onward through the fog to style sheets, wherein you discover how to govern your HTML documents using remote control.

Chapter 4

Style Sheets in Detail

*I*n the beginning, the Web was a simple communication medium, used mostly by researchers and academia to exchange information. The information didn't have to be pretty or perfectly arranged, it just needed to be correct. As the Web spread to the business world, organizations developed a true understanding of the prowess of the Web and its ability to reach more people using fewer resources. The fact that users could have a measure of control over the layout of information in a Web document baffled those users who had only lived in a world of print and presentations. The inability to create columns and use different typefaces was frustrating to Web page authors. Never mind that HTML and the Web in general weren't really designed to support such detailed layout information — the pages just didn't look right!

Because the Web was not just a passing fad, the major browser developers and the World Wide Web Consortium recognized the importance of meeting this need for more user control of Web pages' layouts— without violating the multiplatform, open-ended state of the Web. *Style sheets* were the answer.

In this chapter, we review the Web style sheet concept, give a complete overview of the syntax behind style sheets, look at the three different ways you can include style information in your Web pages, walk you through three different style sheets, and point you to several style sheet resources on the Web. Whew! Just saying all that was hard . . . let's do it!

Understanding Style Sheets

The style sheet concept is not new, but in fact has been borrowed from word processing and page layout programs. In general, a style sheet defines a set of layout parameters for a document to ensure that similar elements in the document appear uniformly. In English, this statement means that all instances of the same element, such as a heading or bulleted item, look alike—the *style* applies the same font, margin, and paragraph specifications to each occurrence of that element.

For example, why should you have to work through five different menus each time you want to create a level one heading? Simply choosing Heading 1 from a style list (and having the text rendered in red, Times 24, a half inch from the base margin, and with an 18-point space afterward) is much easier and more reliable.

This advantage also applies to HTML documents. Before style sheets, you could only change the size and color of text in a Web page and you had to use the <FONT> tag every time. HTML style sheets are like any other style sheet: They define how certain elements in a Web page should appear.

Style sheets also include already established HTML tags such as <H1> and <H2> and <STRONG> — your style sheet definitions override existing browser rendering for any tag, so you can take advantage of existing tags and just alter their appearance.

Taking another cue from standard style sheets, in HTML you can store style sheets individually, outside of the pages that reference them, and apply them to a collection of Web pages, which allows you to create one style template and apply it many times. These style sheets are called *external style sheets*. This flexibility creates a uniform look and feel throughout a large collection of Web documents.

To make style changes on the individual page level, you can include style markup within the document. Style markup works with (or overrides) any specifications in a referenced external style sheet. You can use style markup to customize the color, text font, and other attributes of a specific element, or create separate instances of an element, each with its own specific style.

Style sheets are not limited to one set of specifications per tag in a document. For example, you can have three separate level one headings defined in a style sheet, each with a different CLASS name, and apply whichever you want throughout the document. In the following section, we show you how to create multiple style definitions for a single tag, along with everything else you need to know to create your own style sheets.

Before we go any further, it's important to mention that style sheets are not fully implemented across all browsers and are not 100 percent backward-compatible with existing browsers. The style sheet information we present in the rest of this chapter is based on the Cougar specification (the latest HTML proposal). This means that all the style sheet elements and options we present in this chapter may not be usable right now. We can say with strong certainty that in the next few months, you will be able to use all the information and instructions in this chapter.

For the latest information, it's best to check the most recent Web resources at the following URLs:

✔ The World Wide Web Consortium Style Sheets page at:

```
http://www.w3.org/pub/WWW/Style/
```

✔ The Cougar HTML and Style Sheets specification at:

```
http://www.w3.org/pub/WWW/TR/WD-style
```

Discovering the Syntax of Style Sheets

After we've thrown out just enough information to make you really hungry for the how to's of style sheets, you're probably ready to satiate that desire and get down to the nitty-gritty. Style sheets are not difficult to understand if (and this is a big *if*) you've ever worked with other kinds of style sheets, you understand how HTML works, and you understand how browsers display Web pages. These are not easy prerequisites, but we're assuming that since you picked up this *MORE* book, you know something about HTML basics. (See *HTML For Dummies,* 3rd Edition, if you need to find out the fundamentals of HTML.)

By the book: style rules

Style sheets are essentially collections of rules that tell a browser how a document should appear. As with all other things HTML, these rules have a specific syntax. You can link these rules to your Web pages in multiple ways, but we get to that in few pages. The good news is that both external and embedded style sheets use the same rule syntax, and that individual tags have attributes to help you assign style specifics. When you learn the rule syntax, you're over the biggest hurdle.

Every rule has two components:

- ✔ **A selector:** Usually an HTML element such as <STRONG>, <H1>, or <ADDRESS>.

- ✔ **The style for the selector:** A selector's style can contain one or more predefined properties and their values. In the style font-family: Times the property being defined is font-family, and the value is Times.

You can create a rule by using the following syntax:

```
selector {property: value }
```

For example, the rule for a blue level one heading is:

```
H1 {color: blue}
```

You can include multiple properties and values for any one selector by separating the property-value pairs with semicolons. The syntax looks like this:

```
selector { property1: value1; property2: value2}
```

For example, the rule for a blue level one heading in Helvetica font is:

```
H1 {color:blue; font-family: Helvetica}
```

These rules can apply to HTML elements (ones already defined by the DTD) and elements that you create yourself (new markup that you create for your own specific needs). If you want to create a custom style called "heading" that appears in blue Helvetica, rather than defining a style for the standard <H1> element, the style notation is:

```
heading {color:blue; font-family: Helvetica}
```

The preceding code creates a class called "heading," which you can reference throughout your pages. You can also create multiple versions of an HTML tag by creating multiple classes. The following HTML code alters the standard <H1> tag and creates two new tags, one of class red, as well as one of class blue:

```
H1.red {color:red; font-family: Helvetica}
H1.blue {color:blue; font-family: Helvetica}
```

To specify which one you want to use in any given instance, use the CLASS attribute, as in the following code:

```
<H1 CLASS="red">
```

Pretty nifty, huh?

Properties

Properties can be divided into categories, which makes remembering them easier. The following sections look briefly at each family and any special syntax rules that a property might have.

Color and background properties

The following properties define the color scheme used within a document:

- ✔ Background Attachment specifies whether the image defined in background-image will scroll with the page or be fixed on the canvas. Here is an example:

  ```
  P { background-image: url(http://www.site.com/⤶
        background.gif); background-attachment: scroll }
  ```

- ✔ Background Color defines the background color using one of several predefined colors (discussed in the "Units" section later in this chapter) or the #RRGGBB color code. Here is an example:

  ```
  P { background-color: blue}
  ```

- ✔ Background Image identifies the URL for a background image that appears on the page. Here is an example:

  ```
  P { background-image: url(http://www.site.com/⤶
        background.gif) }
  ```

- ✔ Background Position specifies where a background image will appear on a page, using the keywords top, center, bottom, left, middle, or right. Here is an example:

  ```
  P { background-image: url(http://www.site.com/⤶
        background.gif); background-position: center }
  ```

- ✔ Background Repeat determines how a background image will be repeated. By using repeat, the image tiles in the standard fashion; repeat-x only repeats the image horizontally; repeat-y is limited to vertical repetition; and no-repeat ensures that the background image is not repeated at all. Here is an example:

  ```
  P { background-image: url(http://www.site.com/⤶
        background.gif); background-repeat: repeat-y }
  ```

- ✔ Color defines the color of an element by using a predefined name or #RRGGBB notation. Here is an example:

  ```
  P { color: blue}
  ```

✔ Background incorporates all of the other background properties into one value. Here is an example:

```
P { background: url(http://www.site.com/⤶
        background.gif) scroll blue center no-repeat }
```

Box properties

The following properties define margins and borders for text blocks. The measurements may be a little unfamiliar to you, but never fear, we explain them all in the section entitled "Units."

✔ Top Margin specifies the top margin of a text block by using length or percentage. Here is an example:

```
P {margin-top: 5em}
```

✔ Right Margin specifies the right margin of a text block using length or percentage. Here is an example:

```
P {margin-right: 5em}
```

✔ Bottom Margin specifies the bottom margin of a text block using length or percentage. Here is an example:

```
P {margin-bottom: 5em}
```

✔ Left Margin specifies the left margin of a text block using length or percentage. Here is an example:

```
P {margin-left: 5em}
```

✔ Margin uses four values to assign top, right, bottom, and left margins in that order. The following example assigns a margin of 5 to the top and bottom and 2 to the left and right sides:

```
P {margin: 5em 2em 5em 2em}
```

✔ Top Padding defines how much space should be inserted between the top border and the text using length or percentage. Here is an example:

```
P {padding-top: 10%}
```

✔ Right Padding defines how much space should be inserted between the right border and the text using length or percentage. Here is an example:

```
P {padding-right: 10%}
```

✔ Bottom Padding defines how much space should be inserted between the bottom border and the text using length or percentage. Here is an example:

```
P {padding-bottom: 10%}
```

✔ Left Padding defines how much space should be inserted between the left border and the text using length or percentage. Here is an example:

```
P {padding-left: 10%}
```

✔ Padding uses four values to assign top, right, bottom, and left border padding in that order using length or percentage. The following example assigns a padding of 10 percent to the top and bottom and 20 percent to the left and right sides:

```
P {margin: 10% 20% 10% 20%}
```

✔ Top Border Width defines how wide the top border should be using thin, medium, thick, or a defined length. Here is an example:

```
P {border-top-width: medium}
```

✔ Right Border Width defines how wide the right border should be using thin, medium, thick, or a defined length. Here is an example:

```
P {border-right-width: medium}
```

✔ Bottom Border Width defines how wide the bottom border should be, using thin, medium, thick, or a defined length. Here is an example:

```
P {border-bottom-width: medium}
```

✔ Left Border Width defines how wide the left border should be by using thin, medium, thick, or a defined length. Here is an example:

```
P {border-left-width: medium}
```

✔ Border Width uses up to four values to assign top, right, bottom, and left border widths in that order, using thin, medium, thick, or a defined length. Here is an example:

```
P {border-width: medium thick medium thick}
```

✔ Border Color uses up to four values to assign top, right, bottom, and left border colors in that order by using a predefined color or #RRGGBB notation. Here is an example:

```
P {border-color: blue red white green}
```

✔ Border Style uses up to four values to assign top, right, bottom, and left border styles in that order by using none, dotted, dashed, solid, double, groove, ridge, inset, or outset. Here is an example:

```
P {border-style: double solid solid solid}
```

✔ Top Border sets the width, style, and color of the top border. Here is an example:

```
P {border-top: thin dotted blue}
```

✔ Right Border sets the width, style, and color of the right border. Here is an example:

```
P {border-right: thin dotted blue}
```

✔ Bottom Border sets the width, style, and color of the bottom border. Here is an example:

```
P {border-bottom: thin dotted blue}
```

✔ Left Border sets the width, style, and color of the left border. Here is an example:

```
P {border-left: thin dotted blue}
```

✔ Border sets the width, style, and color of all borders. Here is an example:

```
P {border: thin dotted blue}
```

✔ Width defines in length or percentage the width of the space that the text will occupy. Here is an example:

```
P {width: 50%}
```

✔ Height defines the height of the space that the text will occupy in length or as automatically assigned. Here is an example:

```
P {height: auto}
```

✔ Float allows text to wrap around an element to the left, right, or not at all by using none. Here is an example:

```
P {float: left}
```

✔ Clear determines whether an element allows other elements to float on one or more sides using none, left, right, or both. Here is an example:

```
P {clear: both}
```

Classification properties

These properties provide information about how white space, lists, and other elements should be treated by a browser:

- ✔ `Display` creates one of four elements to be displayed in conjunction with the element it affects. These elements include `block`, creating a line break before and after the element; `inline`, which removes line breaks before and after the element; `list-item`, creating a bullet for the element without creating a list; and `none`, which turns off any display. The following example adds line breaks before and after the paragraph:

```
P {display: block}
```

- ✔ `Whitespace` defines how white space will be treated within the element. Choices include `normal`, collapsing all white space into one line; `pre`, rendering all hard returns regardless of the number; and `nowrap`, preventing line-wrapping without a `<BR>` tag. Here is an example:

```
P {white-space: pre}
```

- ✔ `List Style Type` identifies what type of marker is used with a list item, including `disc`, `circle`, `square`, `decimal`, `lower-roman`, `upper-roman`, `lower-alpha`, `upper-alpha`, and `none`. Here is an example:

```
P {list-style-type: square}
```

- ✔ `List Style Image` identifies an image that is used as a list item marker. Here is an example:

```
P { list-style-image: url(bullet.gif)}
```

- ✔ `List Style Position` defines how a list marker is placed relative to the list item. The `inside` value forces text to wrap under the marker; `outside` indents text. Here is an example:

```
P { list-style-position: inside}
```

- ✔ `List Style` defines the list style type, list style position, and list style image for any given list. Here is an example:

```
P { list-style: inside url(bullet.gif) square}
```

Font properties

These properties affect the way fonts appear and include everything from typeface to size:

- ✔ Font Family defines the typeface family or generic font type. The font family may be any named family, such as Times, Helvetica, or Geneva. Five generic font types exist, which include serif, sans-serif, cursive, fantasy, and monospace. You should include a generic font type whenever you define a specific font (in case the font you defined isn't installed on a user's machine). Any family name that includes spaces, such as "New Century Schoolbook", must be enclosed in quotation marks. Here is an example:

```
H1 {font-family: "New Century Schoolbook", sans-serif}
```

- ✔ Font Size specifies the size of the text. You can choose to specify one of these absolute sizes: xx-small, x-small, small, medium, large, x-large, or xx-large. Other options include larger, smaller, or a percentage relative to the base font size. You can also define the size in length. Here is an example:

```
H1 {font-size: xx-large}
```

- ✔ Font Style defines the style in which a font should be rendered. Choices include normal, italic, and oblique. Here is an example:

```
H1 {font-style: italic}
```

- ✔ Font Variant renders the text in either normal or small caps. Here is an example:

```
H1 {font-value: small-caps}
```

- ✔ Font Weight defines the lightness or darkness of the text. Your choices include normal, bold, bolder, lighter, 100, 200, 300, 400, 500, 600, 700, 800, and 900. Then numbers represent the actual darkness of the font weight, with 100 being lightest and 900 darkest. Here is an example:

```
H1 {font-weight: lighter}
```

- ✔ Font incorporates all of the other font properties into one value. Here is an example:

```
H1 {font: Helvetica, sans-serif xx-large italic small-
        caps lighter}
```

Text properties

These properties determine text spacing, alignment, line spacing, and more:

- ✔ Letter Spacing uses the length format to define the spacing between letters. Here is an example:

```
P { letter-spacing: +.05em}
```

✔ `Line Height` specifies the amount of space between baselines using length or percentage. Here is an example:

```
P { line-height: +2em}
```

✔ `Text Alignment` defines the alignment of text. Choose from `left`, `right`, `center`, or `justify`. Here is an example:

```
P { text-align: right}
```

✔ `Text Decoration` assigns one of five text modifications, including `none`, `underline`, `overline`, `line-thorough`, and `blink`. You can use this property to remove underlining from links. Here is an example:

```
A.visited { text-decoration: none}
```

✔ `Text Indentation` specifies the text indentation using length or a percentage. Here is an example:

```
P { text-indent: 5em}
```

✔ `Text Transformation` changes the case of text using `capitalize`, `lowercase`, `uppercase`, or `none`. The `none` value instructs the browser to leave the text as it was originally created by the author. Here is an example:

```
P { text-transform: capitalize}
```

✔ `Vertical Alignment` alters the alignment of text relative to the baseline. Choose from `baseline`, `sub`, `super`, `top`, `text-top`, `middle`, `bottom`, and `text-bottom` — or you can specify a percentage. Here is an example:

```
P { vertical-align: super}
```

✔ `Word Spacing` uses the length format to define the spacing between words. Here is an example:

```
P { word-spacing: +.05em}
```

Units

The lengths and percentages that we discuss in the preceding sections have specific rules that apply to them, as well as to URL and color notation. This section contains the information that you need in order to use all these units correctly in your style sheets:

✔ **Length Units:** You can use one of three relative length units in your style sheets: `em` is a measurement relative to the height of the element's font, so it adds or subtracts the specified number of ems from the actual height of the element's font; `ex` refers to the height of the letter *x*. The unit `px` stands for pixels as related to the height of the screen.

You can use a number to set the number of ems, exs, or pxs. Another option is to include the + or - sign with a number to indicate the base size plus or minus the supplied number. The legal absolute values are `in` (inches), `cm` (centimeters), `mm` (millimeters), `pt` (points, which are $1/72$ of an inch), or `pc` (picas, which are equal to 12 points).

✔ **Percentage Units:** Percentages can also be stand-alone numbers with the percentage sign (%), which represent a certain percentage of the screen or any other predefined value, such as the width of a text block. You can also use the + and - signs with percentages.

✔ **Color Units:** The predefined colors recognized by style sheets and most browsers are aqua, black, blue, fuchsia, gray, green, lime, maroon, navy, olive, purple, red, silver, teal, white, and yellow. If you want use any other color, you must use #RRGGBB hexadecimal color notation. If you want to brush up on your hexadecimal notation, be sure to read the sidebar "A Hex Upon That Color" in Chapter 2.

✔ **URLs:** To link to a URL in a style sheet, use this notation: `url(url.here.)`

Whew, we bet you thought the properties were never going to end. The good news is that you have a wide variety of options to work with when creating style sheets. Remember that all of these properties may be used in external or embedded style sheets.

Linking to External Style Sheets

When you have all of the pieces and parts of a style sheet, how exactly do you link style definitions to your Web pages? It's so simple that it's scary. After you put together a style sheet, you can reference the style sheet from any HTML page by using the `<LINK>` tag. The HTML code looks like this:

```
<LINK REL=StyleSheet HREF="mystyle" TYPE="text/css"⤴
         MEDIA=screen>
```

In the preceding code example, the `REL` attribute defines the link as a connection to a style sheet, `HREF` gives the actual location of the style sheet file, and the `TYPE` attribute defines a style sheet as `css` or *cascading* — browsers that don't support cascading style sheets will ignore the style. Cascading refers to a specific type of style sheet, one that can work well with other style sheets and embedded style information. Other types of style sheets have their own designations, such as text/dssl for the Document Style Semantics and Specifications Language (DSSL). The large majority of the style sheets you create will be cascading. If you choose to use another type, you must read its documentation to find out its specific TYPE value. (***Remember:*** Most browsers that support style sheets also support css, but if you're using some other type of style sheet, you will definitely want to include type information.) Finally, the MEDIA attribute in the preceding example defines the medium to which the style sheet is best suited. Most Webmasters create their pages to be viewed primarily on a computer screen, but this attribute will allow you to specify what medium your information is best presented in by using one of the following values:

- ✔ print is used for pages that should be printed.

- ✔ screen is used for pages that should be displayed on a computer screen.

- ✔ projection is used for pages that should be displayed in a projection format.

- ✔ braille is used for pages that should be output as Braille.

- ✔ aural is used for pages that will be read using a text-to-speech reader.

- ✔ all is used for pages that can be used by all output devices (this is the default media).

Many of these media values, aural and braille for example, are geared toward making Web information more accessible, whereas the print and projection media allow Web information to be formatted specifically for those output devices rather than trying to force a screen-oriented page to print well or show up clearly on a large presentation screen. In the future when these different media are better supported by the Web, you may have multiple style sheets for each kind of media. For now, it's just important to know your options.

To use the styles you've defined within your Web pages, you can use the CLASS attribute with any tag, or use the <SPAN> or <DIV> tags with the CLASS attribute to apply a style you've created to a section of your document. <SPAN> is a text-level element used to assign a style to text only, just like <STRONG> or <CITE>. If you create a style called .introtext, for example, that applies to only the first few words of a page, you can use this HTML code to reference the style:

```
<SPAN CLASS=introtext>
These are the first few</SPAN> words of the paragraph.
```

The words within the <SPAN> tags then have the .introtext style applied to them, but the rest of the text is left alone.

The `<DIV>` tag is a block-level element, one that separates text into logical groups, that can contain multiple paragraphs, headings, and other divisions. For example, if you create the style `.address`, use this HTML code to reference it in your document:

```
<DIV CLASS=address>

Your address information here

<P>

Your URL here

</DIV>
```

Embedded and Inline Style Specifications

Although you use the `<LINK>` tag to reference an external style sheet, you can use the `<STYLE>` tag to include style information directly within your HTML document, which is also known as an inline style. Any style information you include in an external style sheet can be written directly into an HTML page, but the style information cannot be referenced by other pages. You can, however, use an *inline style* to override or complement an external style sheet that an HTML page references. This enables you to write general style sheets that create an overall look and feel for your pages, but also retain page-level control by adding page-specific styles using the `<STYLE>` tag. To include an inline style, use this HTML code:

```
<HEAD>
<STYLE TYPE="text/css" MEDIA=screen>
<!@hy
  BODY  { background: url(foo.gif) blue; color: white }
STRONG{ background: white; color: blue }
.address { margin-left: 5em; margin-right: 5em }
@hy>
</STYLE>
</HEAD>
```

You use the `<SPAN>` and `<DIV>` attributes to access these inline styles just as you would with an externally referenced style sheet.

Using Tags to Define Style

Several HTML tags have style built into their attributes, most notably the <FONT> and <BODY> tags. The <FONT> attributes include the COLOR, FACE, and SIZE, attributes for altering the type on a case-by-case basis. The <BODY> tag includes the ALINK, BACKGROUND, BGCOLOR, and VLINK attributes for page-level body style.

These two tags do not have the flexibility or extensive list of properties that style sheets have to offer. However, you can use these tags with external or embedded style sheets for specific style needs.

Setting a Good Example: Sample Style Sheets

In the preceding sections, we have described all the components of style sheets, but haven't really shown you a complete one yet. The best examples are those that actually work, so we include the following examples to show you some real-world applications of style sheets.

Back when we were learning HTML (when there were two whole books on the market to help us out), we learned by doing and by imitating others. The View Source command was the key to finding out how other people used HTML to create pages. Now, so many pages are created on-the-fly from databases or use complicated scripting that learning from other people's work isn't so easy anymore. When you view the source code of these pages, you will find quite a bit of code but very little HTML, if any at all. That makes it difficult to learn from other people's work.

When you create style sheets, taking what already works and then modifying it to fit your needs is always easier than starting from scratch, especially when the technology is new. Because so many style sheets are external (and the files not available to the world at large), in this section we include three separate style sheets, each with a slightly different style implementation, to give you a place to start.

You can use any of the elements in these sheets to build your own style sheet. Mix and match and modify to your heart's content. Remember, practice makes perfect. See the "Finding More Style Sheet Information" section for a rundown on what browsers support style sheets so that you can check your work and see whether you've accomplished what you set out to do.

News.com

This popular news site, run by the folks at C|Net, makes use of many different style techniques, including embedded style and tag style. This Web site's home page uses an embedded style sheet (see Listing 4-1) to establish parameters for the various types of information included in the page. The page itself a good example of how to combine scripting, embedded tables, and style sheets to create one great page.

We suggest that you visit the News.com page (found at http://www.news.com/) and view its source code to see the exceptional work. The code is clean, correct, well-written, and uses the best combination of HTML tags to combine several types of information into one coherent page. The content of the page changes daily, but the style sheet remains the same — an excellent example of how to use style sheets for pages that have frequently changing content. With styles already defined, all you have to do is update this page daily by replacing the actual information — the styles on the page remain consistent.

Listing 4-1	The C/Net Style Sheet

```
<STYLE>
<!@hy
.headline      {font-family: Arial;
   font-size: 12pt;
   font-weight: bold;
   text-decoration: none;
   line-height: 100%;
   color: black
                     }

.headline2   {font-family: Arial;
   font-size: 11pt;
   font-weight: bold;
   text-decoration: none;
   line-height: 100%;
   color: black
                     }

.newsheadline     {font-family: Arial Black;
   font-size: 18pt;
   font-weight: normal;
   text-decoration: none;
   line-height: 100%;
   color: black
                     }
```

```
.shorttakes     {font-family: Arial;
   font-size: 9pt;
   font-weight: medium;
   text-decoration: none;
   margin-left: 4pt;
   margin-right: 4pt;
   line-height: 12pt;
   color: black
                    }

.shorttakesbold    {font-family: Arial;
   font-size: 9pt;
   font-weight: bold;
   text-decoration: none;
   margin-left: 4pt;
   margin-right: 4pt;
   line-height: 12pt;
   color: black
                    }

.text       {font-family: Times;
   font-size: 12pt;
   font-weight: normal;
   text-decoration: none;
   line-height: 13pt;
   color: black
                    }

.date       {font-family: Arial;
   font-size: 9pt;
   font-weight: medium;
   text-decoration: none;
   line-height: 11pt;
   color: black
                    }

.byline       {font-family: Arial;
   font-size: 9pt;
   font-weight: medium;
   text-decoration: none;
   line-height: 11pt;
```

(continued)

(continued)

```
        color: black
                    }

.menu        {font-family: Times;
    font-size: 12pt;
    font-weight: normal;
    text-decoration: none;
    line-height: 14pt;
    color: black
                    }

.services    {font-family: Times;
    font-size: 9pt;
    font-weight: normal;
    text-decoration: none;
    line-height: 14pt;
    color: black
                    }

.attribution    {font-family: Arial;
    font-size: 9pt;
    font-weight: medium;
    text-decoration: none;
    line-height: 11pt;
    font-style: italic;
    color: black
                    }

.quote       {font-family: Arial;
    font-size: 9pt;
    font-weight: bold;
    text-decoration: none;
    line-height: 10pt;
    color: black
                    }

.search      {font-family: Arial;
    font-size: 9pt;
    font-weight: medium;
    text-decoration: none;
    line-height: 16pt;
    color: black
                    }
```

```
.navbar        {font-family: Times News Roman;
    font-size: 10pt;
    font-weight: medium;
    line-height: 14pt;
    color: black
                        }

.navbar2    {font-family: Times News Roman;
    font-size: 7pt;
    font-weight: medium;
    line-height: 14pt;
    color: black
                        }

.jointext    {font-family: Arial;
    font-size: 10pt;
    font-weight: bold;
    text-decoration: none;
    line-height: 12pt;
    color: green
                        }

A:visited    {color: green;
                        }

A:link    {color: blue;
                        }

@hy>
</STYLE>
```

Rather than alter existing HTML tags, this style sheet creates new style categories based on the type of information being displayed, whether it's a byline, attribution, a shorttake, or any of the other defined styles. In the following HTML excerpt from the same page, the shorttakes style is referenced using the <SPAN> tag and the CLASS attribute, and then modified using the <FONT> tag.

```
<SPAN CLASS="shorttakes">

<FONT FACE="Arial" SIZE="-1">
NEWS.COM readers say free speech must be protected.

<A HREF="/SpecialFeatures/0,5,10190,00.html">Click here</A>
            for full results.
```

(continued)

(continued)

```
<P>

</SPAN>

</FONT>
```

This code is a perfect example of using an embedded style sheet and a style tag together to implement a global style and then modifying it slightly to meet the needs of the page. The page has several different types of information, including headlines, shorttakes, and other specific content. The style sheets create a different style for each kind of information, providing the Webmaster with a quick, easy, and consistent way of presenting the information.

The Alertbox

The Alertbox is a semi-monthly article about the usability of the Web. The article is written by Jakob Nielsen, an engineer with SunSoft, the software division of Sun Microsystems. The Web page itself, located at http://www.useit.com/alertbox/, references an external style sheet called useit_style.css using the <LINK> tag in this bit of code:

```
<LINK TITLE="Useit House Style" REL=STYLESHEET HREF="/
      useit_style.css" TYPE="text/css">
```

View the page source to see this link for yourself, it's the first <LINK> tag after the <META> information. We dug around a bit and found the actual style sheet useit_style.css so you can have a good look at its innards (refer to Listing 4-2).

Listing 4-2	The Alertbox Style Sheet

```
BODY     {font-family: "'Times New Roman', Georgia, Times,
            'New York', serif" ;
   background: white;
   color: black;
                 }

CODE     {font-family: "'Courier New', Courier, Monaco,
            monospace" ;
                 }

SMALL    {font-family: "Verdana, 'Lucida Sans', Arial,
            Helvetica,
```

```
            Geneva, sans-serif" ;
                    }

HR              {color: gray ;
                    }

.navbar     {font-size: 100%;
    font-family: "Verdana, 'Lucida Sans', Arial, Helvetica,
            Geneva, sans-serif";
    background: #FFFF66 ;
                    }

.notrecommended {color: #666666 ;
                    }

.deemphasized {color: #666666 ;
                    }

TABLE    {font-size: 90% ;
    font-family: "Verdana, 'Lucida Sans', Arial, Helvetica,
            Geneva, sans-serif" ;
                    }

TABLE.densetable {font-size: 80% ;
                    }

TR.summaryrow { font-size: 90%;
    background: #00FFFF ;
                    }

CAPTION {font-size: 100% ;
                    }

.embeddedfloat {float: right; margin-left: 3em
                    }

H1, H2, H3, H4, H5, H6 {font-family: "Verdana, 'Lucida
            Sans', Arial,
    Helvetica, Geneva, sans-serif" ;
                    }

UL.referencelist, .footnote {margin-left: 4em;
    text-indent: -4em ;
    font-size: 83%;
    font-family: "Verdana, 'Lucida Sans', Arial, Helvetica,
            Geneva, sans-serif";
```

(continued)

(continued)

```
    list-style: none ;
                    }

A:link, .simulatedlink {color: blue ;
                    }

A:visited    {color: purple ;
                    }

A:active    {color: aqua ;
                    }

A.notrecommended:link {color: #6666FF ;
                    }

A.notrecommended:visited {color: #CC66CC ;
                    }

A.deemphasized:link {color: #6666FF ;
                    }

A.deemphasized:visited {color: #CC66CC ;
                    }

.overline {font-family: "Verdana, 'Lucida Sans', Arial,
            Helvetica,
    Geneva, sans-serif";
    margin-bottom: -2ex ;
                    }

.updatecomment {font-size: 100%;
    background: #00FFFF ;
                    }

.outsidecomment {font-size: 100%;
    background: #E9E9E9 ;
                    }
```

The preceding style sheet uses a combination of altered standard tags such as `<CODE>`, `<SMALL>`, and `<CAPTION>`, as well as several specific styles that include `navbar`, `notrecommended`, and `embeddedfloat`. The navigation bar is really a table with the assigned style class, as this bit of markup shows:

```
<TABLE BGCOLOR=FFFF66 BORDER=1 COLS=1 WIDTH="100%"↩
            CLASS=navbar>
```

To find out more about tables, be sure to read Chapter 2.

The page also incorporates tag-based styles (those that use attributes such as `BGCOLOR` and `FONT` to define style) and tags defined in the style sheet that work together, as shown in this code snippet:

```
<FONT FACE="Verdana, Lucida Sans, Arial, Helvetica, Geneva,
        sans-serif">

<SMALL>

How you can subscribe and
<A HREF="subscribe.html">get update notifications</A>
when a new Alertbox goes online

</SMALL>

</FONT>
```

`<FONT FACE="Verdana, Lucida Sans, Arial, Helvetica, Geneva, sans-serif">`, a standard HTML tag and attribute, supplies the font face, and `<SMALL>`, which was redefined in the referenced style sheet, changes the size of the text. This example shows how a tag-based style and a style defined by a style sheet can work together to create a combination style for a text block.

You can define and combine styles in many different ways. Planning your page layout and style sheets before actually implementing them is important. In the preceding example, the designer could have redefined the `<TABLE>` tag to meet the `navbar` specifications, rather than defining `navbar` and applying it to the `<TABLE>` tag. However, he would have to create a separate style specification each time he wanted to create a new table that wasn't a navigation bar. Better to leave a much-used tag alone and create classes to use when the standard style just won't do.

The Richmond Review

This literary magazine from the UK is an entirely Web-based publication. Even though it is not distributed in print, the magazine must still maintain the same consistency and standards to which print publications adhere. To maintain this consistency, the *Richmond Review* uses external style sheets, as well as embedded style sheets. Point your browser at this URL to visit the *Richmond Review*:

```
http://www.demon.co.uk/review/
```

Volume II, Issue #4 was the current edition posted to the site when we wrote this chapter. But regardless of the content, the external style sheet remains the same from issue to issue. View the source code and again you see the inevitable ⟨LINK⟩ tag, referencing the governing style sheet (style0.css in this case). The HTML code looks like this:

```
<LINK REL=STYLESHEET TYPE="text/css" HREF="style0.css"⟳
            TITLE="style0">
```

Once again, we tracked down the actual style sheet; Listing 4-3 shows what we found.

Listing 4-3	The Richmond Review Style Sheet

```
BODY       { font-family: "Times New Roman";
               background: white;
               color: black;
               border: black;
               margin-left: 10%;
               margin-right: 10%
               }

DIV.header       { color: purple;
                   font-family: "Arial";
                   font-size: 85%;
                   }

DIV.content      { font-family: "Times New Roman";
                   color: black;
                   font-size: 100%;
                   }

DIV.footer       { color: purple;
                   font-family: "Arial";
                   font-size: 85%
                   }

DIV.footer A:link { font-family: "Arial";
                    font-size: 85%
                    }

CITE         { font-weight: bold }

HR           { color: green
                   }
```

```
HR.sub      { color: navy
                    }


A:link      { color: navy;
                    font-weight: extra-bold
                    }

A:visited      { color: maroon;
                    font-weight: bold
                    }

A:active    { color: red;
                    font-weight: light
                    }


H2             { align: center;
                    color: teal;
                    font-family: "Arial";
                    font-size: 120%
                    }

H3             { align: center;
                    color: teal;
                    font-family: "Arial";
                    font-size: 110%
                    }

SPAN.mailto      { color: green
                    }

SPAN.isbn         { font-weight: bold
                    }
```

In Listing 4-3, you see several classes defined for the same tag, such as the DIV.header, DIV.content, and DIV.footer, or the SPAN.mailto and the SPAN.isbn classes. These classes are all referenced in various places within the actual HTML document. The header class is used right after the </HEAD> tag to begin the document:

```
<HEAD>

<DIV CLASS=header>

<BODY>
```

(continued)

(continued)

```
<H1 ALIGN=CENTER>

<IMG SRC="images/banner.gif" WIDTH="460" HEIGHT="50"
   ALT="The Richmond Review"></H1>

<H2 ALIGN=CENTER>
Vol. II, Issue #4

</H2>

<P>

</DIV>
```

The footer class ends the document and contains document and author information:

```
<DIV CLASS=footer>

<HR>

<P ALIGN=CENTER>

<A HREF="features/index.html">Features</A> |

<A HREF="library/index.html">Library</A> |

<A HREF="reviews.html">Reviews</A> |

<A HREF="scripts/search.html">Explore</A> |

<A HREF="rattler.html">RattleBag</A> |

<A HREF="http://www.bookpages.co.uk/twist/twist.plx?
   form=home.htx&SID=9">Bookshop</A> |

<A HREF="whoweare.html">WhoWeAre</A>

<P ALIGN=CENTER>

<CITE>The Richmond Review</CITE>
```

```
<P>

</DIV>
```

The externally referenced style sheet is not the only source of style information this page draws upon. Embedded style information is also included with
`<STYLE>` markup within the `<HEAD>` tags.

```
<STYLE TYPE="text/css">

<!@hy        @import url(style0.css);

H1 { color: blue }

BODY { background: white } @hy>

</STYLE>
```

Notice that the externally referenced style sheet has also been imported into
the `<STYLE>` tag, so all the information contained in the external style sheet
is effectively contained in this embedded style sheet, even though it is not
listed line-by-line. The `H1` and `BODY` styles have been added to the style
sheet for this page only. The `BODY` background specification is redundant
because it is also included in the imported style sheet, but the `H1` information is new and adds to the imported specification.

This *Richmond Review* Web page shows how embedded and external style
sheets can work together to create a consistent look and feel for a group of
pages, but still retain page-level control. The way style sheets have been
created, you are not forced to pick one way or the other, but can utilize all
three methods for defining styles in your pages.

Finding More Style Sheet Information

The examples and preceding style syntax and linking sections give you solid
information on how to create and implement style sheets in your pages.
Many other Web resources contain information and links that you may find
useful as you create your own style sheets. One useful site is the Web Design
Group's Cascading Style Sheets Guide, which provides a tutorial and in-
depth discussion of all aspects of style sheet design and implementation.
They also have a great HTML tutorial that we have bookmarked. Here's
the URL:

```
http://www.htmlhelp.com/reference/css/
```

As always, we can't overemphasize how useful the World Wide Web Consortium site is. For good measure, here is the URL one more time:

```
http://www.w3.org/pub/WWW/Style/
```

That's it for style sheets, as if it wasn't enough. After you create your first style sheet, the rest will be easy. The current full-release versions of Netscape and Internet Explorer support some parts of style sheets but not all. The newest versions, 4.0 for both, which are still in beta, will have full style sheet support, and you'll be seeing style sheets more and more on the Web. Be one of the pioneers and add them to your site today.

Chapter 5

Of Applets, Scripts, and Other Extensions

· ·

In This Chapter

▶ Including Java applets in Web pages

▶ Discovering the myriad benefits of `<EMBED>` markup

▶ Understanding the emerging `<OBJECT>` tag

▶ Considering some closing comments about `<EMBED>`

· ·

A great deal of the Web's explosive appeal rests on its graphical capacities. Basic text and images are inherently static; even so, Web users expect the same kinds of interactivity they get from CD-ROMs and Playstation games. Webmasters want to include more than plain HTML-formatted information and GIFs in their pages. Audio, video, Java, scripts, and more satisfy both users and developers, but only the latest versions of HTML can support true inclusion of non-HTTP data (other than HTML) within Web pages.

When Sun created Java, it had to find a way to embed applets directly within HTML files. Its answer was the `<APPLET>` tag, used in conjunction with `<PARAM>` to pass document-specific variables to an applet. But the first attempt to include objects of any kind in Web pages was Netscape's `<EMBED>` tag. `<EMBED>` supports Director film strips (`DIR` files) as well as QuickTime movies, audio files, and VRML worlds. The `<OBJECT>` tag will eventually replace the `<EMBED>` tag, but `<OBJECT>` has yet to gain wide browser support. This chapter takes a look at each of these tags and their attributes, how to include them in HTML, and the role each plays in Web development.

Caffeinating Your Pages: The <APPLET> and <PARM> Tags

The <APPLET> tag is present in HTML 3.2 to make the inclusion of Java possible. This tag's attributes allow you to define an applet's path, the area of the screen it should use, its alignment, and alternative text for non-Java-compatible browsers or those who have Java turned off. We also cover additional scripting alternatives in Chapter 11.

The applet tag's syntax is:

```
<APPLET>Alternative Text</APPLET>
```

You probably expect this tag to be a singleton because it simply calls an applet, but it is a tag pair because the text non-Java browsers see is contained within the tags. However, you can't use just any markup within the <APPLET> ... </APPLET> tags: The <PARM> tag provides information to the applet itself. Text contained within the applet tags is rendered as regular text. You can also use the ALT= attribute within the tag to define alternative text.

Applet attributes

Several attributes are at your disposal to control the size and placement of the applet within your pages:

✔ ALIGN=("LEFT"|"RIGHT"|"TOP"|"MIDDLE"|"BOTTOM")

ALIGN defines how the applet is justified within the document relative to the page and text. The following is the syntax for this attribute:

```
<APPLET ALIGN="RIGHT"> Alternative Text </APPLET>
```

✔ CODE="text"

Use the CODE attribute to specify the applet's name. The browser assumes that the applet is located in the same directory as the HTML pages. If it isn't, you need to use the CODEBASE attribute, which is explained in the next bullet.

```
<APPLET ALIGN="RIGHT" CODE="myapplet">
  Alternative Text </APPLET>
```

✔ CODEBASE="text"

The CODEBASE attribute defines the full path to the directory that the applet specified by the CODE attribute resides in. The following shows how to add this attribute to the example:

```
<APPLET ALIGN="RIGHT" CODE="myapplet"
CODEBASE="web/applets/> Alternative Text </APPLET>
```

✔ DOWNLOAD="number"

The DOWNLOAD attribute specifies the order an applet is downloaded in if more than one applet is on a page. The following shows how to add this attribute to the example:

```
<APPLET ALIGN="RIGHT" CODE="myapplet"
CODEBASE="web/applets/ DOWNLOAD="2">
Alternative Text </APPLET>
```

✔ HEIGHT="number"

The HEIGHT attribute defines the applet's height in pixels. The following shows how to add this attribute to the example:

```
<APPLET ALIGN="RIGHT" CODE="myapplet"
CODEBASE="web/applets/ DOWNLOAD="2" HEIGHT="250">
Alternative Text </APPLET>
```

✔ HSPACE="number"

The HSPACE attribute specifies horizontal white space on either side of an applet in pixels. The following shows how to add this attribute to the example:

```
<APPLET ALIGN="RIGHT" CODE="myapplet"
CODEBASE="web/applets/ DOWNLOAD="2" HEIGHT="250"
HSPACE="10"> Alternative Text </APPLET>
```

✔ VSPACE="number"

The VSPACE attibute specifies vertical white space above and below an applet in pixels. The following shows how to add this attribute to the example:

```
<APPLET ALIGN="RIGHT" CODE="myapplet"
CODEBASE="web/applets/ DOWNLOAD="2" HEIGHT="250"
HSPACE="10" VSPACE="10" > Alternative Text </APPLET>
```

✔ WIDTH="number"

The WIDTH attribute defines the applet's width in pixels. The following shows how to add this attribute to the example:

```
<APPLET ALIGN="RIGHT" CODE="myapplet"
CODEBASE="web/applets/ DOWNLOAD="2" HEIGHT="250"
HSPACE="10" VSPACE="10" WIDTH="175" >
Alternative Text </APPLET>
```

As the example grew, it specified more and more information related to the applet's source and its placement. The final tags and contents call an applet named myapplet from the web/applets directory that is 250 pixels high and 175 pixels wide, has horizontal and vertical white space of 10 pixels, and whose alternative text is Alternative Text. Wow, that's quite a bit of information, and it's all rendered neatly in HTML.

Adding parameters to applets

Often developers want to use an applet on many pages and have the applet draw on values specific to each page. This approach allows them to leverage an applet in many ways without having to completely recode it each time. To accomplish this task, page-specific information is contained in the <PARAM> tag. A named variable is passed from the <PARAM> tag to the applet after that applet is downloaded. The <PARAM> tag must be contained within the <APPLET> tags that define the applet to which it passes information. You can pass multiple parameters to any given applet using multiple <PARAM> tags.

The <PARAM> syntax looks like this:

```
<APPLET ALIGN="RIGHT" CODE="myapplet"
CODEBASE="web/applets/ DOWNLOAD="2" HEIGHT="250"
HSPACE="10" VSPACE="10" WIDTH="175">
<PARAM NAME=eyes VALUE="blue">
<PARAM NAME=hair VALUE="red">
Alternative Text </APPLET>
```

The NAME attribute matches a variable name within the applet itself and the VALUE attribute provides the document specific value for that variable. The inclusion of applet and parameter information within a tag is simple, even if creating applets isn't.

About <EMBED>

The <EMBED> tag describes plugins in HTML pages in much the same way that the <IMG> tag describes images. The <EMBED> tag lets you embed different kinds of documents of varying data types into HTML documents by showing the browser where special content should appear. When a capable browser (such as Netscape 3.0) encounters the <EMBED> tag, it knows that the material requires a plugin, and it loads whatever plugin is indicated by the file's extension and its corresponding MIME type.

The <EMBED> tag also behaves like the <IMG> tag in terms of static graphic placement on a Web page, especially when it's used in conjunction with Netscape's <IMG> tag extensions — namely, WIDTH and HEIGHT. <EMBED> can take arbitrary attributes. Like the <IMG> tag, the <EMBED> tag can be placed inside other HTML tags, such as tables.

EMBED has several advantages over other extensions. Because <EMBED> doesn't restrict itself to a limited class of media handlers or types, it allows portable compound document markup, as well as modular design of user agents. Proposed extensions, such as <APPLET> and <FIG>, are more restrictive than <EMBED>, especially because extensible user agents are becoming the norm. Unlike those other two tags, <EMBED> doesn't constrain HTML to any particular set of specialized functions.

Because <EMBED> is a container element, it also offers rich alternative text with links and images. <EMBED> provides excellent extensibility as well and encourages structured enhancement of SGML content models rather than dependence on the proliferation of attributes for individual tags. The backward compatibility between <EMBED> and <IMG> is also a strong feature, as this example demonstrates:

```
<EMBED SRC="movie.mpg">
<IMG SRC="movie.001.jpg"> <!-- first frame -->
</EMBED>
```

Even if a user agent doesn't know to react to the <EMBED> tag or doesn't have a video MPEG handler, the movie's initial frame still shows.

From the point of view of compound document architecture, <EMBED> is useful because it:

- Conditionally creates a presentation resource as a subordinate in the presentation hierarchy below the presentation of whatever HTML entity contains the <EMBED> element.
- Declares a link for which the tail anchor's target implicitly uses the newly created presentation resource. This link creates a direct mechanism to instruct the browser where to find the resource and how to display it.

The World Wide Web Consortium's proposal to include <EMBED> in HTML 3.0 argues that <EMBED> is sufficiently "broad and intuitive" to define generic embedding. The proposal also states that <EMBED> has the potential to reduce implementation-dependent markup. This possible reduction makes <EMBED> very attractive for multimedia content developers.

HTML <EMBED> Markup

The `<EMBED>` link is activated as soon as an HTML entity's parent presentation is made; in English, this means that after the document where the `<EMBED>` tag occurs is displayed, the browser follows the link to the embedded resource. If that link somehow fails or the embedded content can't be created, then the `<EMBED>.BODY` element's content must be rendered instead of the `<EMBED>` element itself.

Netscape's initial implementation of `<EMBED>` was as an empty element, not as a container. Although this implementation results in forward-compatibility problems, the content model for `<EMBED>.BODY` permits error recovery to occur after the first paragraph break, as long as the `</EMBED>` closing tag is omitted.

In Netscape's initial implementation, arbitrary attributes are employed to pass parameters. You can use a combination such as the following for compatibility in the interim (but be aware that it's not legal SGML!):

```
<EMBED SRC="sample.app" ALT="simple alt text"
    FOO="3" BAR=9>
<PARAM NAME="foo" VALUE=3> <PARAM NAME="bar"
    VALUE=9>
</EMBED>
```

Because plugin options vary, the syntax for the `<EMBED>` tag must also vary according to the plugin employed. This variability allows particular input requirements for parameters as well as plugin behavior and content, to condition how the content is displayed.

For information on particular plugins, you are well-advised to investigate their individual characteristics. A good place to start is the Netscape plugins page, which you can find at:

```
http://www.netscape.com/comprod/products/navigator⊃
                /version_2.0/plugins/plugin_download.html
```

<EMBED>'s default attributes

`<EMBED>` takes three default attributes:

- SRC="text"

    The SRC attribute specifies the source document's URL, as in the following example:

    ```
    <EMBED SRC="movie.mov">
    ```

✔ HEIGHT="number"

The HEIGHT attribute defines the object's height in pixels, as in the following example:

```
<EMBED SRC="movie.mov" HEIGHT="150">
```

✔ WIDTH="number"

The WIDTH attribute defines the object's width in pixels, as in the following example:

```
<EMBED SRC="movie.mov" HEIGHT="150"
WIDTH="150">
```

<EMBED>'s other attributes

In addition to the three default attributes, <EMBED> can contain optional parameters in the following format:

```
PARAMETER_NAME=<PARAMETER_VALUE>
```

These parameters can be sent to the plugin that handles the embedded data type. Parameters are specific to each plugin and no limit exists on how many parameters can be passed into a plugin. Here are some examples of parameters:

```
CONTROLS=FALSE
PLAY_LOOP=TRUE
```

Some additional <EMBED> attributes include (remember, this list isn't exhaustive):

```
PARAMS; TITLE, URN, REL, REV; ACCEPT, ACCEPT-CHARSET
ACCEPT-ENCODING; ALIGN, HSPACE, VSPACE, FLOWTO
```

<NOEMBED>

If you want to be loved by the masses, use Netscape's <NOEMBED> tag. Using <NOEMBED> lets you include HTML statements that appear only in browsers that do not support plugins. Using <NOEMBED> is nice because it lets you create HTML pages enhanced for browsers that do support plugins, but that also work for browsers that don't.

If Netscape encounters a `<NOEMBED>` tag, it ignores everything from that point until the `</NOEMBED>` tag. Most other browsers ignore both the `<NOEMBED>` and `</NOEMBED>` and execute the HTML contained between the two. The upcoming "Shockwave for Director" section shows how you can use `<NOEMBED>` for a savvy work-around.

Here's `<NOEMBED>`'s syntax:

```
<NOEMBED> HTML to be ignored </NOEMBED>
```

And here's an example (HTML for both a plugin and a helper application):

```
<EMBED SRC="sample1.rpm" WIDTH="250" HEIGHT="150">
<NOEMBED> <A SRC="sample1.ram">Play the audio!
</A></NOEMBED>
```

For all the details on the `<NOEMBED>` tag, try the Netscape Search engine, available through this URL:

```
http://home.mcom.com/
```

General examples of <EMBED> tag markup

The following code shows a couple of illustrations of how the `<EMBED>` tag is used based on a popular video animation format (`MOV`) and on an even more popular interactive game. In the following example, the `<EMBED>` tag is used to size a window for video playback:

```
<EMBED SRC="CSMovie.mov" WIDTH="150" HEIGHT="250"
    CONTROLS="TRUE">
```

In the following example, `<EMBED>` is used to size a window for game playing:

```
<EMBED SRC="DoomGame.ids" WIDTH="400" HEIGHT="300"
    SPEED="SLOW" LEVEL="12">
```

Specific examples of <EMBED> tag markup

The following sections explore the syntax for some of the most popular plugins. These plugins include Macromedia Shockwave for Director, RealAudio, and ViewMovie.

Shockwave for Director

Here's the standard `<EMBED>` syntax for Shockwave for Director movies:

```
<EMBED WIDTH="x" HEIGHT="y" SRC="myfile">
<EMBED SRC="path/filename.ext" WIDTH="n" HEIGHT="n"
    TEXTFOCUS="focus">
```

To use the `<EMBED>` tag to plant a Shockwave for Director movie on an HTML page, substitute the stage height in pixels for y, the stage width in pixels for x, and the file name or URL in quotation marks after `SRC`.

A super Shockwave work-around

You may need to use a few work-arounds to successfully play Shockwave content. A particular work-around, courtesy of the Macromedia development staff, tailors itself to whatever kind of browser it encounters. For Shockwave- and Java-enabled browsers, the Macromedia work-around for Netscape 3.0 does the following:

- ✔ Reveals the `<EMBED>` tag so that a Shockwave movie appears if the plugin is loaded; a broken icon appears if the plugin isn't loaded.
- ✔ Hides the `<NOEMBED>` block so that the "consolation HTML" shown to nonenabled browsers doesn't appear.

If you're using a browser other than Netscape 3.0 — that is, one that cannot handle Shockwave and Java plugins — this work-around enables your users to skip the "broken graphic" icon they would otherwise see whenever they encounter Shockwave content. In this case, the work-around works its magic like this:

- ✔ It hides the `<EMBED>` tag so that a Shockwave movie can't appear.
- ✔ It reveals the `<NOEMBED>` block so that the consolation HTML appears instead.

This work-around hides `<EMBED>` inside a short routine written in JavaScript, a programming language built into Navigator 3.0. Because JavaScript routines are hidden inside HTML comment tags `<!--` and `-->`, and only Navigator 3.0 understands JavaScript; any other browser thinks that the `<EMBED>` tag is just a comment, and ignores it.

Okay, enough explanation already! Here's the work-around:

```
<SCRIPT LANGUAGE="JavaScript">
<!-- Hide this script from non-Navigator 2.0 browsers.
document.write( '<EMBED WIDTH="x" HEIGHT="y"
    SRC="myfile">' );
<!-- Done hiding from non-Navigator 2.0 browsers. -->
</SCRIPT>
```

Don't remove the comments within the tags; they are necessary for the script's proper functioning.

If you want to display an image or text in place of the "shocked" Director movie on browsers other than Netscape 2.0, use `<NOEMBED>` like this:

```
<SCRIPT LANGUAGE="JavaScript">
<!-- Hide this script from non-Navigator 2.0 browsers.
document.write( '<EMBED WIDTH="165" HEIGHT="145"
        SRC="mymovie.dcr">');
<!-- Done hiding from non-Navigator 2.0 browsers. -->
</SCRIPT>
<NOEMBED>
<IMG WIDTH=50 HEIGHT=85 SRC="mystill.jpg">
</NOEMBED>
```

If a user visits your site running a Netscape 3.0 browser, the browser executes a JavaScript routine when it encounters this markup. With the Shockwave plugin installed, the movie that we call `mymovie.dcr` in the preceding HTML code can play. If the user doesn't have the plugin, the browser displays a broken icon instead.

When a browser other than Netscape 3.0 encounters this script, its first reaction is to ignore the JavaScript routine because it thinks that the routine is a comment. When it comes across `<NOEMBED>`, it ignores that, too. However, the browser ultimately displays `mystill.jpg` because it doesn't know that it's supposed to skip over anything between `<NOEMBED>` and `</NOEMBED>`. Tricky, huh?

RealAudio

Although many options exist for use with Progressive Networks' RealAudio and the `<EMBED>` tag, the basic tag for RealAudio contains only these three attributes:

```
<EMBED SRC=source_URL WIDTH=width_value
HEIGHT=height_value>
```

The `SRC` attribute specifies the RealAudio file's URL, whereas the `HEIGHT` and `WIDTH` attributes specify the embedded component's size. URLs for plugins use the `RPM` extension rather than the normal `RAM` extension; this extension avoids backward compatibility conflicts with the RealAudio Player.

Before your Web browser can correctly identify `RPM` files, you (or your system administrator) must configure the associated MIME type. Except for this extension, files with an `RPM` extension are identical to `RAM` files.

Here's an example:

```
<EMBED SRC="sample1.rpm" WIDTH="300" HEIGHT="134">
```

That example produces the following result:

```
<SRC="sample1.rpm" WIDTH="300" HEIGHT="134">
```

For more information about RealAudio's plugin, please visit:

```
http://www.realaudio.com/
```

ViewMovie

A peculiarity is produced in Netscape 2.0, owing to the peculiar nature of QuickTime movies (and particularly the QuickTime movie controller). That is, the HEIGHT property specified in the tag must be the height of the movie itself plus 16. Sound bizarre? It may be, but this specification accounts for the size of the movie controller. So, if you want to place a 320 x 220 movie on your page, you use this markup:

```
<EMBED SRC="mymovie.mov" WIDTH="320" HEIGHT="236">
```

As of ViewMovie version 1.0a6, however, if you hide the controller without a badge, you can indicate a movie's real size (using a badge can show the controller if it's hidden). In that case, the preceding markup looks like:

```
<EMBED SRC="mymovie.mov" WIDTH="320" HEIGHT="220"
    CONTROLLER="FALSE">
```

In general, name movies with a MOV extension because that's what the plugin uses to identify files with a video/quicktime MIME type. However, if your server is configured differently (that is, if it specifies QuickTime files as QT for video/quicktime MIME type), you can use the extension your server is configured for as well.

ViewMovie Version 1.0a10 supports these attributes within the <EMBED> tag:

> AUTOPLAY
> CONTROLLER
> HREFABS
> ISMAP
> KEEPASPECTRATIO
> LOOP
> PLAYEVERYFRAME
> PLAYRATE
> PLUGINSPAGE
> QUALITY
> VOLUME

You can get more information about <EMBED> and ViewMovie from the following URL:

```
http://www.well.com/~ivanski/viewmovie ⤴
/viewmovie_info.html
```

An <EMBED> Replacement?

The <EMBED> tag will be replaced in future standards and browsers with the new and improved <OBJECT> tag. Although this tag is not yet widely supported, look for it in future implementations. Just so you're not totally clueless about the <OBJECT> tag, here's a quick overview, courtesy of *MORE HTML For Dummies*.

<OBJECT> ... </OBJECT>
Non-HTTP object

The OBJECT tag embeds a non-HTTP object, such as a sound clip, movie, script, or image — into an HTML document.

Attributes:

```
ALIGN=("LEFT"|"TEXTTOP"|"MIDDLE"|"TEXTMIDDLE"
      |"BASELINE"|"TEXTBOTTOM"|"CENTER"|"RIGHT")
```

Specifies the text alignment relative to the text and page. The alignment values are a bit different from those we discuss in earlier sections. LEFT, MIDDLE, and RIGHT flow text around the object, and TEXTTOP, TEXTMIDDLE, CENTER, and TEXTBOTTOM do not produce flowing text, only text aligned with the top, middle, center, or bottom of the object. BASELINE aligns the image with the baseline of the surrounding text. The default value is LEFT.

```
BORDER="number"
```

Indicates whether a border appears around the object and, if so, how many pixels wide it is. BORDER="0" forces no border, and BORDER="10" renders a border 10 pixels wide on all sides of the object.

```
CLASS="text"
CLASSID="URL"
```

Identifies the type of object.

```
CODEBASE="URL"
```

An object's codebase is the URL of the directory the object sits in. This attribute tells the browser where to get an object, and the DATA attribute specifies which object.

```
CODETYPE="text"
```

Identifies the object's Internet code type.

```
DATA="URL"
```

Identifies the object's source file.

```
DECLARE
```

Downloads the object but does not activate it. Use DECLARE when referencing the object later in the document or as a parameter for another object.

```
DIR=("ltr"|"rtl")
HEIGHT="number"
```

Defines the object's height in pixels.

```
HSPACE="number"
```

Provides for horizontal white space, measured in pixels, on either side of the object to set it apart from the text.

```
ID="name"
LANG="name"
NAME="text"
```

Gives the object a name that identifies it to other objects on the page.

```
NOTAB
```

Removes the object from the tabbing order.

```
SHAPES
```

Indicates that the object has shaped hotspots with URL references. Use SHAPES for client-side image maps.

```
STANDBY="text"
```

Displays specified text while the object is loading.

```
STYLE="text"
TABINDEX="number"
```

Defines the link's position in the tabbing order.

```
TITLE="text"
TYPE="text"
```

Identifies the object's Internet media type.

```
USEMAP
```

Indicates which <MAP> information stored in the document should be used with the object to create a client-side image map.

```
VSPACE="number"
```

Provides for vertical white space, measured in pixels, on the top and bottom of the object to set it apart from the text.

```
WIDTH="number"
```

Defines the object's width in pixels.

Context:

<OBJECT>...</OBJECT> is legal within the following markup tags:

```
<A>, <ADDRESS>, <B>, <BIG>, <BLOCKQUOTE>, <BODY>,
        <CAPTION>, <CENTER>, <CITE>, <CODE>, <DD>,
        <DFN>, <DIV>, <DT>, <EM>, <FIELDSET>, <FONT>,
        <FORM>, <H*>, <I>, <KBD>, <LABEL>, <LI>, BB
        <OBJECT>, <P>, <PRE>, <S>, <SAMP>, <SMALL>,
        <SPAN>, <STRONG>, <SUB>, <SUP>, <TD>,
        <TEXTFLOW>, <TH>, <TT>, <U>, <VAR>
```

You can use the following markup within <APPLET> ... </APPLET>:

```
<A>, <ADDRESS>, <APPLET>, <B>, <BASEFONT>, <BIG>,
        <BLOCKQUOTE>, <BR>, <CENTER>, <CITE>, <CODE>,
        <DFN>, <DIR>, <DIV>, <DL>, <EM>, <FIELDSET>,
        <FONT>, <FORM>, <H*>, <HR>, <I>, <IMG>, <INPUT>,
        <ISINDEX>, <KBD>, <LABEL>, <LISTING>, <MAP>,
        <MENU>, <OBJECT>, <OL>, <P>, <PARAM>, <PRE>,
        <S>, <SAMP>, <SCRIPT>, <SELECT>, <SMALL>,
        <SPAN>, <STRONG>, <STYLE>, <SUB>, <SUP>,
        <TABLE>, <TEXTAREA>, <TT>, <U>, <UL>, <VAR>,
        <XMP>
```

Suggested style/usage:

Objects extend HTML so you can include almost any type of data in a Web page. Keep in mind that older versions of most browsers do not support <OBJECT>, and the current implementation in many browsers is not stable.

<OBJECT> works much like <EMBED> but has many more attributes. For a full rundown on the future of the <OBJECT> tag, check the World Wide Web Consortium's Inserting Objects into HTML Working Draft at:

`http://www.w3.org/pub/WWW/TR/WD-object`

Getting Underneath <EMBED>

<EMBED> is a tag that enhances the Web's potential to represent graphics and other high-impact information. It lifts restrictions that you encounter with the <IMG> tag or with specific tags such as APPLET. Why? Because it tells your browser that a plugin is required, without needing to specify exactly what that plugin's functions may be.

Instead, <EMBED> allows the file extension and corresponding MIME type to make things clear. But now, it's time to leave <EMBED> behind and investigate the pleasing power of HTML forms and the CGIs that support them.

Chapter 6

Encouraging Interaction with HTML Forms

In This Chapter

▶ Understanding the limitations of forms

▶ Exploring how Cougar overcomes form limitations

▶ Making use of forms and scripting

*T*he basics of forms — text areas, radio boxes, check boxes, and selection lists — create nifty-looking user feedback forms, but today's Webmasters want more from their forms. Forms are the key to true user-Web interactivity because they are the only HTML convention that allows for user input. In this chapter, we look at some of the limitations in the markup that have prevented forms from living up to their true potential. But wait, we have good news. The new Cougar standard works hard to overcome those limitations, and it does a pretty darn good job. We walk you through the Cougar additions to forms to give you a full overview of their potential.

It's Just Not Enough: The Limitations of Forms

Forms, as you know them, are great for soliciting user feedback. If you don't believe us, check out Chapter 15 in *HTML For Dummies*, 3rd Edition. Standard forms are structured to receive user input and report it back to the Webmaster, usually after CGI or another script translates it into usable information. More advanced iterations are used for online shopping, searching, and creating user-specific pages on-the-fly. Still, these advanced forms require complicated scripting and some major HTML tweaking to make them work.

Forms markup has several inherent weaknesses that make facilitating true user interactivity difficult. A user filling out multiple forms is not really interactive; the process is more like a one-way street. The limitations of form markup (see the following list) prevent an ongoing exchange between the user and the form.

- **Form fields cannot be made read-only.** Current form markup allows users to change any information in form fields. Any information you want "frozen" in a field, such as merchandise prices or order totals, can be changed by the user unless they are forced to constantly resubmit a form to the server and work with a new form (using valuable server resources and trying a user's patience).

- **Checking values as users enter them isn't possible without submitting the form to the server.** Many forms require fields and data formats — the date in mm/dd/yy format, for example — before they can be successfully processed. Currently, the only way to check user input is to return an error page after the form has been submitted to the server and ask the user to go back to the form and change the information.

- **Markup limits form buttons to "submit" and "reset" only.** Form markup doesn't provide for more than two buttons. This restriction forces the data to be sent to the server in only one way or be canceled entirely. Multiple CGI scripts and server paths are not supported.

- **The labels associated with radio buttons and check boxes are not sensitive.** When a user clicks the label next to a radio button or check box, the state of the control does not change. To activate or deactivate a radio button or check box, the user must click the small control itself. This requirement deviates from standard software interfaces that allow a click on a label to change the state of a control.

- **Form markup does not support keyboard shortcuts.** Users have become accustomed to using hot keys to move through software interfaces, menus, and commands. You can't assign keyboard shortcuts to form fields and controls.

- **Webmasters and programmers cannot specify what type of data file to expect when a user uploads a file via a form.** Form markup allows users to submit data files via a form, but there is no way to identify the type of data the user should be sending. This limitation leaves servers open to virus corruption, as well as failed file transfers.

- **Related fields in a form cannot be marked as a group.** Often, you can break the fields within a form into related groups, such as user contact information, user comments, files requested, and so on. Currently, no way exists to mark related fields as groups, a function that would be especially useful to speech-based browsers.

✔ **Form controls cannot be made insensitive at initialization time.**
Controls, such as the Submit button and radio buttons, can be made
insensitive, based on user input or by using a script, but not until the
user submits an initial form to the server. You can't make a control
insensitive from the first appearance of a form.

Clearly, many of these missing elements would work together. The Submit
button could be made insensitive until the user enters required information
that could be verified without sending the form to the server. Or multiple
buttons would send user data through different CGI scripts, depending on
the user's goals and needs. We bet you didn't notice any of these limitations
until we pointed them out to you, but now you can think of all kinds of cool
form-based pages you could create if only you could overcome the limitations. Never fear, Cougar is nearly here.

We Shall Overcome: Cougar Forms Markup

The HTML standards committee recognized that Webmasters use forms far
beyond the capabilities of the markup, not an unfamiliar story in the world
of HTML. To make up for the limitations we list in the preceding section, a
few new attributes and even a new tag have been added to form markup.

As we write this chapter, available no-beta browsers do not support the new
Cougar additions (the primary reason you won't see any screen shots in this
chapter). However, we are confident that the next full releases of both
Netscape and Internet Explorer will have full Cougar form markup support.
However, please note that many of these new forms additions will not be
backward-compatible with earlier versions of the various browsers because
they will require scripting that older browsers do not support.

Because we introduce you to the newest additions to forms markup by way
of the list of limitations of the current markup, we discuss each new element
in the context of the limitation it overcomes.

Rendering text areas read-only

We can think of at least a dozen instances where a read-only input field
would be extremely useful in a form: the merchandise pricing and totals we
mention earlier in the chapter, user information carried over from another
form, the current date and time, and many more. To create read-only text
fields, the Cougar specification includes the READONLY attribute. Used only
with the TEXT and PASSWORD input types and the TEXTAREA elements, this
attribute prohibits the user from changing or adding text to the field.
However, the information in the field is still valid and returned to the server
when the form is submitted.

The actual HTML for a read-only field looks like this:

```
<INPUT NAME="product_price" TYPE="TEXT" SIZE="10"
        MAXLENGTH="10" READONLY>
```

You can change the read-only status of any given field by using an associated script.

Checking values without the server

Control over the type of data users enter into your form fields is limited. You can let them know the format the data should be in and put an identifier of some type next to required fields; but in reality, neither they nor you will know if they have entered the required data correctly until the form reaches the server. If the data is incorrect, you have to route users back to the form they just filled out with instructions on which fields to correct.

A new set of attributes that work in conjunction with scripts can check the information that a user enters into a form without sending the form to the server. This innovation allows you to set flags and warn users when their data is incorrect or missing. They can correct their mistakes and add any missing data before they submit the form to the server the first time. This capability conserves valuable server resources and helps reduce user frustration. The new attributes include the following:

- ONCHANGE calls a script when the control changes (a user enters text in a field, selects a button, and so on).
- ONCLICK calls a script when the control is clicked.
- ONFOCUS calls a script when the control becomes the focus of the browser.
- ONBLUR calls a script when the control loses the browser's focus and the value changes.
- ONSELECT calls a script when the control is selected.

The scripts associated with each attribute can do much more than check the data a user enters. They can call other HTML pages, load non-HTML objects, and fill out other portions of the form based on the user's input.

Two buttons are not enough

Submit and Reset are nice and all, but sometimes you need another button or two to process form data. You can devise script work-arounds to overcome this limitation, but with the advent of the <BUTTON>, a work-around is unnecessary. `<BUTTON> ... </BUTTON>` is a container that can include text, graphics, and any other noninteractive content. This element is designed to work with the `ONCLICK`, `ONFOCUS`, and `ONBLUR` attributes to call a script when the button is selected.

You can create a new-fangled button with an image and formatted text using HTML similar to the following:

```
<BUTTON>
    <IMG SRC="index.gif" ALIGN="BOTTOM">
    <STRONG>Click this button to create an index of pages on
            our site related to the interests you described
            in the form above.</STRONG>
</BUTTON>
```

Clicking in the general vicinity: hot labels

Nothing is more frustrating than missing a radio button or check box because your click wasn't right on the mark. Again, standard user interfaces have made users accustomed to certain things, and hot labels are one of them. A click on a label in most user interfaces causes the associated button or box to be selected or deselected. Unfortunately, this functionality is missing from earlier versions of forms markup.

Cougar provides for this with the `<LABEL> ... </LABEL>` tag. Previously, labels for form elements were just text sitting near the control but not directly associated with it. `<LABEL>` creates a clear association between the label and the control. This association ties the label text to the control, allowing the label to activate the control in the same way clicking the control would. Pretty cool as far as we're concerned.

Two types of label markup exist — implicit and explicit. Implicit labels contain the control with which they are associated within the tag pair, while explicit labels identify the control they are associated with but do not contain it. This arrangement allows labels and controls to be separated in tables and columns. The difference between the two becomes abundantly clear when you look at them together.

Markup for an implicit label:

```
<FORM>
<LABEL>User Identification Number
    <INPUT TYPE="TEXT" NAME="IDNUMBER">
</LABEL>
</FORM>
```

Markup for an explicit label:

```
<TABLE>
<TR>
  <TD><LABEL FOR="USERID">User Identification Number
          </LABEL>
  <TD><INPUT TYPE="TEXT" NAME="IDNUMBER" ID="USERID">
</TR>
</TABLE>
```

In the explicit example, you see two new attributes the implicit example doesn't show. The FOR attribute in the <LABEL> tag identifies the control the label is associated with, and the ID attribute in the <INPUT> tag assigns that identification to the control.

Explicit associations allow you to separate labels and their associated controls, giving you more control and flexibility in your design. But you have two new attributes to keep track of for each control and label you create. If the strings in the FOR and ID attributes do not match, the label breaks and leaves you with an incomplete form.

Getting there faster: keyboard shortcuts

Users are accustomed to navigating a user interface with the Alt (PCs) or Command (Macs) key in combination with one or more keys (hot keys). This method makes accessing familiar and common commands quick and easy. Moving through an interface is easier if the user can access fields via a series of keystrokes rather than having to go from mouse to keyboard and back again. Current forms markup does not include this functionality, but Cougar forms markup does.

You can add the ACCESSKEY attribute to any <LABEL> tag to create a hot key for the element to which the label is associated. The markup looks something like this:

```
<FORM>
<LABEL ACCESSKEY="I"> User Identification Number
  <INPUT TYPE="TEXT" NAME="IDNUMBER">
</LABEL>
</FORM>
```

The commands ALT+I or COMMAND+I automatically move the cursor to this User ID text field. The access key is case-insensitive, and only one character can be specified to act as the hot key. Basically, you are limited to 26 hot keys per form; if you need more than that number, break your form into multiple forms to make life a little easier for your users.

Selective data acceptance

Many different kinds of data files move over the Web these days. Everything from straight text to fully formatted documents. Audio, video, and multimedia files are almost as common as HTML. Although forms allow you to request that a user submit a file to the server, no way exists to verify that the file they actually send matches what you requested. One harmless consequence is that their submission is incomplete, but a much more dangerous consequence occurs if a virus is accepted by your server, and you lose all your data. Although we would like to believe that everyone on the Web has everyone else's best interests at heart, this altruism isn't always so.

The ACCEPT attribute has been added to the list of attributes for the <INPUT> tag. Use this attribute to define a list of MIME type data files to be accepted by the server. Users can only submit files of the types defined on your list. For example, if users are submitting Shockwave movies as part of a creative Web interface contest, the following is the form markup to limit the data files to Shockwave movies:

```
<FORM>
<LABEL> Submit your movie
    <INPUT TYPE="CDATA" NAME="MOVIE" ACCEPT="shockwave/
            .dcr">
</LABEL>
</FORM>
```

The server refuses any data types other than Shockwave files. Note a couple of caveats here: Good virus programmers can get past even this barrier. Always scan all computers regularly for viruses. Also, some users may not understand how to create file names that agree with your MIME definition. If you are accepting limited file types, include good instructions on a help page to guide your users in preparing files that your sever will accept.

For more information on MIME types and file acceptance visit:

```
ftp://ds.internic.net/rfc/rfc1867.txt
```

Disabling form controls

On many occasions, having a form control disabled from startup would be nice. Having the Submit button disabled until required information is submitted is just one example. You can use scripts to dynamically disable a control, but you can't disable a control from the initial presentation of the form.

The DISABLE attribute was created to work with the <INPUT>, <TEXTAREA>, <SELECT>, <OPTION>, <OBJECT>, <LABEL>, and <BUTTON> elements to make any of them inactive from word one. The control appears but it isn't usable until a script changes its disabled state. Unlike the READONLY attribute, the DISABLE attribute causes the server and any associated scripts to effectively ignore any values presented by a disabled control.

The following input control is disabled:

```
<FORM>
<LABEL>User Identification Number
   <INPUT TYPE="TEXT" NAME="IDNUMBER" DISABLE>
</LABEL>
</FORM>
```

A user name field could have a script called by the ONCHANGE attribute that would enable the ID field after an acceptable user name was entered. Using this combination of attributes and scripts, only certain users could even fill out a form, much less submit it.

Forms and Scripting

Throughout this chapter, we refer again and again to scripts that can be used with the new form attributes and tags, but we don't actually show you any of those scripts. We'll be honest; scripting is programming, and this ability can't be picked up overnight. However, scripting isn't as difficult as object-oriented Java programming, and it can be mastered with a little perseverance, a bit of reading, and a bunch of practice.

In the last chapter, we gave you a good introduction to scripting and applets. Review it and its resources to find out how to make those scripts work with your forms. Chapter 11 presents a more detailed look at scripting languages and how to include scripts in your Web pages.

The World Wide Web Consortium site is also a gold mine of information on HTML and scripting. To review their materials, point your browser at:

```
http://www.w3.org/pub/WWW/TR/WD-script
```

This chapter brings us to the end of our discussion of advanced HTML. You've probably noticed that advanced HTML usually requires more than just HTML to make things click. Next, we move on to a discussion of non-HTML additions to your site. It's time to make your site sing and dance!

Part II

Beyond HTML: Extending Your Web

"ALL RIGHT, WHICH ONE OF YOU CLOWNS IS RESPONSIBLE FOR THURSDAY'S DOWN TIME?"

In this part . . .

This part introduces some wild and wonderful Web extension technologies, beginning with a discussion of helper applications and plugins in Chapter 7. Each of the four following chapters covers a different technology. In Chapter 8, we tackle Macromedia's animated Shockwave for Director and its related Afterburner tool. Next, in Chapter 9, we examine the Virtual Reality Modeling Language (VRML) that can be used to create complete, three-dimensional virtual worlds for Web access. Following that comes Chapter 10, where we jump into Sun Microsystems' exciting Java programming language and explore its potential uses on the Web. Then, in Chapter 11 we examine several of the various scripting languages that you can use to extend ordinary HTML documents with all kinds of layout controls and input widgets.

Chapter 7

Extending and Improving the Web Experience

*U*nless you've been hiding under a rock lately, you've heard about all kinds of technologies to extend the Web's capabilities. Today, you can find Web extensions for everything from audio to video, with quite a few points in between. And if the buzz in the developer community is any indication, these extensions are pretty hot stuff!

This chapter surveys the available Web extensions. It dips into underlying terminology and technology and discusses the pros and cons of extensions that aren't available to all users, including how to design them into your Web pages and how to steer your audience through (or around) them. This chapter is intended to prepare you for the next five chapters, which cover various Web extension technologies in greater detail.

If Your Browser Can't See It, Is It Really There?

Before we launch into a discussion of Web extensions, we want to remind you of a basic aspect of Web browser behavior. Please remember that the convention is for browsers to ignore markup that they can't recognize. In other words, some browsers cheerfully pass over certain Web extensions because they are unable to recognize the extensions and, therefore, are blissfully ignorant of their existence.

Throughout this part of the book, you can see how this browser behavior (that is, ignoring unrecognized extensions) is exploited by Web authors who develop content by using those extensions that rely, in part, on specialized HTML markup. You find out some clever techniques to deliver one set of materials to users whose browsers can handle special extensions and another set to those whose browsers can't.

We encourage you to provide alternate materials to users whenever possible. This extra effort ensures that you always reach the broadest audience — if only to evangelize them to adopt the new software and technologies necessary to appreciate your other work! But more importantly, this approach recognizes that not all users bring the same capabilities to the Web and doesn't try to discriminate between those who have the right stuff and those who don't.

Keep from alienating part of your audience by always providing alternate materials whenever you use an extension or some other advanced HTML feature. Whether to include alternatives is entirely up to you, but reaching out to those users who can't immediately appreciate your stunning multimedia work or your cool applications is as important as catering to those who can.

Beyond HTML . . .

As Web browsers and related technologies continue to evolve, HTML appears less and less able to handle the sophisticated display and interaction requirements that new capabilities so often foster and demand. That advancement is why we tackle two of the most important Web extension technologies in the sections that follow: *helper applications* and *plugins*. Read on to find out how these tools can open your browser up to new worlds of capability!

Assisting the browser: helper applications

A long tradition on the Web supports the linking of so-called *helper applications* to certain file types. These file types are usually identified by their extensions (for example, MOV for animated movie files and WAV for wave table audio files) or by their associated MIME types. The approach to identifying the files that need helper applications works like this:

1. When a URL points to a resource that a user has selected, the browser requests that source to be delivered.

2. The server returns the selected information with a header that indicates the MIME type for the resource. You can view this header as a form of "explicit labeling" because the server tells the browser exactly what's going on.

3. The browser looks up the MIME type in a built-in associations table. By using this table, the browser determines whether it can handle that data itself or whether it must involve another application. You can view this process as a form of "implicit labeling" because the file extension tells the browser how to handle incoming data.

When the browser requires another application to deliver a selected resource, that application is *helping* the browser. And thereby, you get the name *helper application*. One unfortunate side effect of running a helper application, however, is that a program other than a Web browser takes control of your display. After users finish with the materials delivered by the helper application, they must exit that application and explicitly return to the browser to pick up where they left off.

Hooking up with plugins

As technologies go, the helper application method is workable and not terribly inconvenient. But with the release of Netscape Navigator 2.0, Netscape introduced a more tightly integrated way to extend the browser's functionality without forcing it to surrender control to another application. This technology is called a *plugin*, and it works the way its name suggests: Instead of relinquishing control to an external application, a plugin permits third parties to write programs that extend the browser's functionality directly, while maintaining the same familiar interface and behavior. Most modern browsers support this architecture today, leaving helper applications only for unusual or complex capabilities.

The plugin architecture is also quite intelligent: Although plugins may be installed at any time (or even preconfigured with a browser in some cases), they're not actually loaded into your computer's memory until materials that require the plugin's attention arrive at the browser. This feature lets users add an arbitrary number of plugins to their browsers without causing the browsers to become bloated memory hogs.

For those of you familiar with the Macintosh, Netscape plugins work very much like the operating system extensions called *INITs* that appear as icons when a Macintosh is booting up. In much the same way, Netscape's Help subsystem provides an "About Plugins" document that you can peruse at any time to see which plugins are installed.

After Netscape relinquishes control to a plugin, that plugin does its thing within the same overall framework as the native browser. This framework enables users to interact with content and extensions without necessarily knowing that the browser is no longer running the onscreen display. Even when a plugin is active, though, the browser maintains overall control of the interface and information delivery. An added benefit suggests that an infinite number of content types and resources are theoretically available through the same window. That benefit is why most Web browser vendors now use plugins to extend their software.

The bottom line is that a Web browser no longer needs to be conceived of as, more or less, an HTML rendering service. The addition of plugin technology opens the door to all kinds of built-in services and lifts the barriers to functionality that HTML is unable to support. Although this phenomenon introduces a certain amount of disparity among Web-user communities (along the lines of those who have certain plugins versus those who lack them), plugin technology promises to add significant new and useful capabilities to the overall Web environment.

What's in Store for Your Web Pages?

Assuming that you've got a properly enabled browser, the answer to the question posed by the section heading is "Almost anything." Because plugins are usually available by download over the Internet and include their own installation programs, adding a plugin is as easy as following these steps:

1. **Grab a file.**

2. **Unpack the file's contents.**

3. **Run the proper installation program.**

This simple sequence of steps puts all kinds of interesting capabilities within your reach. Today, you can find about a dozen Netscape plugins that range from the Adobe Portable Document Format (PDF) and its Amber reader to the PaperSoft WebFX plugin for VRML. The list of available elements includes all the topics that we discuss in the next four chapters — namely, Shockwave for Director, VRML, Java, and a variety of document display engines. For a list of Netscape plugins, visit the Netscape home page at:

```
http://home.netscape.com
```

From there, click the Netscape Search icon from the image map at the bottom of the page and use *plugin* as your search term. You should find a variety of background and information documents on this subject including:

```
http://home.netscape.com/comprod/mirror/
         navcomponents_download.html
```

At this URL, you find a set of lists of all the plugins currently available for Netscape Navigator. (The list may change as Netscape introduces new versions of Navigator, so be sure to use the search engine to find the latest and greatest information.)

With the right set of plugins in place, you can use your browser to view fascinating multimedia animations, watch a variety of video formats, listen to high-fidelity audio, and more. One word of warning, however: The more complex or richer the data you seek to display, the bigger the underlying files typically are. If you up the ante on what you view, you must wait longer for the results!

Although Internet Explorer supports its own plugins, it can also support Navigator plugins, too (in a shrewd backhanded endorsement of the concept that indicates just how far Microsoft is willing to go to grab market share from Netscape). What this means in English is that you can use Navigator plugins that you may have already installed with Internet Explorer as well as "the other major browser…."

The Hottest Plugins . . .

A quick trip to the plugin list mentioned earlier in this chapter shows you that this book doesn't cover every known plugin. Instead, we choose four categories that have generated the most buzz (and have seen the most use). We cover these in detail in the next three chapters, and you can expect to discover more about:

- **Macromedia's Shockwave for Director:** A plugin that permits Director content to be delivered over the Web. Because Director is the tool of choice for game, CD-ROM, and interactive multimedia developers, the use of this plugin opens the Web up to a great deal of interesting content. Shockwave is an excellent tool for delivering new multimedia content; we cover this plugin in Chapter 8.

- **The Virtual Reality Modeling Language (VRML):** A full-fledged computer programming language designed for the creation and navigation of fully-realized three-dimensional graphical spaces called *virtual worlds*. Many pundits believe that this kind of interface and data presentation technology represents a major step from current two-dimensional graphical user interfaces to something much more intuitive and realistic. We cover VRML in Chapter 9.

✔ **Java:** An object-oriented programming language from Sun Microsystems. Java includes the capacity to run on a wide variety of computers from a single set of source code and can deliver small programs, called *applets*, to Web users on demand. Users can execute these applets on their local workstations. Not only does Java deliver client-side capability to Web users, but it also provides a technique to extend browser functionality on-the-fly! Of the four examples we look at, this one has generated the most buzz. We cover Java in Chapter 10.

In the upcoming chapters, we explain how to use plugin technologies in your Web pages. We tell you how they work, where to get them, and how to incorporate them effectively in your Web sites.

The Perils of Incompatibility

Okay, so we sound like a broken record. But remember that not everyone in your audience will be able to appreciate the work you put into content that requires a plugin. That's why we suggest alternatives where possible; we describe site and page design techniques that permit you to educate less fortunate users about the benefits of plugins and point them to the resources they can use to remedy their deficiencies (if they're so inclined and circumstances permit).

The most important thing to remember about the Web is that "content rules." Where plugins are concerned, this rule has two profound implications:

✔ **Provide multiple alternatives.** Wherever possible, don't deliver critical content in a plugin-dependent form. Plugin-dependent content keeps those members of your audience who don't have the plugin from seeing your content — the more important that content is, the more essential alternate forms become.

✔ **Provide ample warnings.** If your site includes plugin-dependent content, warn users on your home page and provide end-arounds on the pages that feature such content. The initial warning lets users know what to expect; the end-arounds provide a graceful way for disadvantaged users to skip what they can't view properly anyway.

Both techniques demonstrate a degree of concern for your entire user base. Providing alternatives and warnings shows the users that you care and provides them with pointers for dealing with plugin-dependent materials.

Designing for Extended Capability

Even those users who do have the right plugins won't always appreciate your enhanced content, unless you follow some basic rules of design and delivery. The following list gives our top recommendations for including plugin-based content on your pages:

- **Small is beautiful:** Whether you're delivering audio, video, or multimedia, bigger files take longer, and users hate to wait!

- **Give users a choice:** Don't force users to download materials if they don't want to. If you have bigger files, give the users control over whether they see them. Tell the users how big the files are and let them click a link if they choose to download.

- **Use plugin content sparingly:** Animation, video, and other dynamic formats have a great deal of sex appeal, especially for Web authors in search of excitement. Always ask yourself, "Is this material really necessary?" before using a plugin. After you're convinced (that the material is necessary), ask your beta testers, too. If the beta testers find the material superfluous, other users probably will, as well.

- **The download alternative:** If you can find a way to let users download materials for display offline, give them that option. Users may not want to wait for a download for immediate viewing; offering a self-contained alternative reaches a broader audience and lets everyone keep surfing while the file downloads in the background.

If you follow these four basic rules, you will get the most benefit from your plugin-based content. You may be tempted to stray from these rules because this stuff is so much fun, but remember that your main function is to deliver quality content to your audience!

Serving the Audience

In some cases, you can assume that your audience is homogeneous — for example, on an organizational intranet where policy dictates that everyone uses the same advanced browser. If you're offering Web pages in this environment, you can use plugin-based content with a bit more abandon than if you're serving the general public. But even then, the four principles we list in the preceding section still apply.

If you're dealing with the general public, you never know who's likely to visit your site. Because the primary goal of a Web site is to communicate with all visitors, do as much as you can to avoid excluding anyone. If you follow this simple suggestion, you can design your site to serve everyone with similar, if not identical, materials.

Trends in Web Extension Technology

As we mention at the beginning of this chapter, the plugins we introduce represent only a fraction of what's available. Our investigations have turned up hundreds of other plugins for capabilities that range from database access to local system and desktop management to a variety of stunning visualization and idea-mapping tools.

Although we don't know exactly which plugins will fit your browsing needs, you'll probably have at least several in your working environment. As usual, your best source of information in this area is the Web itself: Stay tuned to your browser vendor's "What's New" and news pages so that you find out about newly released plugins and enhanced or updated older plugins.

Although we explore some of the more mature and exciting plugins in the upcoming chapters, remember that you've by no means seen it all. Plugin technology should keep the Web an exciting place to be for some time to come!

Chapter 8

Shocking Your Web Site

● ●

In This Chapter

▶ Defining Shockwave for Director

▶ Understanding Shockwave's underpinnings

▶ Installing and using Shockwave technology

▶ Configuring your Web server for Shockwave

▶ Using Shockwave content in your Web pages

▶ Designing effective "shocked" pages

▶ Finding the top Shockwave resources online

● ●

Shockwave for Director is a technology that's paving the way for the Web to become a more interactive, multimedia-oriented arena for information exchange. Shockwave possesses the unprecedented capacity to convert a multimedia creation into an Internet-ready work without using a general-purpose programming language, such as Java, Perl, or C. The implications are significant; Shockwave enables thousands of multimedia professionals to convert content previously viewable only on CD-ROM into Internet-ready material. Shockwave has helped to change the look and feel of the Web.

With Shockwave's capabilities, text-based and static Web documents can become dynamic, multimedia works. We want you to recognize that Shockwave is not a new authoring tool for the Internet; it is a technology that enables you to deliver existing multimedia content via the Internet (that is, it's ready for inclusion in your Web pages!). All in all, Shockwave technology is appealing because it's accessible, impressive, Web-savvy, and, best of all, *free* (as long as you own Macromedia Director, that is).

A Shockwave Overview

Shockwave for Director is not a monolith; it's actually a collection of capabilities, all of which must be present to make Director movies available over the Internet. In fact, three ingredients are essential to creating and delivering Shockwave content:

> ✔ A working copy of Macromedia Director is necessary to create the content that will be converted into Shockwave format.
>
> ✔ The content developer must also obtain a copy of the Macromedia AfterBurner software to transform and compress native Director movie files into a more compact form, better-suited for Internet delivery.
>
> ✔ Users must have a Shockwave-enabled browser that can accommodate and play back Shockwave content. Currently, either Netscape Navigator or Internet Explorer 2.0 or better is necessary.

With these ingredients in place, authors can create Shockwave content, and users can appreciate their efforts.

Shockwave was developed by Macromedia, a cutting-edge multimedia company that rules the realm of digital arts and multimedia software tools. Macromedia's most important contribution to multimedia is Macromedia Director, considered to be the industry's preeminent software for authoring and animating multimedia. Not coincidentally, Shockwave supports only Director materials, used by over a quarter million multimedia professionals. Because the majority of the multimedia industry already uses Director, Shockwave claims a viable niche on the Web as well.

A few words from Macromedia Director

As authoring tools go, Macromedia Director is considered to be quite powerful. For example, Director is relatively platform-independent, which makes it pragmatic for the Internet's multiplatform demands. But please understand that Director is a large and complex program. This complexity doesn't mean that using Director is impossible, but that fully appreciating all its features and capabilities may take some time.

Director's creators based the program on a theater metaphor; its main components are a Stage, a Cast, and a Score. The Cast is where you store items for a project (the actors, as it were, which could be anything from titles to animate for credits, to graphical shapes or figures, or even sound files, that you can manipulate on the Stage). The Score is used to control what Cast members do on the Stage. The Stage itself is, of course, the arena where the multimedia is played out for the audience, your viewers.

Macromedia developed Director with accessibility in mind, but this attribute doesn't prevent Director from offering excellent expandability. The two features that make Director impressively expandable are Lingo, its scripting language, and Xobjects — external, custom files that you can program to extend the program's built-in functionality.

Doing the Lingo limbo

Lingo is a scripting language that can be used in conjunction with Shockwave when you observe certain limitations. Because Shockwave does not support linked media — basically, multimedia files that embed calls to other multimedia files within themselves — you can't use any Lingo commands that create media linkages. You certainly can create multimedia Web content with Shockwave without ever using Lingo, but you should consider using Lingo if you want more complete control over your Shockwave content (or if you enjoy working with complex programming).

If you were accustomed to working with Lingo before Shockwave hit the scene, be aware that certain Lingo commands were modified for Shockwave use. Also, you may have to remove some Lingo commands from files that you want to convert to Shockwave (this removal is particularly necessary for those commands that interlink media files or resources).

Shockwave's bright future

To further ensure Shockwave's success, Macromedia has partnered with some of the most pivotal companies in the computer industry, including Netscape, Microsoft, Silicon Graphics, and Navisoft. By agreeing to integrate Shockwave technology into their browsers, these companies have endorsed Shockwave and made it broadly accessible.

Macromedia's development of Shockwave brings dramatic new options for high-powered multimedia to the Web. Before Shockwave was available, a programming language (such as VRML or Java) was needed to create multimedia effects. Macromedia developed Shockwave specifically for individuals who are more interested in the creative end of multimedia than its programming aspects. The fact that Java requires its users to be familiar with an object-oriented syntax (such as C++) burdens it with an intense learning curve. Shockwave's learning curve is light by comparison, as is Director's.

Interestingly, Macromedia does not view Java as a competing technology, but as a complement to Shockwave. Recognizing that Java's system-level language can serve as a basis for network-based applications and multimedia tools, Macromedia has licensed Java and plans to integrate these two technologies. The next planned versions of Director and Authorware (another Macromedia multimedia authoring product that represents a usable subset of Director's capabilities) will feature Java applet playback.

In addition, Macromedia seeks to create a new *continuous publishing tool* by combining Shockwave and Java. Continuous publishing means that any changes to source materials are automatically propagated to consumers over the Internet. This combination is intended for Web authors looking for high-bandwidth, cutting-edge multimedia. Shockwave may ultimately act as a front-end to Java-based, custom Internet applications.

Shockwave is an industry darling for another reason as well — Macromedia did not release Shockwave in an alpha or beta form, but instead, as a completely developed package. In addition, its developers actually delivered on time. Although its growth as a product is ongoing, Shockwave hit the market in a relatively stable form and has enjoyed heavy use since its introduction in December of 1995.

What you need to use Shockwave

Obviously, the first thing you need to run Shockwave is a computer. In addition to this key component, you need the following:

- Macromedia Director
- Afterburner
- A Web browser that supports the Shockwave plugin
- A Web server that delivers multimedia content
- The necessary information to configure your Web server for Shockwave
- A working knowledge of HTML

Our prior discussion of Macromedia Director should help you understand the program's role; we discuss Afterburner and the intricacies of Web server configurations later in this chapter. Currently, the only Web browsers capable of handling the Shockwave plugin are the 2.0(+) versions of Netscape and Internet Explorer, and Silicon Graphics Web Force. Macromedia has recently announced partnerships for use of Shockwave at America Online, PointCase, and in the Castanet Marimba technology.

Installing and Using Afterburner

Afterburner is one of Shockwave's three essential components (the other two are Director and the Shockwave plugin). Afterburner's role is to enable you to play, over the Internet, movies that you create with Director. Director saves documents in a format called a film strip. Afterburner takes film strip files, denoted by a `DIR` suffix, and converts them into `DCR` files. During conversion, Afterburner analyzes the files and applies the most efficient compression possible. Through this process, Director files become ready to be embedded into HTML documents and, therefore, playable at Shockwave-enabled Web sites. A `DCR` extension means that a file was converted with Afterburner.

Afterburner's compression technology can take a film strip created with Director and compress it significantly — an average file shrinks 60 percent. This compression doesn't affect the quality or the look of a film strip; the file simply becomes more manageable for Internet transport. A file that begins at 4M can potentially be reduced to 100K after conversion with Afterburner. Because Afterburner can apply compression schemes that are tailored to each element's specific media type, files compressed with Afterburner are sometimes smaller than the original `GIF` images that they may include!

Afterburner's compression technology is most beneficial for Internet users with 9.6 Kbps or 14.4 Kbps modems, because delivering compressed files is so much faster. This extra speed from compression allows developers to build larger, more complex files, yet still share them with modem-based users. Animation appears at around 8 Kbps a second for these users, so decreasing the file size makes a tremendous difference. Ultimately, Afterburner's high-quality compression makes accessing Web graphics more efficient and enjoyable.

Running Afterburner on a Macintosh

To run Afterburner on a Mac, your system must meet these minimum requirements:

- ✔ 2MB (or more) of free hard disk space
- ✔ Macintosh computer with 68030, 68040, or PPC processor
- ✔ 640 x 480 display with 256 colors
- ✔ 8MB (or more) RAM memory
- ✔ Macintosh OS System 7.5 or later

Installing Afterburner on a Macintosh

The basic instructions for installing Afterburner on a Macintosh appear in the following list. Although new versions of Afterburner include new sets of instructions, this set of instructions explains the installation process and demonstrates how easily you can install and use the software.

1. **Download the most recent version of Afterburner.**

   You can get the most recent version from:

   ```
   http://www.macromedia.com
   ```

2. **Double-click the afterburner.sea file (if prompted for a destination, choose an appropriate location in the dialog box and click OK).**

   The Afterburner file is uncompressed onto your hard drive. The resulting folder contains the Afterburner drag-and-drop compressor and an Xtras subfolder.

3. **To initiate compression, drag and drop any completed Director film strips onto the Afterburner icon.**

Running Afterburner for Windows

To run Afterburner on Windows, your system must meet these minimum requirements:

- ✔ IBM-compatible PC
- ✔ Intel 80386 processor running at speed of 25 MHz or greater (80486/66 or better recommended)
- ✔ VGA or better graphics resolution
- ✔ 8MB RAM
- ✔ 5MB free hard disk space
- ✔ Microsoft Windows 3.1 or later (Windows 95 or NT preferable)
- ✔ Microsoft DOS 6.00 or later (except for Windows NT)

Installing Afterburner on Windows

Here are the basic instructions for installing Afterburner on a Windows computer. Although new versions of Afterburner include new sets of instructions, this set of instructions explains the installation process and demonstrates how easily you can install and use this software.

1. **Download the most recent version of the Afterburner software.**

   You can get the most recent version from:

   ```
   http://www.macromedia.com
   ```

2. **Move AFTBURN.EXE from the download directory (folder) to an empty directory (folder) on your hard drive. Double-click AFTBURN.EXE.**

   The file decompresses and deposits several files, including SETUP.EXE, in the current directory.

3. **Double-click SETUP.EXE to install Afterburner.**

   This step launches a standard Windows Setup program, which asks for the installation directory and deals with previous versions, if any are present. Then, the program copies all the necessary files and makes necessary environment changes to make it work.

4. **Drag completed Director film strips onto the Afterburner icon for compression.**

Implementing Afterburner

The following are the four basic steps for using Afterburner:

1. **Create a movie by using Macromedia Director.**

2. **Test the movie on your local computer system and on any other platforms available.**

3. **Use Afterburner to post-process the movie title.**

   That is, create a compressed file by dragging and dropping your movie file's icon onto the Afterburner icon. This effort creates a file with the DCR extension alongside the original one with the DIR extension.

4. **Put the compressed file on an HTTP server that has been properly configured to deal with Shockwave materials.**

After a Director file is processed with Afterburner, the resulting DCR file is said to be *burned*. After you "burn" a file, you can't use it as a regular Director film strip.

If you're creating any kind of content with Macromedia Director, always save a copy of your work as a film strip (a DIR file). The DIR format is the only format that can be reopened and reedited after its initial creation. If you want to leave the door open for future changes, always make sure that you keep a film strip version of your work available on your main system, on removable media, or on a floppy disk.

Configuring a Web Server for Shockwave

To share your Shockwave creations with the Internet community, you must post those creations on a Web server. You won't find many servers today that aren't capable of being configured to handle Shockwave — operating systems such as UNIX, Windows NT, MacOS, or OS/2 all qualify. Many variables affect the process of posting Shockwave content to a Web server (such as connection type, server/client software, and server hardware), and as a result, giving exact directions for Web server configuration is difficult. Our goal in this section is to give you a general overview of the important Web server considerations that you must address to make a server "Shockwave-enabled."

The type of Web server you select depends on your specific needs. Obviously, the slickest, speediest connectivity is ideal, but the price of such technology can often be prohibitive (and many people find issues of cost most crucial). If you have the time, the money, and the technical knowledge to house your Web site on your own server, you must decide what kind of connection is most effective. If having your own Web server isn't feasible, you can pay an Internet Service Provider (ISP) to post your content on its server. For a more in-depth discussion of Web server issues, see Chapter 19 in this book.

Shockwave configuration for specific Web servers

The process of configuring your Web server for Shockwave consists primarily of telling the server what to do with Shockwave content and then placing that content onto the server. Because HTTP (HyperText Transfer Protocol) has an intelligent design that can incorporate new media types, configuring a server for Shockwave is pretty easy.

Although configuration specifics vary, remember that you use three pieces of fundamental data when configuring Shockwave for all HTTP servers:

- ✔ MIME type: application
- ✔ Sub Type: x-director
- ✔ Extensions: DCR, DIR, DXR

Shockwave and MIME

MIME (Multipurpose Internet Mail Extensions) formats are a key ingredient for transmission of Web documents between clients and servers, and vice-versa. As an IETF standard, MIME facilitates Web server configuration for new types of media. All HTTP-based media handling and identification is founded on this standard, and through MIME information, requesting software (such as an e-mail package or, more likely, a Web browser) knows how to process incoming data.

All HTML image files and documents on the Web are identified by their MIME types. When you are on the Web and you request a document, the server responds by sending both the page's contents and a MIME header, which contains information about the data type for each element that composes the page. This header is called *Content-type*. To properly display a page, your Web browser must receive the MIME information telling it that the page is an HTML document. If you request an image file from a server, the MIME header similarly identifies the data as JPEGs or GIFs.

Just as HTML files need unique Content-type headers (which look like this: `Content-type: text/html`), and image files need header values (`Content-type: image/gif`), Shockwave files need their own MIME type in order to function on the Internet. The Shockwave MIME type is:

```
Content-type: application/x-director
```

In the preceding header, `application` is the document's type, and `x-director` is the primary subtype. The `x-` before `director` indicates that the data type is external and requires help from another application (a Shockwave plugin, in this case) for successful delivery.

After Shockwave files have the proper MIME types assigned, make sure that the server knows how to recognize Shockwave content and provide the correct MIME type when a browser requests this information. Although too many Web servers exist for us to give configuration examples for all of them, the examples of specific server configurations in the following sections give you some idea of the structure and activities involved.

Shockwave configuration for NSCA httpd

The NCSA's UNIX Web server system, `httpd`, accounts for a large number of the servers on the Web and provides a good example of how to configure your server. NCSA `httpd` identifies MIME file types by mapping between MIME types and file extensions. This method enables files sporting an `HTML` extension to be identified as `text/html` while setting the correct Content-type header values. This mapping takes place in a file named `mime.types`, which lives in the `conf` directory, found under the server's root directory.

Each line in this file begins with a type/subtype pair and has a comma-delineated list of extensions after spaces or a tab. In HTML, the entry appears like this:

```
text/html html htm
```

To add support for a Shockwave movie, simply add this line to the `mime.types` file:

```
application/x-director dcr dir dxr
```

DIR is the extension for Director film strip files, DCR is the extension for Shockwave-compressed Director files, and DXR isn't currently used by Shockwave — but DXR may eventually be used for adjusting file content. This configuration isn't case-sensitive, so files with extensions such as dcr, DcR, DCR, and other variations are all equally legal.

Shockwave configuration for tenants

If you have *tenant* status on a server that's running NCSA httpd (tenant status means that you pay for space on the server, but don't control the machine), we doubt that you have direct access to the mime.types file. But even if you don't have administrator access, you can still add support for Shockwave by using one of two approaches.

The first method to add Shockwave support is to ask your server's system administrator to make the changes outlined in the preceding section. The second method is more hands-on, but is only viable for an NCSA server and its offspring (such as Apache): Go to the directory that houses your Shockwave files and add support for the MIME type directly through an access control file. Check to see whether a file of this type already exists (or ask your system administrator). The file name varies from server type to server type, but the default name for NCSA httpd and its derivatives is .htaccess.

No matter what naming convention your server uses, you must create an access control file in the directory where Shockwave DCR files reside. In addition, you must add directives to allow you to map from file suffixes to the correct MIME type, and set the necessary privileges to make these settings world-readable. With default naming in a UNIX system, you can create an access control file by typing

```
cat >.htaccess
```

followed by these directives for `httpd`:

```
AddType application/x-director dcr
AddType application/x-director dir
AddType application/x-director dxr
```

Then type ^D (press Ctrl+D) to end input to the file. After creating this file, you must also set the file's permissions so the server software can read the `.htaccess` file (or its equivalent) whenever the server looks for one of your Shockwave files in the directory. You can perform this action in UNIX with the following command line:

```
chmod 644 .htaccess
```

Shockwave configuration for W3C httpd

W3C `httpd`, formerly called CERN `httpd`, is the most frequently used UNIX server after NCSA `httpd`. W3C `httpd` puts all server directives in a single configuration file, which takes the default path `/etc/httpd.conf`. The following lines add Shockwave support:

```
AddType .dcr application/x-director 8bit
AddType .dxr application/x-director 8bit
AddType .dir application/x-director 8bit
```

The W3C `httpd` syntax differs somewhat from NCSA `httpd` and can only process one extension per line. In addition, the syntax specifies the encoding type (`8bit`) and reverses the order of listing the MIME type and file extension. You must use the keyword `AddType` at the beginning of the line to identify the MIME directive, because the World Wide Web Consortium `httpd` configuration file includes every kind of server directive allowed.

Because all the system configuration information is in one place in this file, the chance that you'll be allowed to make changes is unlikely, unless you're a system administrator. Therefore, be prepared to share this configuration information with your Webmaster or the system administrator who's in charge of your Web server.

Shockwave configuration for Quarterdeck's WebSTAR

WebSTAR offers CGI-based remote administration that performs some necessary configuration functions on your behalf. The most complete method to perform administrative functions in WebSTAR is to use the adminstration package, called WebSTAR Admin. WebSTAR Admin enables you to use a graphical interface for most common server administration tasks. The Macintosh version of WebSTAR Admin uses a complex Macintosh interface that controls servers running on your machine or on other machines accessible through AppleTalk.

Do the following to configure the Macintosh version of WebSTAR for Shockwave:

1. **Launch the WebSTAR Admin application.**

2. **Select your server in the dialog box that appears.**

   Your server has to be running locally or must be accessible via the network in order for this process to work.

3. **Choose Configure⇨Suffix Mapping from the menu.**

   The Suffix Mapping dialog box appears.

4. **Fill out the Suffix Mapping dialog box.**

   This box is where you create the collection of file associations between extensions and file type, just as in the MIME extension files discussed earlier in the chapter.

5. **Click the Add button and then click the Update button to complete the configuration settings.**

6. **Repeat these steps for the** `DIR` **and** `DXR` **suffixes.**

   Repeat steps 4 and 5 to add all of the file extensions and application associations you think that you'll need.

Today, a version of WebSTAR is available for Windows NT. Because of interface differences, the menu names and sequence of instructions is a little different, but otherwise, both versions behave in much the same way.

Placing Shockwave Files on Your Server

After you've configured your server to deal with Shockwave, the next step is to upload your Shockwave content. If your Web server is connected to the development machines on your LAN, post your content just as you copy any other normal files over the network.

If your machines are linked to a UNIX server through a PPP or ISDN connection, uploading content onto your Web server is slightly more complex. You must use FTP (File Transfer Protocol) or a similar program to collect and upload your files. FTP is available in a variety of freeware, shareware, and commercial versions, so getting a copy of FTP shouldn't be too difficult.

However, the process of uploading your Shockwave files may be slow if you don't have a speedy connection to your server. You may want to construct an archive of the content you've created, compress it, and upload it during the hours you're normally sleeping. Another idea is to break your archive into smaller parts before you upload it. This piecemeal upload allows you to transfer files in manageable chunks, and if anything goes wrong while you're transferring the data, you won't have to resend the entire collection.

If you transfer files across platforms — for example, from Macintosh or PC to UNIX — keep in mind that not all compression standards work on all platforms. Utilities to create and handle tar and ZIP formats are available for Macintosh, UNIX, and Windows platforms, so they're a good overall choice. No matter what compression technique you choose, you must have all the software you need on both sending and receiving sides to ensure that you can work with your files before and after you transfer them.

Using Shockwave Materials

Before you can deliver your Shockwave masterpieces to any users, you must embed your Shockwave files within valid HTML code. You can accomplish this embedding by using a number of approaches.

Netscape introduced a proprietary HTML tag to support Director movies (as well as QuickTime movies and VRML worlds) that has now become part of the HTML 3.2 recommendation. This tag, <EMBED>, tells the browser that the material associated with the tag requires a plugin. The embedded file's extension and its corresponding MIME type determine what plugin loads.

Because the options that plugins support can vary, the syntax for the <EMBED> tag varies according to the plugin that's referenced, and depends on its particular content. However, the standard <EMBED> tag for Shockwave Director movies looks like this:

```
<EMBED SRC="path/filename.ext" WIDTH="n" HEIGHT="n"
    TEXTFOCUS="focus">
```

The URL for this example is specified through the SRC option; this URL may be local, remote, relative, or absolute. The file's extension is usually DCR, to indicate that the file has been *burned* with Afterburner compression, although the Shockwave plugin loads if the browser notices DIR or DXR file extensions as well. The WIDTH and HEIGHT options determine the dimensions (in pixels) for your project's display window. Remember to verify that the Stage size you choose for your Director movie corresponds to the desired height and width, because if your browser finds a discrepancy, it may position the image awkwardly.

The final attribute, `TEXTFOCUS`, is optional. This attribute controls Shockwave Director content by indicating how the plugin should react to user keyboard input. This attribute has three possible values: `onMouse`, the default value, indicates that the plugin may accept keyboard input after a user clicks at any place in the movie. The second value, `onStart`, enables the plugin to accept input from the keyboard as soon as the movie begins to play. The final value, `never`, ensures that the plugin cheerfully ignores keyboard activity.

The `<EMBED>` tag behaves like the `<IMG>` tag in terms of static graphic placement on a Web page, especially when used in conjunction with the `<IMG>` attribute extensions, `WIDTH` and `HEIGHT`. As with the `<IMG>` tag, you can place the `<EMBED>` tag inside other HTML markup, such as table tags (`<TABLE>` ... `<TR><TD>content here</TD></TR></TABLE>`). If your project requires precise positioning, you may want to wrap your movie inside a table, where you have more control over position and layout.

Do's and Don'ts for Designing Shockwave Materials

We intend for the following suggestions to help you use Shockwave as effectively as possible. Because Shockwave technology is progressing quickly, not all of these recommendations may be necessary in the future.

To stay current on Shockwave technology, be sure to visit the Macromedia Web site at:

```
http://www.macromedia.com
```

Many of these tips relate to reducing file size. Because the majority of Internet users cruise cyperspace with a 14.4 Kbps modem, they, understandably, aren't interested in downloading gargantuan movies. The amount of download time a user is willing to invest is often determined by the value of a file; most people are not as eager to download a superfluous animated banner as they are to download something more rewarding, such as a game. This fact leads us to two specific size-related warnings:

 ✔ If you use large files, warn users about how big they are; hyperlink the files to your pages so users can choose whether to download those files.

 ✔ Whether files are large or small, make triply sure that they're essential to your content; then make sure that your beta testers agree!

Failure to heed either warning leads to audience defections to sites more sensitive to their users' needs — and limitations!

Do

Here's a list of things that you should do to ensure a successful site:

- Do make your images as small as possible. Big is not better when you're talking about download time.

- Do keep your target audience in mind. Think of what entices and intrigues the people who may view your Shockwave movies.

- Do rescale your images after importing them into Director. You can make them appear larger or smaller while saving valuable file space.

- Do test your work on multiple machines, especially on a Macintosh if you're on a PC, and vice-versa.

- Do avoid shading artwork. Flat colors are more effective, because the computer treats each gradation as a separate color, and this treatment slows the ease and speed of a download.

- Do create backgrounds with tiling (this tip is for color Macintosh users only, because creating backgrounds with tiling requires QuickDraw). Tiling is an effective, undemanding way to imbue your movies with custom backgrounds.

- Do use Ink Effects within Director. Employing this technique saves significant amounts of memory in the Cast (Director's storage area for elements in your movies) while providing access to complex looks.

- Do use the Text tool in Director instead of rendering or saving bitmapped text. Using the program's Text tool makes Shockwave movie sizes more manageable because Director won't save each pixel for a text image (as with bitmapped text); Director saves only the information that defines the text.

- Do think carefully about what fonts you use. Computers substitute other fonts when a selected one isn't available. If you're concerned about achieving specific effects through fonts, choose standard ones.

- Do lower sampling rates to reduce audio file sizes. The sampling rate that gives the best sound is 22.050 KHz. Although slower rates work, dropping to 11.025 KHz causes distortion on Windows machines.

- Do indicate to your users whenever they must activate a Shockwave movie that you include on your pages. The most effective way to tell your users about a movie is through an attention-grabbing graphic or notice that appears in their browser early, while your page is loading.

- Do position your content within the boundaries of an average Web browser window — playing movies on the edge of a browser window is useless. Test your pages with a 14- or 15-inch monitor.

✔ Do think about including a top-level *Welcome* page that displays only text and graphics. It should warn users about special content — such as Shockwave — and inform them about file sizes and potential download delays. Users with slower modems appreciate information about file sizes and the type of content you offer.

Don't

Here's a list of things that you should NOT do to ensure a successful site:

✔ Don't think of Shockwave as a general-purpose programming language — it isn't. Coupled with Director, Shockwave gives you great animation and interactivity possibilities, but these features don't mean that Shockwave is "just like" a general-purpose programming language, such as Java or VRML.

✔ Don't let your Shockwave movies overpower your page's content. Yes, Shockwave *is* exciting and fun to play with, but the movies at your site shouldn't overwhelm your viewers or be superfluous or irrelevant.

✔ Don't make your total page sizes too enormous. You don't need to get carried away and put twelve Shockwave movies on a single page. Although the chosen few with T3 connections may stay around long enough to be impressed, the time necessary to load such a page will repel many other users.

✔ Don't forget that some users are still using non-Shockwave-enabled browsers. Check out your page to see how it looks if it loads minus your fantastic movies. Think about providing alternate ways to view your work (for example, a download page with equivalent Director Projector files that a user can view on any Macintosh or Windows PC).

The bottom line for creating Shockwave presentations is to make effective use of the technology. Be sure that movies add to your pages, without imposing unnecessary delays on your users or penalizing those users who don't have high-speed Internet access.

The Top Shockwave Resources

The ultimate Shockwave resource online is, not surprisingly, the Macromedia Web site, located at:

```
http://www.macromedia.com.
```

This site features an extensive list of complementary services and products for Shockwave and also contains answers to specific questions about using the application.

Within the Macromedia site, you can find additional pages that contain interesting materials; the Gallery Guide is a great place to go looking for examples of "shocked" Web sites:

```
http://www.macromedia.com/shockzone/guide/
```

When you're designing content for the Web, keeping your knowledge fresh about how people view your site is a good idea. The following site supplies current information about how people are navigating through the Web:

```
http://www.e-land.com/e-stat_pages/e-stat_main.html
```

Another quality Web page featuring Shockwave is DreamLight Multimedia's page at:

```
http://www.dreamlight.com/webshop/software/scrnbts.htm
```

The following sites also provide interesting information for following Shockwave links:

```
http://www.teleport.com/~arcana/shockwave/
http://www.ld.ucsf.edu/shockme.html
```

For detailed information on Shockwave, refer to *The 60-Minute Guide to Shockwave for Director*, by William H. Hurley III, W. Preston Gregg, and Sebastian Hassinger (IDG Books Worldwide, Inc.).

One of the things that Macromedia most hopes to see in Shockwave's future is the use of linked media over the Internet (which Shockwave's first release doesn't support). Macromedia also hopes that future versions of Shockwave will be able to support QuickTime (this support is currently unavailable due to the lack of support for linked media). The development of support for QuickTime would be especially nice because Netscape Navigator and Internet Explorer both support the QuickTime plugin. Perhaps future versions of Shockwave may also decipher the mysterious DXR extension.

After reading this chapter, we hope that you have a better idea about the exciting possibilities that Shockwave brings to the Web. The Web has already been recognized as the premier attempt to distribute multimedia all over the world through a series of networked computers. The revolutionary development of Shockwave may well represent a big step into a new realm of multimedia technology.

Chapter 9

Virtual Worlds with VRML

● ●

In This Chapter

▶ Defining VRML

▶ Delving into VRML's fascinating past

▶ Creating thrilling VRML content

▶ Using VRML-enabled Web browsers

▶ Configuring your Web server for VRML

▶ Designing VRML

▶ Finding the top VRML resources online

● ●

*V*RML (pronounced *vermul*) is the acronym for Virtual Reality Modeling Language. VRML is an object-oriented programming language that renders scenes modeled in 3-D graphics. HTML (HyperText Markup Language) challenges our ideas of how text is represented — VRML does the same for space. By bringing the possibility of 3-D representation to the Web, VRML literally adds a whole new dimension to the Web experience and promotes a more interactive future.

VRML's presence on the Internet scene pushes the Web toward a more realistic appearance by allowing information to be structured with everyday symbols. Instead of telling your users to follow the third link of a home page and the fourth link after that, VRML's advent enables you to give instructions such as, "Go into the site's living room and open the red door on your left."

VRML was developed not only to push the Web toward a more human-oriented structure, but also to give normal, nonprogramming folks the chance to create virtual spaces without having to learn a complex programming language. Supporters hope that VRML becomes a standard language for interactive Web documents. Some pundits argue, however, that VRML hasn't lived up to its hype and assert that VRML is not as accessible as it claims to be, because a powerful computer is nearly mandatory to run VRML successfully. We see merits to both sides of this discussion and cover issues related to this debate in the following sections.

VRML's Brilliant History

When it officially hit the market in April of 1995, VRML had barely been in the works for a year. In May of 1994, Mark Pesce, a developer interested in bringing a virtual reality interface to the Web, attended the first World Wide Web conference in Geneva, Switzerland, and presented a paper entitled "Cyberspace." That presentation set VRML's creation in motion.

Pesce, whose views about making the Web a more sensual, human place mark him as a sort of cybervisionary, was working with another developer, Tony Parisi, to manufacture a language capable of rendering 3-D on the Web. By the time the first World Wide Web conference rolled around, the pair had succeeded in creating an interface called *Labyrinth* (`http://www.well.com/user/caferace/labyrinth.gif`) that does render 3-D.

Their presentation was a tremendous success and turned other industry professionals on to the power of the 3-D space metaphor for the Web. The presentation also led to an agreement that developers should adopt a single, unified programming language — leading to the creation of VRML. In fact, numerous conference participants elected to lend their contributions to the project and put together a working group on the spot!

In the spirit of true Net collaboration, Pesce set up a mailing list as a forum to support VRML's initial development. The response to the topic was fast and furious, and the forum witnessed a great deal of excited debate over what an initial VRML requirements document should contain.

Pesce moderated the discussion generated via the mailing list personally. He was convinced that VRML would be most effective if it were not a totally new language, but a modification of established programming metaphors that people were already comfortable with. The group decided that an ideal language would be accessible, analogous to HTML, and capable of expressing everything that a professional 3-D designer's heart desires.

You can find the archives of this mailing list at:

`http://vrml.wired.com/`

This group's goals are listed at:

`http://www.gold.net/oneday/render/index.html`

And the winner was . . .

The language ultimately selected for VRML development was Open Inventor, an object-oriented 3-D toolkit from Silicon Graphics, Inc. (SGI). The set of programming libraries for Open Inventor enables users to control objects like trackballs, cubes, polygons, materials, cameras, and text.

Open Inventor emerged as the preferred choice for several reasons. One important reason was its ASCII-based structure that enables Open Inventor to work seamlessly with HTML. Other winning points included its professional-level quality, its expandability, and its previous debugging through commercial testing and implementation.

Pesce requested that the language be placed in the public domain, which was a heady demand. SGI eventually complied even though this placement means that the company no longer *owns* Open Inventor in the traditional sense. This generous action allows anyone to build on Open Inventor without having to worry about paying royalties or being sued.

Tony Parisi and Gavin Bell, one of Open Inventor's chief creators, presented VRML 1.0 at the second World Wide Web conference in November of 1994. The presentation was a successful, standing-room-only event that alerted much of the industry to VRML's exciting potential. The ball kept rolling — QvLib, a quick VRML parser, appeared within a few months, and the WebSpace and WorldView browsers came along soon after. News of VRML hit the news media in April of 1995, and the hype (aided by SGI's potent marketing engine) was thick enough to make *Newsweek* give VRML its own cover.

VRML and HTML: What's the difference?

In case you're wondering about the exact differences between VRML and HTML, the following few pointers may help out:

- ✔ HTML deals with text and was designed as a common text delivery system for the Web. VRML was also designed to be a common delivery system for the Web, but for visual and graphic presentations, instead of primarily textual data.

- ✔ VRML and HTML work similarly, except VRML documents represent 3-D spaces, and HTML only displays text and graphics in 2-D.

- ✔ VRML and HTML are neither mutually exclusive nor in competition. In fact, some say that HTML space *lives* within the grander confines of VRML space.

- ✔ Although HTML is easy to do manually, doing VRML manually is much harder. The reason for this difference is pretty clear when you think about it: HTML uses text to make a textual document, but VRML uses text and numbers to produce graphical objects. Consequently, using authoring tools is the norm for VRML (but not for HTML).

So, what's VRML good for?

With the release of the 2.0 version in mid-1996, VRML is beginning to realize its full potential, especially in its attempts to conform more closely to human standards of interaction. It added support for interactivity, complex navigation, and other types of advanced functionality. VRML 2.0's API specifies what kinds of interactions can transpire in a browser, but does not specify how interactions themselves occur (except for establishing default behaviors). This arrangement gives users freedom to determine their own interactivity and behaviors. In other words, users can build interactions based on data gloves, joysticks, or keyboard, with accompanying different styles of feedback to boot!

The incorporation of audio support for MIDI and spatialized audio into VRML is also exciting. Just as Web pages now have backgrounds (garnered by HTML extensions), VRML spaces use background audio. This innovation does more than enhance the auditory surfing experience; it can also give directions and allow two-way communication. Another exciting technology that VRML 2.0 uses is *video streaming*, which combines video texture mapping with spatialized audio. Taken together, all this multimedia support adds to the reality of the user's virtual experiences.

The following are just a few examples of the virtual worlds that VRML enables:

- **Medical and scientific research:** Check out NCSA's server (`ftp://ftp.ncsa.uiuc.edu`) for examples displayed in VRML format.

  By using VRML, researchers can implement experiments that can't be visualized or performed in real life. VRML's possibilities as a teaching tool are very exciting: Students who can't deal with the idea of dissecting a real animal appreciate the option of cutting 3-D VRML models instead.

- **Online conferencing:** The notion of virtual meetings with clients thousands of miles away has excited businesses for years. Telecommunication companies are developing virtual phone booths that use VRML for public networking.

- **Virtual shopping:** As roads become more crowded and people find their lives becoming that way, too, virtual shopping becomes ever more attractive. VRML applications enable you to examine objects from all angles and, at the same time, provide a wealth of instantly accessible product information.

- **Real estate and architecture:** VRML's future in the areas of real estate and architecture is great, because building on land (or land covered by concrete) is much more expensive than building on screen. By using VRML, builders get a look and a feel for proposed edifices. They can implement custom-building choices quickly and painlessly and have lots of room for experimentation and adjustment.

✔ **Entertainment:** The possibilities are endless here. VR (virtual reality) games and interactive movies are two areas under intense development, and online gambling is making a killing on the Web.

Check out the Virtual Vegas site at:

```
http://www.virtualvegas.com/
```

Many die-hard MOOers and MUCKers (and other denizens of virtual realities habituated by acronymophiles) find that VRML versions of fantasy land are still a little cheesy, but these lands are quickly becoming more believable. Virtual communities, such as the one at `http://www.cybertown.com/`, make interesting use of VRML too.

VRML's characteristics

In technical terms, VRML is an object-oriented programming language that provides methods to group 3-D graphical objects. VRML's objects are called *nodes*. These nodes, which can contain practically any type of information, can have offspring, called *children*, which represent modifications to the parent node. Nodes may also be reused through *instancing*, which allows new nodes to inherit an original node's attributes and is ideal because it enables programmers to reuse code fragments efficiently. Instancing also means that display is faster, because another instance of a node simply repositions its descriptive data elsewhere on the display, without needing to create an additional copy in memory.

Unlike most object-oriented languages, VRML's individual components aren't nonlinear, or randomly organized. Instead, its source file resides in a *scene graph*, a hierarchical file that indicates the order in which nodes must be parsed. Every entry in a VRML scene graph is classified as a node object. Because scene graphs give programmers control over the order of a scene's rendering, they also imbue VRML with ideal precision and control.

Nodes

Nodes are divided into three classes in VRML: shape, property, and group. The only way that an object can appear in a scene is through the use of a shape node. On the other hand, property nodes control lighting and material and determine how an object is drawn within a scene. Group nodes are responsible for organizing and enveloping nodes through *containment*. When a node has children or other objects (like surfaces, textures, light sources, and so on) contained within its parent node, the node is classified as a group node.

The following is a basic definition statement for a node:

```
[DEF objectname]  objecttype  {  [fields]  [children]}
```

Only the type declaration and the curly braces are required for the definition to work; including the fields, name, and children is optional. Use DEF only if you're specifying a name for a node.

Nodes have a great flexibility in their design specifications, and likewise, node characteristics are rather loose. A node's properties include the following:

- **Fields:** Fields are variables with parameters, and they describe a node's characteristics (such as color, size, or rotation). A node may contain zero or more fields.

- **Object type:** VRML has 36 types of nodes; these nodes can be either actual shapes or influences that affect the way the shapes are drawn (such as an angle rotation or a light source).

- **Name:** Naming is optional because a node can work without a name. However, naming makes a node more flexible and powerful, because knowing a node's name enables you to manipulate the object at will.

As is recommended, you can use one of two nodes in VRML as the foundation for VRML worlds that work with a variety of platforms. LOD, the level-of-detail node, is one, and the other is WWWInline. These two nodes work well together, because they facilitate *lazy loading* (also called *on-demand loading*), which lets a VRML browser decide at what level of detail to load objects and when to load them. When you're loading an object *lazily,* you see an empty box with the object's dimensions before the object appears. Lazy loading is nice because users can start navigating through a VRML world before all objects are completely loaded — which can be a big deal if they're dealing with hundreds of objects.

Field types

Rendering objects in 3-D requires a variety of mathematical operations that, in turn, demand many data types. VRML's 16 field types are drawn from the 42 types used in Open Inventor and fall into two categories: single-value and multiple-value.

Single-value field types can be images, Booleans, vectors, or numbers (integers or real). You can discern single-value fields by an *SF* prefix; multiple-value fields are trickily prefixed by *MF*. Single-value field types can consist of an arbitrary number of individual parameters (which makes them seem rather underserving of their name). But the classification comes from the fact that, unlike multiple-value field types, single-value field types can describe or act on only a single object or property. Through the use of field types, you have the power to describe practically any kind of 3-D object.

Creating VRML Content

The following sections discuss the various issues involved with creating VRML worlds. We examine the preliminary steps involved and move on to discuss some content creation tools that are available to make creating good VRML a piece of cake!

A virtual world in seven easy steps

In his book, *VRML — Browsing and Building Cyberspace,* VRML guru Mark Pesce gives a list of seven steps toward creating effective VRML. These are the steps:

- ✔ **Conception:** Pesce identifies *conception* as the step that may take the longest, especially if you're attempting to create worlds that aren't grounded in reality as we know it. This step gives you the room to imagine, to fantasize, to consider artistic ideas.

- ✔ **Planning:** After the conception stage has ended, you can move into the more realistic stage of *planning*. At this point, create a physical plan of your project and consider questions of finance, time, and execution. If you're creating a project at the professional level, this stage is the time to investigate applications, such as Autodesk 3-D Studio or Walkthrough Pro, that could help your work.

- ✔ **Design:** How you *design* a project is dependent on how you conceive it. Do you see your creation as architecture, art, public space, or something else? If you're modeling a building, you probably want to create a series of surfaces to represent walls, ceilings, and floors, with cutouts for windows and doors. Add further objects to represent fixtures, furniture, carpets, and other elements within the spaces you define. In other words, your approach is to re-create the characteristics of a building or room and to populate that room with representative objects that a user would expect to find within that space.

- ✔ **Sampling:** *Sampling* is the process by which you convert real-world objects into virtual equivalents. You handle this process by creating texture maps from actual drawings and wrapping them around idealized or artificial 3-D objects, or you can make 3-D scans of real objects and use those scans as a framework.

- ✔ **Construction:** *Construction* is the stage where you start building things. During this stage, the focus is on tools.

Make sure that the tools you select are appropriate by running a test with a simple model. If you experience conversion problems, note the problems and attempt to find work-arounds. Because many VRML tools are still new and immature, construction is often messy — but hey, that's part of the game!

> ✔ **Testing:** You can never *test* too much, especially because VRML is a new technology, and people approach a creation from many different platforms and viewpoints. Try as many different browsers and plat-forms as you can: Start locally and then expand across the Web.
>
> ✔ **Publishing:** Ah, the final glory! When your creation's in optimum shape, it's time to *publish* or perish. The initial publication is a test in itself, because you find out how people viewing at different connection speeds respond to your world.

Your job as a Web developer isn't over just because you've published your virtual world — now you get to respond to people's feedback and make adjustments accordingly.

Creation tools for your VRML world

VRML creation tools come in two basic forms. Object creation tools, such as Caligari trueSpace, are the first type. They provide a sculpture studio of sorts, in which you can design arbitrary objects. The second type is space creation tools, such as Virtual Home Space Builder. This type is ideal if you're interested in constructing VRML spaces. These types of construction tools are complementary — in fact, creating objects (with an object creation tool) and then putting them into a virtual space (with a space creation tool) is the customary order for building virtual worlds.

Virtual Home Space Builder

One of the easiest ways to create VRML content is with an entry-level VRML authoring tool such as Virtual Home Space Builder (VHSB) from Paragraph International. As the name indicates, VHSB was created to enable you to make your own space, which you do by clicking and dragging. The VHSB interface is colorful and easy to use; these features make VHSB ideal for first-time VRML users with programming anxiety.

If you have questions about any interface feature of VHSB, hold the mouse over the feature to invoke a pop-up blurb of explanatory text. Although VHSB is limited in the 3-D items that it offers and handles, its tradeoff between simplicity and ease of use is worthwhile (especially if you're experimenting or exploring, rather than doing professional-quality work).

One of VHSB's nicest features is its Walk View window, which gives a real-time rendering of the world you're creating. In this window, you see a fairly accurate view of how your world looks to a VRML browser. The Walk View window has nifty buttons such as a magnifying glass, which magnifies your work, and crosshairs, to shift an image's perspective to head-on.

You can download a free beta version of VHSB at:

```
http://www1.paragraph.com/products/i3dfamily/vhsb/
```

Virtus Walkthrough Pro

Walkthrough Pro is another authoring tool that provides an interface for building 3-D worlds. James Cameron, director of *The Abyss*, found this tool to be useful when he was making this movie — he used Walkthrough Pro (actually, an earlier version) to view movie sets in cyberspace before he spent the time and money to build them.

Walkthrough Pro, which works on both Macintosh and Windows platforms, is a more complex and professional tool than VHSB and, consequently, has a steeper learning curve. With Walkthrough Pro, you can create QuickTime and Windows AVI movies. You can also make texture-mapped scenes by using textures from the hundreds of choices found in its library or any textures that are scanned in or imported from clip-art libraries. Walkthrough Pro offers a great selection of furniture with which you can decorate your spaces, as shown in Figure 9-1.

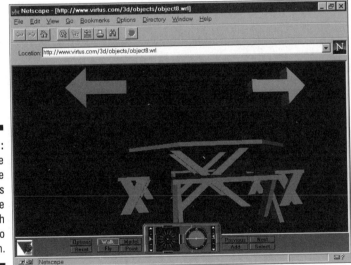

Figure 9-1:
An example of furniture objects from the Walkthrough Pro selection.

Installing and Using VRML-Enabled Browsers

By early 1997, most Web browsers compatible with a Macintosh (if the system had a 68000-based processor or better) or a Windows-based PC (Windows 95, NT, or 3.1) supported VRML plugins. Unfortunately for most people, the best VRML browsers available are designed for UNIX platforms, particularly for SGI machines.

In general, VRML browsers serve as helper applications for standard HTML browsers. A few stand-alone browsers don't require assistance from other applications to display VRML files. But if you're going to look at anything other than VRML content, you want to use such browsers as helper applications, because those same browsers pick up only the VRML portions of Web documents when you use them alone. With Netscape's 2.0 release, VRML plugins became big news, and they define the norm for browsers today.

WIRL (short for Web Interactive Reality Layer) is regarded as one of the best and brightest of these plugins. By using its inline extensions architecture, Web users experience fully interactive virtual reality on the Web, as shown in Figure 9-2. That's why we think that the plugin approach is the right way to go: They're available when you need them, and get out of the way when you don't!

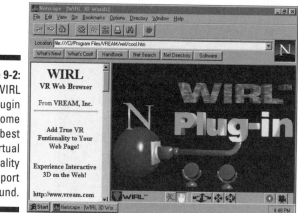

Figure 9-2: The WIRL plugin offers some of the best virtual reality support around.

Check the list of Web sites at the end of this chapter for links to sites that discuss other VRML plugins.

Stand-alone PC browsers

The following sections discuss some of the better stand-alone VRML browsers available for PC users.

WorldView from InterVista

WorldView is the only browser that currently works with every one of the Windows platforms. Hypothetically, WorldView should work with a 14.4 modem and a standard PC, because part of its goal is to provide a browser for people running only modest hardware. The minimum processor that you can use is a 50 MHz 80486, with at least 8MB of RAM (12MB of RAM is more realistic for Windows 3.1 or 3.11, and for Windows 95 or NT, you need at least 16MB). For more information, visit:

```
http://www.intervista.com/
```

CosmoPlayer

CosmoPlayer comes from the fertile breeding ground of SGI, the creators of the Open Inventor rendering language. If you're interested in running this plugin for Navigator or Internet Explorer, you need at least the following hardware:

- A 75 MHz Pentium processor (faster is preferable)
- 16MB RAM (more is better)
- A 256-color SVGA display system (or better, preferably)

For more information on CosmoPlayer, visit the following URL:

```
http://webspace.sgi.com/cosmoplayer/download.html
```

Helper applications for standard HTML browsers

The following browsers work only as helper applications within standard HTML browsers, such as Netscape Navigator or Internet Explorer. Whenever possible, make sure that you're running the most recent version of the browser, as well as the most recent version of the corresponding plugin.

VRwave for Windows

VRwave for Windows was developed for VRML 2.0 by the same three power players who built VRweb for VRML 1.0: NCSA (The National Center for Supercomputing Applications), the Gopher development team from the

University of Minnesota, and IICM (the Institute for Information Processing and Computer-Supported New Media). Because all these organizations are non-profit, this browser is available as freeware at:

```
http://www.iicm.edu/vrwave
```

Live3D

Live3D is based on the earlier VRML add-in developed by Paper Software, purchased by Netscape in late 1996. Live3D is a convenient plugin that embeds itself (as a plugin) in Mosaic, Netscape Navigator, or Internet Explorer. Live3D handles both HTML pages and VRML files with the greatest of ease. For more information on Live3D, go to the following URL at the Netscape site:

```
http://home.mcom.com/comprod/products/navigator/⊃
          version_3.0/multimedia/live3d/index.html
```

Configuring your browser for VRML

Your first priority in the VRML arena is to make sure that your Web browser knows what to do with VRML files when they arrive. To do so, modify the Preferences settings (or whatever configuration utility the browser uses; if you're in doubt check out its Help utility with the term "MIME" or "MIME types" — it should tell you what you have to do to add support for a new MIME type) so that your browser is able to handle a new MIME type (in this case, x-world/x-vrml). In addition, let your browser know what default extension to use for VRML files. WRL is the extension most commonly used for VRML files, but VRML is used as the extension on occasion. Instead of changing defaults stored in your home directory, change the browser's defaults directly. (In Navigator, alter the .usr/local/lib/netscape/ .mime.types file, instead of changing your personal ~/.mime.types file.)

To get the MIME types file configured properly after you've successfully integrated your VRML plugin, do the following:

✔ Edit your .mime.types file by adding the following line:

```
x-world/x-vrml   wrl
```

✔ Edit your .mailcap file by adding the following line:

```
x-world/x-vrml;  /install_directory/vrweb   %s;
```

If these changes don't work, you may need to talk to your system administrator to make system-wide VRML-enabling changes, especially if you don't have *root privileges*. (This level of file access lets you change basic system definitions; for security and control reasons, it's not a common end-user privilege.)

Configuring your Windows browser for VRML

To successfully run a browser such as VRwave on your PC, you need:

✔ At least a 75 MHz Pentium processor

✔ A minimum of 16MB RAM

✔ A 256-color SVGA display, video card, and driver

✔ Win32s — if you're using Windows 3.1, it is downloadable at:

```
ftp://ftp.outer.net/pub/mswindows/win32s.zip
```

If you want to use Navigator or Internet Explorer, you must define a new MIME type. If you're doing this with VRwave and Netscape, try the following:

1. **Choose Options⇨Preferences.**

2. **Select Helper Application from the pull-down menu.**

3. **Click the New Type button.**

4. **In the Configure New MIME Type dialog box, enter** x-world **for MIME type and** x-vrml **for MIME subtype.**

5. **Enter** WRL **for the Extensions field.**

6. **Click Launch Application in the Action selection box.**

7. **Select pathToVRwave\vrweb.exe for the application.**

8. **Close the dialog box and continue on with your work.**

Configuring a Macintosh browser for VRML

The first functional VRML browser for the Mac was called Whurlwind. It's been superseded by a Power Macintosh Navigator plugin called Whurlplug, that works with either Mosaic or Navigator to support VRML. We suggest pushing your memory allocation up to 4,000K when you're using Whurlplug (because of its heavy graphical requirements).

The only VRML browser in general release for 68K Macintoshes is Virtus Player. This browser also offers a version for Power Macintoshes (which is much faster than Whurlplug) and a version for Windows 95. ExpressVR is an excellent Macintosh VRML plugin for Navigator and Internet Explorer.

You can find ExpressVR at:

```
http://www.andrew.cmu.edu/user/anderson/vrml/
```

This site also has excellent pointers to all kinds of other Macintosh VRML resources as well.

Configuring Your Web Server for VRML

Adding VRML to existing Web sites is easy because it doesn't require any change in the way servers operate. The essential thing to tell your Web server is that VRML documents take the extension `WRL` and a MIME type of `x-world/x-vrml`. After your server has this information, it can detect VRML documents and let your browser know whenever a VRML document is on its way.

To prepare your Web server for your VRML masterpiece, analyze the VRML files you've created so that you can give the administrator an idea of what's in store. If you've created a gargantuan world, the administrator may need to distribute your world across several servers or reorganize it to decrease the burden on any individual server.

Related VRML object files should be identified (usually because they occur in the same scene or are "nearby" — as in "the other side of a doorway" and a doorway) and placed on different hosts if possible. This effort helps ensure optimal performance. If the processing load associated with delivering large numbers of objects isn't spread out, server loads may be inconsistent. This inconsistency can sometimes cause a *cascade effect* — where a call to one object results in an immediate call to another object, and so on — that could overload a server and cause all your users to lose touch with your virtual reality!

Because *object inlining* use — that is, where objects are rendered within the framework of a particular scene graph — is heavy in VRML, we recommend that you use professional VRML publishing tools to analyze any document set. Then, you can use the results to give the site administrator any publishing recommendations offered by these tools. Even though some VRML publishing tools are still in development, you can also adapt Web server analysis tools (available on the Web) for use in VRML publishing.

Design Do's and Don'ts for VRML

The following lists detail what you should and should not do when creating VRML. Trust us...we figured these out the hard way!

Do

Here are some good practices to follow to ensure a successful VRML world:

- Do make your graphics as small as possible — 100 to 200K is ideal. VRML's precision is sometimes counterproductive, because the language can describe an object's mathematical qualities so accurately that the object is impossible to handle.

- Do keep your target audience in mind. Think of what may entice and intrigue the people who view your VRML site.

- Do check the following site for cutting edge information about VRML and troubleshooting help:

  ```
  http://www.meshmart.org/vrml.htm
  ```

- Do use GZIP. The VRML community has agreed that you should compress VRML files with GZIP. Using GZIP can reduce file sizes by up to 80 percent — and it's free! Try it, you'll like it. You can find it in many places on the Web, so we recommend going to your favorite search engine and typing in the keyword GZIP to see what turns up.

- Do view your work on multiple platforms; for example, view your work on a Mac if you use a PC, and vice versa.

- Do think about how your page may look to non-VRML users. Then check the page with a non-VRML-capable browser to see!

- Do test your page more than once! Try the following Web site for more information on testing:

  ```
  http://www-dsed.llnl.gov/documents/tests/vrml.html
  ```

- Do use LOD (level-of-detail) or WWWInline as a foundation when creating VRML worlds. Using one of these nodes increases your odds of making sure that your creation works with a variety of platforms.

Don't

Avoid these definite no-nos:

- Don't think seriously about coding VRML by hand. Coding VRML by hand is much, much harder than coding HTML by hand. Coding VRML manually is advisable only as a learning experience — or if you've got hundreds of hours to spend.

- Don't forget to test your page from all angles. Make sure that the page loads every time and that it runs at an acceptable speed (even with less-than-killer equipment). Failure to test can mean site failure!

The Top VRML Resources

Check out these resources for more information on VRML.

- *VRML — Browsing and Building Cyberspace,* by Mark Pesce, New Riders Publishing, 1995. This interesting book covers not only the history and scope of VRML, but also Pesce's visionary ideas about VRML and the Web.

- *60 Minute Guide to VRML,* by Sebastian Hassinger and Mike Erwin, IDG Books Worldwide, Inc., 1995. This work is divided into three sections that each take about an hour to read. In addition to being accessible, the guide includes a good list of VRML links.

- The VRML FAQ:

  ```
  http://vag.vrml.org/VRML_FAQ.html
  ```

- Netscape maintains a comprehensive directory of VRML sites at:

  ```
  http://home.netscape.com/comprod/products/navigator/
          version_2.0/plugins/vrml_sites.html
  ```

- Multimedia Gulch is San Francisco's foray into virtualhood:

  ```
  http://www.planet9.com/vrsoma.htm
  ```

- The VRML repository:

  ```
  http://www.sdsc.edu/vrml_repository/repository.html
  ```

- The following site contains good links, information on VRML, and specific system software: `http://www.well.com/www/caferace/vrml.html`

We hope that all this material has given you insight into the possibilities that VRML harbors. In the next chapter, we move from virtual reality to virtual caffeine as we tackle Java, the hot programming language for client-side Web extensions.

Chapter 10

Java Still Jams!

*I*n the words of Sun Microsystems, Inc., Java's developer, Java is "a simple, object-oriented, distributed, interpreted, robust, secure, architecture-neutral, portable, high-performance, multithreaded, and dynamic language." Those of you who aren't walking dictionaries should read on for an explanation of those terms. In its own perverse way, this statement is incredibly accurate, although completely overcome by jargon!

A Java Overview

"Way cool. Stratospheric. White hot. Sizzling." The Web community describes Java with these words. What's so great about this object-oriented language with the funny name? Its multimedia capabilities, for one thing. Many people see Java as the most exciting avenue for bringing interactivity to the Web.

The unique features that Java offers, in combination with browsers such as Netscape Navigator and Internet Explorer, bring to the Web a form of real-time multimedia interactivity that has previously been available only from CD-ROMs. Instead of following hyperlinks, you get information in the form of moving pictures, audio, and video when you surf the Net with a Java-friendly browser. If you're looking for hotel information online, Java lets you walk through rooms on-screen to decide which one you like. You can plan stock or other financial portfolios with live data. And online shopping changes dramatically.

Java's specific features include the following:

- Cartoon-style animation
- Music that plays in the background while a user loads a Web page
- Inline sounds that play in real time while a user loads a Web page
- Real-time video
- Multiplayer interactive games

We've heard people compare Java's potential impact to the advent of the spreadsheet for PCs or the development of Mosaic, the first graphical Web browser. Java's future is regarded brightly in areas as diverse as electronic commerce, software distribution, and gaming. And as a bonus, Java is one of the most secure and virus-resistant languages ever created.

What makes Java different?

Java applets (small Java programs that you can include in HTML documents) are Java's most radical and brilliant creation. Applets greet you at Java-enhanced sites. Instead of viewing a table of contents at a Web site, you may encounter an applet showing a talking head that smiles, laughs, blinks its eyes, and tells you the site contents. As long as you're using a browser that supports Java, downloading specific software to run an applet isn't necessary; the Java environment in your browser automatically picks up the applet and runs it from your desktop.

This last feature sets Java apart from other languages. With a standard Web browser, you can't use a new content type (such as a special image format or game protocol) until the browser is updated to include that new type.

In stark contrast, Java compatibility is a feature that any browser is able to implement. Java sends the browser the requested content and the program needed to view it. Another bonus for you Web authors is that you no longer have to wait until a browser implements support for certain file types to use these types on your Web sites — instead, you can write the code yourself (in Java) and send your file to any user who requests it!

One of Java's most stellar features is its platform independence. A Java application can run on any platform and requires only that a single copy of the master version of that application be stored in a controlled location (on a Web server somewhere on the Internet). This process is truly revolutionary because it transforms the Net into a software distribution system and changes your Web browser into a platform capable of running an infinite variety of software.

Therefore, when you request a Java application over the Internet, the application runs on your local machine — without having to consider what type of hardware or software you use. This omniplatform capacity is a boon for system administrators as well because they need to worry about revising and controlling access to only one copy of the code. A Java-capable user can take advantage of applets from anywhere and everywhere.

Yet even among developers, Java's real power isn't fully realized. Professional developers can exploit Java's thundering power by creating tool kits that sit on top of raw Java. In turn, these tool kits should enable users to create powerful applications that are customized to their needs.

About those terms . . .

Now that we helped you recover from the original Java gibberish that we quoted in the first sentence of this chapter — and we hope that you are just a little excited about its potential — we want to explain those terms. Remember, we said that Java is "a simple, object-oriented, distributed, interpreted, robust, secure, architecture-neutral, portable, high-performance, multithreaded, and dynamic language." In the interests of clarity, the following sections tell you what that *really* means.

Simple

Programmers call Java both *simple* and *elegant*. Java syntax eliminates the unnecessary and esoteric elements that plagued C++. For that reason, many people think that Java will ultimately replace C++ as a programming language of choice.

Object-oriented

Every Java class is directly or indirectly descended from the Object class — the grandfather of all Java classes. (*Class* refers to a method for defining a set of related objects that can inherit or share certain characteristics.) Likewise, everything in Java must be an object, unlike in C++. Only the most basic, primitive Java operations and data types (such as int, while, for, and so on) operate at a subobject level. In Java-speak, every class *extends* directly or indirectly from the Object class, making Java *object-oriented*.

Distributed

From its inception, developers designed Java to be run over a network (to be distributed). Consequently, Java features well-developed, inherent HTTP and TCP/IP capabilities. CORBA-style Interface Definition Language bindings grace Java; in programmerspeak, this statement means that Java programs are able to invoke remote procedures over a network from server-based objects. And in something closer to English, this explanation means that Java programs are able to request remote services across the network, with some reasonable expectation that those requests will be fulfilled.

Interpreted

Java's unique, hard-core compiler converts any Java source code into a machine-independent format. This advanced conversion enables the source to run on any computer that is equipped with a Java Virtual Machine (a special platform-specific program that implements a Java runtime system, allowing the machine to interpret Java code).

The *bytecodes,* which result from the conversion, are the key to Java's impressive application portability. Although this portability is a groundbreaking feature, Java isn't completely different from other programming languages. That is, programmers who are well-versed in Java write application code and save it in files with a JAVA extension. These files, or programs, are then translated into a format that enables your computer to run them.

Robust

Java is considered *robust* because its design completely eliminates *pointer* manipulation from the language (pointers are names or locations of specific memory addresses and are often used by programmers to play games with memory allocation and data access, both of which can be fraught with peril). Eliminating this element removes a big source of runtime errors. Although pointer abstraction in languages such as C and C++ can benefit seasoned programmers, it can also cause memory leaks and other obscure runtime errors.

Another of Java's winning features is its garbage collection mechanism that remembers to deallocate memory. After an object is *thrown away* in the Java runtime environment (that is, after it has been used and is no longer needed in a program), other objects can reclaim and reuse the memory vacated by the thrown-away objects.

Secure

Java is *secure* because it is a client-side technology. Java programs are, in effect, downloaded from a host machine to your client machine by using conventional Web server transports (such as HTTP). Java uses safety precautions to prevent viruses from reaching your machine; before running any applet, the Java runtime system looks at incoming Java bytecodes to make sure that the program code is safe. Any code that is not safe is unequivocally rejected. Although this feature may be the safest thing going, that distinction attracts renegades who revel in code-cracking, so don't count on 100 percent safety. Still, Java's security should only improve as the language matures.

Architecture-neutral and portable

Java's byte-ordering issues (that is, the order in which it interprets bytes in memory when handling numbers and values) are negligible. Also, its bytecodes operate independently of any underlying architecture (the *architecture-neutral* feature means that it doesn't depend on hardware support to represent data). In addition, Java's character sets are Unicode-based for internationally *portable* applications. Today, the portable Java runtime system is available on a wide variety of systems, including Windows 95 and Windows NT, Solaris, HP/UX, SunOS 4.1.3, AIX, OS/2, and Digital UNIX (OSF/1). This availability means that the same program will run on all these operating systems (and their associated hardware) without requiring any modification.

High performance

To call Java a *high-performance* language may be slightly premature, because Java code seems to run 20 to 30 times slower for some CPU-intensive programs. The promise of high performance is definitely apparent, though. Sun Microsystems is committed to making Java's on-the-fly performance rival that of native C or C++ applications. Sun Microsystems' development of a just-in-time class compiler, which is able to provide more dynamic runtime support for Java's unique capabilities, is helping to improve Java performance across the board.

Multithreaded

Multithreaded means that Java can run multiple subtasks (called *threads*) within a single large application. Multithreading usually helps interactive performance. Java can create and manage its own threads and is inherently multithreaded; that is, Java has certain threads (such as the garbage collection system for reallocating memory) that run in low-priority mode.

Java borrowed the idea of synchronized keywords from the Mesa programming language and the Xerox Cedar environment. When code is wrapped with the `synchronized` keyword, its objects and methods may only be accessed by one object at a time. In other words, the `synchronized` keyword makes any associated code single-threaded, rather than inherently multithreaded (the normal Java default).

Dynamic

Java lets you patch applications *dynamically*, so (unlike patching in C++) you have to worry much less about recompilation. Because releasing a perfect piece of software is rare, making adjustments to your application at some point is practically inevitable. Java makes these adjustments much easier by deferring lots of its linkage manipulation until runtime, which basically eliminates C++'s superclass problems.

That's it for the gibberish, but aren't you glad we told you all about Java? If you can simply appreciate the incredible thought and effort that's gone into Java's design and development, we've succeeded in delivering the right message!

Java's history: from seedling to coffee bean

Java came out of the fertile breeding grounds of Sun Microsystems. The growing process began when a disgruntled employee, Patrick Naughton, told Sun Microsystems' chief Scott McNealy that he was leaving Sun Microsystems to go to NeXT Computer, Inc., because NeXT was doing more interesting work. McNealy asked Naughton to tell him (McNealy) what he (Naughton) thought was wrong with Sun Microsystems before leaving.

The list of suggestions that Naughton created was well-received by Microsystems executives, who gave him, along with a team of coworkers, carte blanche to pursue new research projects. The team code-named themselves Green and set to work on developing the fundamental elements of what would eventually become Java. They initially thought the key to success lay in the area of consumer electronics (such as interactive TV). Finally in 1994, after a series of disappointments, they realized that the Web was Java's ideal medium.

In the early days, the development team's metaphors were more organic than caffeinated; not only was the team named Green, but the language that emerged into Java was named Oak (because James Gosling, its creator, gazed on an oak tree from his office). But by 1995, Oak was renamed Java, and Naughton had written a Java interpreter for a Web browser called HotJava.

In May, Sun Microsystems formally announced Java and HotJava at its SunWorld '95 exposition. Netscape, always interested in cutting-edge technology, simultaneously announced its intention to license Java for Navigator 2.0. The buzz was thick from then on, because Java's potential to turn the Web on its ear (and garner a great deal of profit) was obvious. Sun Microsystems agreed to make Java and HotJava available free of charge, banking on the idea of making money by licensing the runtime code and Java development tools for commercial use.

Licensees must pass conformance tests in order to license Java and receive branding from Sun Microsystems, Inc. The purpose of this testing is to ensure that applets work on all branded products. Current Java license owners (besides Netscape) include Macromedia, Inc., Novell, Spyglass, Sybase, Symantec, Mitsubishi Electronics, IBM, Microsoft, and Adobe.

Even with such illustrious licensees, whether Sun Microsystems will make loads of money from Java is unclear (although Java's reputation has already helped Sun Microsystems' stock rise). One thing is sure — the Sun Microsystems' plan to make Java an essential programming language and a crucial part of the Web has already worked.

The 1995 release of JavaScript, a more accessible scripting language that nonprogrammers can use, also increases Java's market power. Microsoft's introduction of its own J++ Java development environment, and its increasingly heated endorsements of Java technology have also helped to legitimize Java in the minds of the largest of all development communities on the Web — the so-called "Wintel" (Microsoft Windows/Intel) developers.

This site contains a timeline of Java's evolution through the end of 1995:

```
http://ils.unc.edu/blaze/java/javahist.html.
```

Java's learning curve

As far as developers are concerned, Java's learning curve is minimal because its syntax is close to C++. However, for mere mortals uninitiated into the complex wonders of C or C++, Java is a complicated — and largely unnecessary — language to learn.

Unlike HTML, Java wasn't designed to be particularly accessible, and you don't really need to know Java just to write for the Web. Writing in Java can be compared to the more complicated and professional realm of creating CGI (Common Gateway Interface) programs.

The *lite* version of Java, called *JavaScript*, is much more viable than Java for most ordinary HTML authors to use (and Chapter 11 of this book covers this subject in brief). Sun Microsystems has also voiced its intentions to develop tool kits for nonprogrammers as well, and interesting development environments are also available from Symantec (Visual Café) and Borland (Latte).

The bottom line is: Nonprogrammers needn't worry about learning Java to enjoy its benefits. The only thing you need to experience Java's full-bodied flavor is a Java-enabled Web browser (such as a recent version of Netscape or Internet Explorer) that lets you install a Java plugin, which delivers Java's runtime interpreter. For those of you who are interested in programming in Java or JavaScript, read on for the exciting details.

Java versus C++ — the differences

Java features the following:

- **Single inheritance:** Keeps object relationships simple and easy to follow.
- **Garbage collection:** Reclaims available memory and lets Java applications run more efficiently.
- **Native multithreading:** Lets Java applications "'divide and conquer'" processing tasks, which also improves efficiency.

C++ features these elements:

- **A preprocessor:** Enables programmers to work with useful abstractions, without building them directly into the language.
- **Operator overloading:** Lets programmers play all kinds of tricks with variables and memory; although risky, this technique can provide substantial power when properly applied.
- **Header files:** Enables programmers to invoke standard collections of type definitions, variables, and library elements.
- **Pointers:** Lets subroutines and modules move addresses around, rather than values, which can speed up program behavior.
- **Multiple inheritance:** Lets programmers combine aspects of existing objects at will; although often confusing, this process is also incredibly powerful.

Creating Java Content

For nonprogrammers, creating Java content isn't nearly as easy as creating Web page content with HTML. But if Java's seductive programming power is too appealing for this information to daunt your interest, we suggest that you do some research before plunging into programming.

The following URL takes you to the Java Message Exchange, where you can ask questions and read about other people's experiences with the language:

```
http://porthos.phoenixat.com/~warreng/WWWBoard
          /wwwboard.html
```

Sun Microsystems has a site that features helpful Java tutorials and covers topics such as writing Java programs, writing applets, creating a user interface, and much more:

```
http://java.sun.com:80/tutorial/index.html
```

Another excellent way to find out about Java is to look at Java source code wherever you can. Study and mimic examples of Java that you find on the Web — imitation is not only the highest form of flattery, but also a great way to understand a subject.

Unfortunately, Java source isn't as easy to see as HTML: You can't simply hit a View Source button and instantly immerse yourself in Java (because applets move as bytecodes across the Internet, not as source code). To look at Java source, you need to find a Java-related newsgroup (such as `comp.lang.java`) or a mailing list, or surf the Web and grab all the code you can find. But don't despair — you can find plenty of Java out there!

About Java programming . . .

You can use any word-processing program or editor to create and edit a Java program, as long as the tool you use can save files in ASCII format. Just remember: You must save all Java programs in a file ending with the `JAVA` extension.

Before you run your Java program, you must compile it with the Java compiler, usually a program named *javac*. The compiler translates Java source code into *bytecodes*, an intermediate form of code that changes Java language statements to machine instructions.

The bytecode doesn't go the final step of adopting a machine language that corresponds to a specific operating system and computer; the Java runtime environment does that step. Completing this final step is Java's key to platform independence and the reason that Java is both *interpreted* and *compiled*. After you compile a program, though, you're ready to roll.

If you encounter any problems with compilation or interpretation of Java code, the following site's troubleshooting tips should quiet your woes:

```
http://sunsite.unc.edu/javafaq/
```

Say "Hello World": creating a Java program

Demonstrating programming concepts with a simple "Hello World" program has been customary for a long time. This program, which prints the string Hello World to the screen, demonstrates the mechanics of writing code and constructing a simple program.

Before you start, make a directory or folder called JAVAHTML and create a subdirectory or subfolder called CLASSES within that directory. (Calling the first directory JAVAHTML isn't actually required, but you do need to call the subdirectory CLASSES.)

The code that we show next is a "Hello World" application written in Java. To run this application, type the following lines into a text file and save the file with the name HelloWorld.java in the JAVAHTML directory.

```
class HelloWorld {
public static void main (String args[]) {
System.out.println("Hello World!");
}
}
```

Compile this program by typing javac HelloWorld.java at the command prompt (make sure that you're in the JAVAHTML directory).

If, for some reason, this program doesn't work, check out the following troubleshooting tips:

- ✔ Did you include the semicolon (;) after System.out.println("Hello World!")?
- ✔ Did you remember the closing bracket?
- ✔ Did you type everything exactly as it appears in the preceding code lines? Precise capitalization is essential because Java is case-sensitive.

The compiler places the executable output in a file named HelloWorld.class in the JAVAHTML directory after the program is successfully compiled. At this point, you can run the program simply by typing java HelloWorld at the command prompt. The program (hypothetically) responds by printing Hello World! on the screen.

Finding and Using Java-Enabled Browsers

You need the following components to use Java:

- ✔ A Java-enabled Web browser: HotJava, Netscape 2.0 or later, Internet Explorer 2.0 or later
- ✔ A Java compiler that turns Java source code into bytecodes
- ✔ A Java interpreter to run Java programs
- ✔ A text editor, preferably programming-oriented, such as BBEdit or Brief
- ✔ A suitable operating system (Windows 95 or Windows NT, Mac/OS 7.5 or better, many flavors of UNIX)

The following components are nice to have for your Java adventure, but not crucial:

- ✔ A Java debugger
- ✔ A Java class browser
- ✔ A Java-capable visual development environment
- ✔ Java documentation, either online information or any of the many books now available on this subject

You can find elements of these components, along with detailed instructions for their use, at the Sun Microsystems page:

```
http://java.sun.com/
```

Before Java's technology emerged, the Web was confined to static pages filled with only images and text. However, now that Java's on the scene, you not only have the same features as a CD-ROM — animation, multimedia, and instant interactivity — but when you're plugged into a network using Java, you also have live data, communication, and instant updates. Java, working with the Web, is a great one-two punch for anyone who realizes the full possibilities of this technology.

Referencing Java Materials in Your Web Pages

Incorporating Java materials into your Web pages can endow them with a whole new look and feel, as well as new potential. By using applets, you can actually walk your viewers through a sequence that you want them to see. The following list gives you tips for effective use of Java applets in your pages:

- ✔ Read about Java before you start trying to program with it. You can find a number of helpful resources on the Web and a number of books on Java as well.

- ✔ Surf to see what's going on in Java programming. The list at the end of this chapter provides URLs for a number of interesting Java sites.

- ✔ Select an applet that you would like to emulate. GAMELAN, at http://www.gamelan.com/, is a directory that offers many sample applets. Study the HTML code from the applets page and consult the code as you create your applet's parameters.

- ✔ Access an applet. You can't use applets in your pages unless you have the ability to access them! You have two paths of access: remote call and local compilation.

- ✔ Do some experimenting with call commands and figure out what HTML tag calls the applet for use on your pages. Directories called CLASSES are the repositories for all compiled applets.

To invoke a Java applet from inside a HTML document, use the HTML <APPLET> tag. The following code shows the general syntax for utilizing the <APPLET> tag:

```
<APPLET
CLASS="class name"
SRC="URL"
ALIGN="alignment"
HEIGHT="height in pixels"
WIDTH="width in pixels"
APPLET_SPECIFIC_ATTRIBUTES="values"
...>
```

To preserve security, applets can't do certain things. The following list shows you some of the things that applets can't do:

✔ Make network connections to any host except the one where they originated.

✔ Read every system property.

✔ Define native methods or load libraries.

✔ Read or write files on the host that runs them.

If you think about these restrictions, most aim at preventing applets from violating system security or data integrity, primarily to discourage hackers from trying to use Java's normal behavior (of moving code from one system to another) for their evil purposes.

Java Design Do's and Don'ts

The following sections examine some areas to explore — and to avoid — when writing Java code.

Do

Do the following things when you design Web page elements with Java:

✔ Do make sure that your applet stops running when it's off-screen. If the browser is iconified (minimized) or displaying a page other than the one containing the applet, the applet generally shouldn't be running — doing so drains CPU resources. Your applet can run off-screen only if your applet code doesn't explicitly launch any threads.

✔ Do implement the stop() method if your applet code launches any threads. The stop() method can halt and destroy the threads you've launched by setting them to null. For example:

```
public synchronized void stop() {
   if (refresh != null) {
      public synchronized void stop() {
      refresh.stop();
      refresh = null;
```

✔ Do give your users a way to stop an applet's behavior, especially when the applet does something that is potentially annoying, such as playing sounds (think of all those people secretly surfing at work!).

One way to stop an applet's behavior is to implement the `mouseDown()` method (in an applet that normally doesn't respond to mouse clicks) so that clicking the mouse suspends or resumes the thread. The following code shows one approach to using the `mouseDown()` method:

```
boolean threadSuspended = false;
        //an instance variable
public boolean mouseDown(Event e, int x, int y) {
if (threadSuspended) {
  myThread.resume();
} else {
  myThread.suspend();
}
threadSuspended = !threadSuspended;
return true;
}
```

Don't

Don't do the following things when you design Web page elements with Java:

- ✔ Don't forget to remove or disable debugging output. Debugging output (usually created with `System.out.println()`) may be useful to you, but it may annoy or confuse users. To give your users feedback, try the status area at the bottom of the window or inside an applet's display area.
- ✔ Don't forget to end source URLs in your `CLASSES` directory with a slash.

Lots of other do's and don'ts exist for doing Java right. Read on for some excellent resources on this topic.

Top Java Resources

Not surprisingly, Sun Microsystems has an excellent collection of Java resources at `java.sun.com/`. In addition to that page, the following Web resources contain helpful and interesting information about Java:

- ✔ The Java Message Exchange is full of questions and answers:

  ```
  http://porthos.phoenixat.com/~warreng/WWWBoard
          /wwwboard.html
  ```

- ✔ Gamelan is an excellent resource for Java applets:

  ```
  http://www.gamelan.com/
  ```

✔ John December offers an impressive collection of Java information:

`http://www.december.com/works/java/info.html`

✔ This page contains useful information about Java, as well as downloads and links:

`http://sunsite.sut.ac.jp/java/`

✔ The following is a great page of Java links:

`http://www.nebulex.com/URN/devel.html`

✔ Sun Microsystems' helpful Java tutorials cover topics such as writing Java programs, writing applets, creating a user interface, and many more:

`http://java.sun.com:80/tutorial/index.html`

✔ Café Au Lait is a superlative resource listing:

`http://sunsite.unc.edu/javafaq/`

✔ If you have compiler or interpreter problems, this site is full of trouble-shooting tips:

`http://java.sun.com/tutorial/troubleshooting/index.html`

✔ The IDG JavaWorld page is an exhaustive Java resource:

`http://www.javaworld.com/`

Java's Future

The idea that Java can automatically improve the quality of Web applications is not a given. Without vision, Java's applets alone can't push Web users into a higher realm of surf-nirvana. However, Java's potential is undeniable, and its possibilities in terms of multimedia and interactivity are staggering. If used well by developers, Java permanently enriches the Web.

Whether development continues with Java or something newer and more exciting comes along, you can't deny the growth and progress that Java has stimulated for the Web. Plus, Java is the world's greatest excuse for lame, caffeine-inspired puns! In the next chapter, we leave Java behind and move into the less rarefied, but more accessible, world of HTML scripting languages, including Java's cousin, JavaScript.

Chapter 11

Scripting Alternatives

● ●

In This Chapter

▶ Understanding scripting languages

▶ Jumping into JavaScript

▶ Venturing forth with VBScript

▶ Doing the Dynamic HTML thing

▶ Exploring new scripting alternatives

● ●

*S*omewhere between the basic capabilities in HTML markup that you know and love and the rich but complex possibilities conferred by CGI and Java programming lies a middle ground. This halfway point is also rife with possibilities to extend your Web site's look, feel, and level of interactivity.

Welcome to the Scripting Zone, an area of Web extension where you'll type bizarre and sometimes incomprehensible text to make your Web pages stand up and do tricks. Like HTML, scripting languages leave traces that anyone who views the source code for a Web page can see. But like the languages you'd use for CGI programs or Java applets, scripting languages confer more power and capability on their makers than does plain, unadulterated HTML.

Most experts believe that power and complexity are related for scripting languages, so it's important to understand that they're not truly general, nor infinitely extensible, as are real programming languages. However, they're also somewhat easier to learn and use than a full-blown programming language.

Best of all, most scripting languages (including all of those in this chapter) include lots of built-in functions, toolbars, widgets, interfaces, and other pre-fabricated goodies so that mere mortals who use a scripting language need do very little low-level, nuts-and-bolts programming. Instead, these tools use the built-in facilities of a scripting language as a set of building blocks to assemble surprisingly sophisticated extensions to Web pages at the cost of very little programming effort. Perhaps that's why scripting languages are quite hot right now—and it also should explain why this topic is in this edition of *MORE HTML For Dummies*!

Although each of the scripting languages discussed in this chapter has its strengths and weaknesses, any of them will provide a significant increase in what you can do with your Web pages, both as a page designer and as a content author.

The Mechanics of Scripting

All scripting languages rely on the presence of a special program, called an *interpreter*, to read the contents of a script while a document is open, and to take action based on that script's contents, immediately after each line is read. Because scripting relies on interpretation while the script is read, script languages depend on something called a runtime system, which means that the script is completely decoded and executed while it's running on a computer.

This system is in direct contrast to programming languages like C or Pascal, where a program called a *compiler* reads and interprets programs in advance. Values can be read or substituted at runtime from an input file or from user interaction, but compilation of the bulk of a program's code greatly reduces the amount of processing.

For this reason, interpreted languages, such as those used for Web scripting, run more slowly than compiled languages, because more processing is necessary to handle the code at runtime. That's also why you'll often see adjectives such as fast, efficient, or lightweight applied to scripting languages, because they indicate that such languages have been optimized to behave well at runtime, to require little in the way of system resources, and to impose no significant additional computing burden on the machines where they run.

Scripting languages are also sometimes called *embedded languages* because they usually appear within text for some other kind of language or text markup. For example, all the scripting languages covered in this chapter are built to appear within HTML documents, marked by the presence of the `<SCRIPT>` tag.

When the browser recognizes a `<SCRIPT>` tag, the following process begins:

1. The browser looks for a value for the `LANGUAGE` attribute (which may be something like `JavaScript`, `VBScript`, or `Jscript`).

2. Based on the value of the attribute, the browser invokes a runtime interpreter for that scripting language and passes control to the interpreter as soon as it's identified.

3. The interpreter takes over and executes the script until it reaches the closing `</SCRIPT>` tag.

4. The interpreter returns control to the browser, which continues with its job of HTML interpretation and rendering.

Because HTML is purely character-based, any scripting language that's embedded within HTML must share that character basis. This character basis means that you can use any text editor to create scripts for inclusion on your Web pages. But in many cases, particularly for VBScript, you'll find a variety of authoring tools that can help you build scripts. (In some cases, tools are available to help you build the HTML documents within which such scripts must occur.)

Programming with JavaScript

JavaScript isn't the same as Java, although the two are closely related. Created as a joint venture between Netscape and Sun, JavaScript is sometimes jokingly called *Java Lite*. (It was named *Mocha* before release — tired of the coffee metaphors yet? Keep reading.) JavaScript is a compact, object-based scripting language used to develop client and server applications. What can it do for you? Well, JavaScript provides a faster and more accessible means (than Java) to incorporate applets and other small programs into your Web site.

JavaScript is frequently regarded as Java's decaf version, which isn't wholly accurate because JavaScript addresses a different market niche. Dynamically typed languages (which permit type definitions to be added at will) that are less complex and more compact than Java, such as dBASE and HyperTalk, are considered to be JavaScript's real predecessors. They, like JavaScript, appeal to a wider audience than a highly specialized language like Java. Their accessibility owes to certain qualities: easy syntax; specialized, built-in functions; and minimal requirements for object creation and use.

JavaScript was explicitly developed for use with Netscape Navigator 2.0, where it provides a set of client-side APIs (Application Program Interfaces). These client-side APIs address the nuisances of static Web text. When JavaScript statements are embedded in an HTML page, they can then recognize and react to mouse clicks, page navigation, and `<FORM>` input. Although JavaScript lacks Java's strong type-checking and static typing mechanisms, it still supports the majority of Java's basic control flow constructs and expression syntax.

When you're working with JavaScript, you needn't use (or know anything about) classes. Instead, you acquire finished script components from a JavaScript resource (perhaps from a commercial product or an online collection of such materials) that make high-level properties (like `color` or `visible`) susceptible to scripting controls. As a result, you can set these properties to achieve the effects you desire in a Web document. JavaScript may offer the next best thing to writing code, and its capabilities enable many Web authors to include capabilities they wouldn't be able to include otherwise.

Differences between Java and JavaScript

JavaScript scripts run more slowly than Java applets because JavaScript interprets each line separately as it reads it from the HTML source file, but Java applets are immediately executed by the Java runtime environment within a browser.

JavaScript doesn't possess all the object-oriented features that Java has; in JavaScript, you can define objects but not object classes. JavaScript also lacks Java's object inheritance. Neither of these omissions is too significant for an average JavaScript user, because JavaScript's shorter scripts don't generally have the same reuse requirements that objects in Java do. In general, these omissions mean that JavaScript writers must content themselves with whatever predefined objects and attributes are available, rather than the richness and flexibility of full-blown Java, especially when it comes to recasting or tweaking objects to add functionality. But because JavaScript has been created to reduce complexity and speed development, anyone who needs to do extensive work with objects will be better served by working with Java directly, rather than using JavaScript.

Because developers created JavaScript specifically to enable HTML writers to support different HTML tags and to allow elements to interact with each other, input from one HTML form can influence HTML information inside another HTML page. In addition, JavaScript may change the text of the HTML page where it resides. By contrast, Java applets don't usually interact with HTML or change the text on a Web page. Instead, Java applets limit themselves to a specific region of a page that's reserved for their exclusive use (much like a separate display frame).

Also, JavaScript can deliver interactive Web forms more efficiently than Java. JavaScript enables you to handle error-checking with built-in event-handling mechanisms that are conveniently based upon user interaction with an HTML form.

The following lists highlight the main characteristics of Java and JavaScript. Comparing these lists should help you understand the differences between the two languages. The first list describes Java characteristics:

✔ Java code is compiled on a server before it's executed on the client.

✔ Java has strong typing requirements, which means that the program code must declare variable data types.

✔ Java applets consist of object classes with inheritance.

✔ Java has *static binding*, which means that its object references must exist when the Java code is compiled.

The following list describes JavaScript characteristics:

✔ The client interprets (it doesn't compile) JavaScript.

✔ JavaScript code is both integrated and embedded in HTML.

✔ JavaScript has loose typing, which means that the JavaScript code need not declare variable data types.

✔ Although JavaScript code uses built-in objects, it doesn't have classes or complete object-orientation.

✔ JavaScript has *dynamic binding*, which means that its object references are checked at runtime.

JavaScript syntax and semantics

The meat of any JavaScript program lies between the `<SCRIPT>` and `</SCRIPT>` tags, which define the program's starting and stopping points. `<SCRIPT>` marks the point where the browser hands control to a JavaScript interpreter, which reads all the lines in the HTML file until it encounters the `</SCRIPT>` tag. Between those two HTML tags is where the syntax and semantics of JavaScript truly reside.

The following line is an example of JavaScript code:

```
document.write("This text should appear before
  the body of the HTML page.<P>");
```

In this block of text, an object named `document` is being accessed, and its `write` attribute is being applied to the text inside the parentheses between the quotation marks.

This example illustrates the `object.attribute` syntax which defines the way that JavaScript statements work. The semicolon (;) marks the end of a statement to tell the interpreter that it's complete. Danny Goodman's *JavaScript Bible* (see the reference information in the next section) covers the syntax in great detail, and includes a terrific Quick Reference in Appendix A.

Viewing source code is a good way to figure out how to use JavaScript, just as it is when you're trying to learn Java. Examine the following JavaScript code:

```
<HTML>
<HEAD>
<TITLE>My First JavaScript Page</TITLE>
<SCRIPT LANGUAGE="Javascript">
<!-- The SCRIPT tag indicates the beginning of a
script; the value supplied for the LANGUAGE
attribute indicates that it's written in JavaScript.
Notice also that the script occurs in the HEAD
section of this particular HTML document.
-->


<!--
document.write("This text should appear before the body
 of the HTML page.<P>");
// -->
<!-- The preceding HTML comment is used to "wrap"
JavaScript code so that browsers that don't under-
stand JavaScript will not display code that they
can't act upon. This is a common scripting trick.
Notice also that the syntax uses the document
object's write method to output literal text
(what's between the double quotes) that includes genuine
            screen output, plus HTML tags.
-->

</SCRIPT>
</HEAD>
<BODY>
<H3> Check out my first JavaScript Web page! </H3>
</BODY>
</HTML>
```

JavaScript resources

As with most other Web-related technologies, you can use a search engine like Yahoo!, Excite, or AltaVista to produce gobs and gobs of JavaScript information by submitting JavaScript as a search string. The following are some of the best JavaScript resources:

✔ The Java Authoring Guide covers a range of information on JavaScript:

```
http://home.netscape.com/eng/mozilla/2.0/handbook ⊃
         javascript/index.html
```

✔ The FAQ (Frequently Asked Questions) for JavaScript:

```
http://www.his.com/~smithers/freq/beta/jsfaq.html
```

✔ Danny Goodman's *JavaScript Bible*, 2nd Edition (IDG Books Worldwide, Indianapolis, IN, 1996, List price: $39.99 with CD-ROM) is one of the best-ever resources on JavaScript. For information on this book, go to the following site:

```
http://www.idgbooks.com
```

There's certainly no shortage of resources on JavaScript, so dive right in if you're interested in learning more. Your Web pages — and your users — will thank you!

Programming with VBScript

Microsoft's full name for VBScript is Visual Basic Scripting Edition. VBScript is a subset of Microsoft's immensely popular Visual Basic development environment, a great favorite of software developers everywhere. VBScript has been implemented as a fast, portable, and efficient interpreter for use in Web browsers and other applications that can use ActiveX controls and Java applets. Support for VBScript is currently bundled with Microsoft Internet Explorer 3.0 (and higher-numbered versions) and with Internet Information Server 3.0.

What about Jscript?

Those of you who follow the latest trends are no doubt aware that Microsoft has floated yet another scripting language, called Jscript, for use with its Internet Explorer browser. So what's the difference between JavaScript and Jscript? And why should you care?

First, JavaScript originated with Netscape and Jscript originated with Microsoft, but the fundamental difference between the two is that JavaScript relies on underlying runtime mechanisms associated with its own interpreter and related mechanisms, but Jscript depends on the presence of ActiveX Scripting support in the runtime environment. Practically speaking, this difference leads to the idea that it's better to use JavaScript where the primary audience for a site uses Netscape Navigator and use Jscript (or VBScript) where the primary audience uses Internet Explorer. Because a subset of JavaScript works with Internet Explorer, and Jscript works on Navigator when ActiveX support is loaded, this idea is not a cut-and-dried matter, but rather, a strong tendency.

Like JavaScript, VBScript programming relies on the use of the `<SCRIPT>` tag pair in HTML. The VBScript interpreter, which reads and reacts to the contents of the scripts that appear within HTML documents, handles everything between the opening `<SCRIPT>` and closing `</SCRIPT>`.

What VBScript supports that JavaScript does not is an intuitive, graphical interface for building and using scripts within HTML documents. For example, if you're working in an environment that supports Microsoft's ActiveX Control Panel, this interface means you can launch this tool and invoke all kinds of tools and wizards to help the process of scripting along at any point in building an HTML document.

VBScript is a strict subset of the Visual Basic for Applications language that's supported in Microsoft Excel, Project, Word, and Access, as well as in the Visual Basic 4.0 development system sold separately by Microsoft. VBScript is designed to be compact and low in overhead, for easy use across a (potentially slow) Internet connection. Because of VBScript's design characteristics, it does not use strict data typing, nor does it support file input/ouput or direct access to a machine's underlying operating system (these assumptions are wise for software that will run across a variety of platforms in any case).

When used in the Internet Explorer environment, VBScript acts just like JavaScript — in other words, it's based on a text interpreter that reads ASCII characters from within an HTML file invoked by the combination of the `<SCRIPT>` tag and the `LANGUAGE = "VBScript"` attribute. Like JavaScript, VBScript does not rely on stand-alone (or rather, stand-apart) applets like those used in pure Java. As with any scripting language, VBScript adds to the contents of the HTML documents in which it appears.

What's the scoop on ActiveX?

At this point, we've slung the term ActiveX enough that it cries out for definition:

ActiveX, which Microsoft once called Object Linking and Embedding, or OLE, is a collection of tools designed to bring audio, animation, and user interaction to Web documents. It is quite similar to the plugin technology developed for Netscape Navigator and used in Java applets. All three technologies make it possible to send small programs to a Web browser without requiring the involvement of any other special software on the desktop or back-end capabilities from a Web server. ActiveX supplies code from Microsoft that allows developers to add dynamic or interactive components or controls to otherwise static Web pages. The general consensus is that ActiveX is Microsoft's competitive response to Sun Microsystems' Java technology (even though Microsoft itself has licensed Java, and offers its J++ Java development environment to its customers).

In short, ActiveX represents important Microsoft technologies necessary to permit Web and other documents to access persistent software objects and exchange information across a network.

Because VBScript can draw on a vast library of ActiveX controls, predefined buttons, toolbars, and other graphical widgets, it offers considerable capability when creating or defining interactive controls or onscreen forms for user input on Web pages. Because so many developers are already familiar with the VB development environment, they can leverage what they already know with VBScript.

The ActiveX Control Panel provides powerful document editing and a helpful graphical programming toolset that is useful when you're programming with VBScript. This tool makes it easy to extend existing HTML documents or author script-enhanced HTML documents from scratch, because of its powerful HTML layout controls and its menu-driven access to immense libraries of predefined functions, buttons, and other graphical objects. The ActiveX Control Panel is likened to "NotePad on steroids," in that it presents a text editor interface to the user, but mouse- and menu-driven development tools are never more than a few mouse clicks or keystrokes away. The ActiveX Control Panel includes Scripting Wizards that can help with script creation, an HTML layout tool that provides precise control over HTML page layout and object placement, and support for HTML authoring.

The only barrier to VBScript's path to world domination is that each VBScript script on a page forces a separate load of the VB runtime system. At around 3MB of memory per incarnation, this memory drain can quickly bring even serious systems to their knees. But performance limitations aside, VBScript offers serious capability and easy page extension to anyone with a modicum of interest in programming. Taken with the large number of books, tutorials, and explanatory materials available for Visual Basic and Microsoft's outstanding support for VBScript, it is a Web extension technology not only to be reckoned with, but worth considering for those environments where Internet Explorer is the dominant (or only) Web browser in use.

As you might expect, Microsoft's Web site provides one of the best points of departure for an investigation of VBScript's multifarious capabilities. Start at the VBScript home page, which you'll find at:

```
http://www.microsoft.com/VBSCRIPT/
```

From this site, you can obtain a copy of the latest FAQ, download the software and documentation, and obtain access to all kinds of related links and examples.

Dynamic HTML

Dynamic HTML is a new development in the area of Web scripting and HTML authoring. An initiative started by Microsoft, Dynamic HTML is now working its way through the W3C to define a standard for inline scripting languages. Microsoft and its supporters dubbed this technology Dynamic HTML, but the W3C has labeled it the Document Object Model (DOM).

The W3C's efforts are focused toward establishing the DOM as a platform- and language-independent or neutral interface that enables programs and scripts to dynamically access and update content, style, and even structure displayed within a browser. Further enhancements may include a communi- cations standard to allow inline scripts to communicate interactively with background CGIs or to incorporate processed data back into a presented page.

Vendors use the term "dynamic HTML" to describe the combination of the DOM (or DOM-like occurrences), HTML markup, style sheets, and inline scripts (such as JavaScript) to animate and dynamically alter Web docu- ments. Microsoft, Netscape, and others have submitted proposals for the ultimate outcome of the DOM standard. Obviously, each vendor's proposal favors its current technology and products, but the W3C is determined to define a standard that offers no native advantage to any vendor.

The work at the W3C has only recently started, so it may be months before any public proposals or drafts of any kind are available. Until the W3C is able to make a declaration of DOM standards, the user community is at the mercy of those vendors who forge ahead and deploy their own versions of these proposed standards. In such situations the double-talk of vendors is highly evident — they claim to work with the W3C by establishing standards for the Internet community, but they persist with and deploy their own proprietary implementations. This tactic can affect the ultimate outcome of a standard by rallying public support and approval for one vendor's solution over another. This questionable policy keeps the user community in a perpetual state of flux. Unfortunately, it's also become one of the rules of the Web world!

Keep an eye on the DOM information page hosted by the W3C for the latest standards developments:

```
http://www.w3.org/pub/WWW/MarkUp/DOM/
```

At the time of publication, the only available document from this page was a preliminary version of standards requirements.

The skinny on DH

The surprising thing about Dynamic HTML is that so much is being made of an interface standard that adds little to the existing inline scripting capabili- ties. Adept programmers can create some of the features touted by Dynamic HTML without invoking a new standard. To be specific, Dynamic HTML is a definition for an interface standard that adds an object model to HTML. This model enables scripts and other programs to interact dynamically with and alter page elements while a browser is displaying them. Dynamic HTML supports most of the common and popular inline scripting languages, including JavaScript, Java, and VBScript. The only really new or improved features that Dynamic HTML offers are the capability to interact with multimedia and database objects, support for the W3C Cascading Style Sheets (CSS) Specification, and backward browser compatibility.

Unless the W3C adds new HTML markup, or severely alters the assumed path to standardization, most Web authors and beginner programmers will be able to take advantage of Dynamic HTML without too much difficulty. Most existing expertise and experience with Web programming applies well to the construction of Dynamic HTML.

Benefits of Dynamic HTML

Although the final standard for Dynamic HTML is somewhere off in the foreseeable future, we can still generalize about its significance and capabilities. The benefits of this new method of Web publishing and design may pan out only as vague hopes and dreams, but today the following highlights gleam within current proprietary extensions. From our current vantage point, the promises of Dynamic HTML include:

- ✔ **Customized creative content:** Web designers and authors alike can alter the appearance and content of documents on-the-fly in response to user activity. Some of the dynamic features include tool tips over images and icons, fly-open contents, and alterations in font, color, or style of text when a user moves his mouse pointer over it. All of these page interactions occur without communication with the server, and operate as long as a page is displayed in a browser.

- ✔ **Rich multimedia:** Special effects, animations, audio mixing, transitions, vector graphics, and moving sprites are new additions that require far less data transfer than previous Web multimedia methods.

- ✔ **Fine layout control:** Just as a programmer can define the position of objects based on absolute screen position, so Web authors can use x, y, and z order absolute positioning to control object placement with Dynamic HTML.

- ✔ **Business data manipulation:** Web documents can manipulate content on-the-fly without communicating with a server or using high-end programming languages. One possible example would be sorting stock prices based on price or company name.

- ✔ **Decreased server load:** With more and more of the processing of Web documents occurring on the client side, servers will be able to handle more simultaneous users without increasing the servers' workloads.

✔ **Improved platform independence and cross-platform compatibility:**
Because Dynamic HTML uses inline scripting directly supported by
browsers, fewer platform-specific issues (such as plugins or helper
applications) can prevent access to delivered content.

✔ **Down-level browser support:** Dynamic HTML features will automatically change themselves to static elements that conform to older
browsers' capabilities.

The big boys

After submitting proposals to the W3C for consideration and standardization, both Microsoft and Netscape have forged ahead and implemented
proprietary solutions into their latest browser versions. You can explore
these respective companies' perspectives on how Dynamic HTML should
function by visiting the following URLs:

✔ Microsoft Internet Explorer 4.0 with Dynamic HTML:

```
http://www.microsoft.com/ie/ie40/browser/dynamic.htm
```

✔ Netscape Communicator 4.0 with Dynamic HTML:

```
http://developer.netscape.com/library/documentation/⊃
       htmlguid/dynamic_resources.html
```

To experience the thrill of Dynamic HTML, you'll have to download the 15-
plus megabytes' worth of files for each of the 4.0 browsers. As we write this
material, both Netscape Communicator and Internet Explorer are still in
beta release, so you are on your own if you install a beta application. We
recommend waiting for a final release, especially if your computer is a
production tool.

To Script, or Not to Script?

The title of this section raises a question that many of you will have to ask —
and answer — where your own Web pages are concerned. Because of the
power and flexibility of the many scripting languages available, you should
take this question quite seriously. Although some effort is involved in
learning a scripting language (or development environment, if you'd prefer),
the results can be nothing short of amazing. Because scripting is such a
wonderful alternative to CGI programming (and requires no interaction with
the ISP that hosts your Web pages), we think it's an important addition to
any Web site. What you decide to do, however, is entirely up to you.

Enough of scripting already, the next chapter moves on to cover enriched
forms of text display, such as Adobe's Portable Document Format (PDF).

Part III
Cool Web Applications

In this part . . .

Part III is completely new to the second edition of
MORE HTML For Dummies. Here, we examine some of
the many categories of Web-based applications that have
become available to extend and expand any Web site's
capabilities since the publication of the first edition. First,
we tackle the ins and outs of using search engines to index
and deliver information to your visitors on demand in
Chapter 12.

After that, we take you through Chapter 13, where we
expose several packages that can turn your users' e-mail
messages into threaded discussion groups called forums
(in honor of the topic-related message groups on older-
fashioned online services like CompuServe or AOL). We
conclude this part of the book in Chapter 14, wherein we
cover Web-focused document management systems that
can help you keep a growing collection of documents,
graphics, programs, and other files under control.

Chapter 12

Using Your Own Search Engine

*T*he best Web sites not only have the best content, but also the best ways to access that content. One of the more popular ways to expand and simplify access to any site's content is to use a search engine to sift through its offerings. If you've been active on the Internet for more than three hours, you have probably used a search engine already to locate sites or data relevant to your needs. Many of the same technologies you've used to search the whole Internet can be toned down to let others search through your Web site. By implementing a search engine on your Web site, you will open your site to greater scrutiny and potentially more visitors, because word that your site is so easy to access and use should spread like wildfire.

What Is a Search Engine?

A search engine is a tool used to locate information. Describing the term *search engine* without using those very words in its definition is not easy, but here goes: A search engine is an application that looks for data based on a set of keywords or other user-defined criteria.

Searches won't usually be performed directly on all the data from the entire Internet, or even just your entire Web site, but rather against a pre-indexed database of search information. This database contains meta-information about what data is stored at which URLs. The meta-information can include just about anything from author name to creation date, to content keywords.

Using a special kind of search algorithm, often called *fuzzy logic*, the search engine compares the keywords that a user provides against its database. It creates a list of any matches or near matches that it finds. A new HTML document is constructed that contains this list of matches and links to related resources, and that new document is what's returned to the user. Search engines like Yahoo!, Excite, or AltaVista use this process to generate the pages of "hits" (or responses to your search request) for display on your screen.

What Makes 'Em Tick?

Search engines consist of just two quintessential components: a database gathering agent and the search engine itself. Both these components must be present in some form for a search engine to be able to do its job.

The database gathering agent can be either robot or human. A human must painstakingly create the entire database that the search engine uses by hand. A human also must update that same database by hand each time changes affect the content at which it is directed. That's probably why very few search engines use humans to create their databases. A robot — also known as a spider, crawler, wanderer, or any number of other terms that describe an intelligent electronic organism — is able to create the database faster and more efficiently than any human. A robot can tirelessly investigate and record electronic information around the clock. Plus, when changes are made to a site, a robot can detect those changes, remove old information from the database, and add new information (and all without complaining that it never gets to spend time with its family).

The search engine itself is a sleek conglomeration of programming code that can take a string of characters or words and compare them with the information stored in its database. But that's still not the whole picture: A search engine usually doesn't perform a query against its entire database because the data set involved is often still too big. Instead, the engine uses an index linked to the database used for the search. This index can be either keyword- or concept-based. (Other types of indexes may exist, but they aren't widely used.)

Keyword indexes are lists of the most commonly occurring words pulled from the data that the robot gathered. Generally, the robot pulls keywords from <META> tags in a document's head, headings within the text, or words that appear repeatedly within the document. To make sure the robot gets the right keywords for your site, you should use <META Keyword ="value"> tags in your documents and heading tags (<H1>, <H2>, and so on) to organize your documents.

The only problem with keywords is that they are context-free. In other words, a search engine cannot tell the difference between multiple meanings or usages of the same word. Some engines attempt to compensate for this limitation by including search support for singular and plural forms of the same word, different verb tenses, cases, and other predictable word transformations, so a query has a greater probability of returning relevant hits.

Concept-based indexing is the result of an artificially intelligent search agent using linguistic algorithms to make "educated guesses" about what a search string means or is intended to find. This type of indexing focuses more on matching general ideas or concepts rather than matching terms word for word. Concept engines often return a probability score for each hit to help users gauge the relevance of their results. Because of the open-ended nature of the concept model, results can stray widely from the desired topic; educated guesses don't always produce the desired meanings, nor the right results.

Both keyword- and concept-based search engines can provide additional control or fine-tuning to the searches they perform. Usually the controls take the form of Boolean operators, such as AND, OR, and NOT. These operators work with language much like the +, -, ×, and √ operators do for arithmetic. By using these Boolean operators and parentheses, you can fine-tune any search request. For example, the following search request would look for a tri-colored object that wasn't a flag, such as a beach ball or a parrot:

```
(blue AND red AND white) NOT flag
```

You may notice that some search engines offer advanced or power user options in addition to standard search features. Generally, these options provide support for Boolean operators or even provide graphical assistance when working with more complex (but precise) search queries. If you have some particular favorites among the engines that you use, explore these advanced capabilities and how they can benefit your Web site.

Two Ways to Use Search Engines

If you don't already recognize the near infinite value of search engines, then take this challenge: Find the name of the 23rd president's favorite pet, but do not use a search engine of any kind. Once you start banging your head against your monitor, you'll understand fully the worth of good search tools.

Where your own Web site is concerned, you have two choices for incorporating search engines:

- ✔ Allow users easy access to full Internet searches by including a query form in a document on your site
- ✔ Offer users the power to search your material by installing a search engine that focuses exclusively on your Web site

You can decide to employ one of these options, both options, or neither option. But remember, your choice may determine your future Web success (as if all the rest of your decisions didn't affect your fate).

Internet-wide search capability

Adding the capability for others to search the entire Internet through your Web site is easy. Many of the top search engines encourage this type of use of their services. Some of them even offer special benefits, free stuff, or software for incorporating their search forms in your Web site. To add Yahoo!, Excite, or even AltaVista's search engine to your Web site, all you have to do is add the proper form markup to an HTML document and you're done. That's it!

Visit your chosen search engine's home site and then look around for a help or "how to" page. This page usually offers some great insights on how to incorporate the engine's search forms quickly and easily. You may also discover that the search engine vendors will pay you (don't get too excited, such payment is usually in kind, not in cash) for letting them know you're linking to their site. If your link causes a significant traffic increase through their site (and ultimately to their advertising sponsors), you are very likely to get something in return.

Follow this quick three-step process to add Yahoo! to your Web site:

1. **Load the** `Yahoo! to Go` **document in your Web browser.**

   You can access it at the following URL:

   `http://www.yahoo.com/docs/yahootogo/search`

2. **Copy the HTML code offered to you.**

3. **Paste the HTML markup into one of your own documents where you want the search engine to appear.**

That's all there is to it! All of your favorite search engines offer this kind of service. Just take a few moments to look through whatever online information they provide about how to include their search form on your site. Doing it their way — that is, by reading the directions — usually results in successful searching.

For those anarchists among you, we know an even better shortcut: Copy the markup from someone else who's already done the work. The best example to use is also the nearly exhaustive list of Internet search engines available at Search.Com. This method may save you as much as 10 minutes of reading the real documentation from the original site, but then instruction manuals are for wimps:

1. **Load the Search.Com page into your browser by accessing the following URL:**

   `http://www.search.com/`

2. **Click the** `A-Z list`, **and then click the link to the search engine of your choice.**

3. **When the relevant Search.Com hosted version of the search engine's form appears, view the HTML source for that document by choosing the appropriate command from your browser.**

4. **Locate the area below the HTML comment** `<!-- main body content begins here -->`.

5. **Copy the entire section from the opening** `<FORM>` **tag to the closing** `</FORM>` **tag.**

6. **Paste this code into your own document.**

If you use this shortcut method, you still need to visit the original site to make sure the vendor doesn't require a license to include its search engine form on your site. If you get into trouble for misusing somebody's engine because you didn't follow their rules, please don't blame us. We just warned you this might happen!

Site-specific search capabilities

Adding search capabilities that focus on your site is much more directly rewarding than adding Internet-wide search capabilities, both to you and the regular users of your site. Adding a link to your site for users to search the entire Internet is just a quick way to get them to leave; adding a search engine that returns only information about your site keeps them around longer.

Many search engine vendors offer "personal" versions of their software for deployment on your own site. But there's usually a catch — many of these products cost money, and those that don't are often hamstrung in their capabilities (which is why this category of software is sometimes cynically called *crippleware*). But we think the cost of this kind of marvelous tool is worth it, especially for large, growing, or frequently used Web sites like yours.

Every search application is different, so you need to pay close attention to the details when selecting a search engine for use on your site. The following are some of the most important aspects to investigate (especially if you're paying for the use of such a product):

- ✔ Compatible hardware platform(s)
- ✔ Compatible network operating system(s)
- ✔ Support for your Web server(s)

 ✔ Additional storage space requirements

 ✔ Special programming language requirements (Java, Perl, ActiveX, and so on)

 ✔ APIs supported (CGI, HTTP, ISAPI, and so on)

 ✔ License and use restrictions

Take your time and do your homework. You're sure to find a search engine that meets your current system parameters and gives you all the search power you need. To simplify your own search process, we've gathered a list of great search engines for your review in the next section.

The Search Contenders

Search engines are everywhere. This section lists our favorites, but don't limit yourself to our selections. Dozens of great search engines that focus on your Web's content are available for you to install or use remotely.

A great place to start looking for other products is to visit Search.Com:

```
http://www.search.com/
```

If a search engine is online and is good enough to offer itself for private use, it will be listed on this site. Or go to Yahoo! (`http://www.yahoo.com/`) and search on `search engine` — you'll get plenty of results.

The following list of search engines provides information about the platform(s) supported and prices:

 ✔ AltaVista Search: $29.95 and up (Windows 95, Windows NT, DEC Alpha)

```
http://altavista.software.digital.com/events/blimp↩
         /index.htm
```

 ✔ Excite for Web Servers: free with limitations (Windows NT, Solaris, UNIX, coming soon: DEC Alpha, Solaris, Macintosh)

```
http://www.excite.com/navigate/
```

 ✔ Fulcrum's Search Server: $5,000 (Windows 3.x, Windows NT, Solaris, UNIX)

```
http://www.fulcrum.com/english/products/server.htm
```

✔ Iconovex's EchoSearch, AnchorPage, WebAnchor, and Indexicon: free and up (Windows 3.*x*, Windows 95, Windows NT, Macintosh)

```
http://www.iconovex.com/
```

✔ Index Server for Internet Information Server 3.0: free with limitations (Windows NT 4.0)

```
http://www.microsoft.com/ntserver/info/indexserver.htm
```

✔ Infoseek's Ultraseek Server: $1,000 and up (Solaris)

```
http://software.infoseek.com/products/ultraseek
         /ultratop.htm
```

✔ InfoSeek's Web Kit: free (no additional information available)

```
http://www.infoseek.com/Webkit
```

✔ NetResults: $995 (Java-based)

```
http://www.netresults-search.com/
```

✔ Open Text's LiveLink Search: $12,000 (Windows NT, Solaris, UNIX)

```
http://www.opentext.com/
```

✔ Pacific Coast Software's WebCatalog: $695 (Windows 3.*x*, Windows 95, Windows NT, Macintosh)

```
http://www.pacific-coast.com/
```

✔ PLS's PLWeb Turbo: $49 (Windows NT, Solaris, UNIX)

```
http://www.pls.com/products/plturbo/
```

✔ The Internet Company's NewsSpace: (no additional information available)

```
http://www.internet.com/
```

✔ Verity's Search97: pricing information not available (Windows NT, Solaris)

```
http://www.verity.com/
```

Providing the capability to search the Internet as a whole or to just search your important collection of documents is a valuable addition to any Web site. But wait, don't put the book down quite yet. You've yet to experience the real thrill of hosting a Web until you've operated a Web forum. That's the topic of the next chapter.

Chapter 13

Cussin' and Discussin' on the Web

*I*f you've spent any time on the Internet, you're sure to have run across at least a few of the Usenet newsgroups—you know, the 20,000+ discussion groups that cover topics ranging from food to computers to auto repair to psychotic fetishes.

But, we aren't here to talk about Usenet newsgroups, exciting though they may be. We're here to talk about a similar messaging technology available for Web sites that usually falls under the heading of Web forums.

An Intro to Forums

A Web forum is a Usenet newsgroup-like discussion group. This revolutionary Web-based interactive communication technology is appearing on Web sites around the globe. Web forums offer your readers an ever-changing and growing database of information built from prior submissions and related to the subject matter and content of your site. Forums provide access to collections of archived, threaded messages to make it easy for readers to review previous postings and add new responses.

Forums permit Web sites to solicit feedback, deliver technical support, and maintain ongoing discussions with an entire site's audience automatically. Everyone who visits a forum-enhanced Web site can read through any or all of its postings. Finally, as the true Webmaster you are — or seek to become — you can guide and control the content of forum postings as needed.

The following are some of the many benefits that Web forums can provide:

- ✔ Instant publishing of posted messages
- ✔ Automated threading and content notification
- ✔ Fully HTTP/HTML-supported forums that are compatible with all (or at least most) Web browsers
- ✔ A fully graphical interface (except for the message text itself)
- ✔ Full control over messages, from authoring to deletion and management
- ✔ An electronic trail for all submitted material

Web-based discussion forums differ from Usenet newsgroups in the following ways:

- ✔ Forums store and administer messages from a central location; newsgroups are globally distributed but non-centralized.
- ✔ Forums use Web browsers and the standard protocols of the Web, but newsgroups require special utilities (often added to browsers these days) and NNTP support (that is, the Network News Transport Protocol).

Web-based discussion forums differ from chat products in the following ways:

- ✔ Forums are not real-time interactive communication systems as are chat systems.
- ✔ Forums use plain or hyperlinked text, but chat systems can use text, audio, and video for interaction.
- ✔ Forums archive posted messages; chat systems usually do not record conversations.

Web-based discussion forums differ from groupware applications in the following ways:

- ✔ Forums are considerably less expensive than groupware products.
- ✔ Forums perform a single task: threaded messaging; groupware products usually perform numerous tasks, including scheduling, task management, shared folders, and workflow, in addition to threaded messaging.

One Lump or Two?

This section takes a quick peek at a few important issues to consider when choosing a Web forum software product. Here, you'll learn about stand-alone and integrated servers, database support issues, multimedia enhancements, and more.

Stand-alone versus integrated servers

Discussion forum software is available in two unique flavors: stand-alone or integrated. The stand-alone flavor acts and operates completely independently of a Web server, which means that the forum application operates at some level as a Web server of its own. When a Web site links to forum material, the forum application takes over all responsibility for interacting with a user's browser. Integrated forums, on the other hand, install themselves in such a way that they become intimate with your existing Web server. The forum software still manages messages, but the Web server handles all interaction with the user's browser (that's what it's there for anyway, right?).

Either of these solutions works well. But there are a few caveats : If you want an integrated solution, you'll have to choose a forum software specifically designed to integrate with your particular make and model of Web server. If your organization's Web site is large and heavily visited, a stand-alone forum solution may provide better performance.

No matter type you choose, make sure that both your Web server and your chosen forum software support the same HTML DTDs, HTTP standards, CGI, and other frills such as ActiveX, ISAPI, or Java. Anything less is an invitation for trouble, plain and simple!

Database: custom or current?

Usually, forum software employs a database of some kind to manage messages and threads. Because these messages and the relationships between messages supply the primary value of a forum, it's essential to make sure that things work smoothly in this area. To that end, the database is a key ingredient for successful deployment.

Most forum packages use a proprietary DBMS (database management system) to manipulate and store all the message and threading data. But a few such systems can work with third-party DBMSes. For most people, the use of a proprietary or a standard third-party DBMS will be of no consequence or concern as long as the stupid thing works. But for those of you who have already spent big bucks on a powerful, name-brand DBMS, you may want to consider forum packages that can use your existing database instead of installing yet another large resource-demanding application on your network.

With or without whipped cream?

Most people won't eat chocolate pie without whipped cream, and most won't drink a shake without a maraschino cherry; you may not want to settle for forum software that doesn't support media or object enhancements. Such enhancements include the capability to offer more than just plain text within the threaded messages that users post.

Often, minimal support for standard HTML markup and GIF/JPEG inline images is all you need. This support enables users to link to other resources such as Web or FTP sites or add in graphics from anywhere on the Internet to give their messages the extra oomph they want. But some forum software can support a wider range of message enhancements, including Java, ActiveX, Shockwave, audio clips, videos, JavaScript, and more. If you want such extra frills in your forums, look for them. But in our opinion, anything beyond HTML support is overkill for this type of communications system.

For your eyes only?

Just because you host a fully public Web site doesn't mean that your forums have to be equally open to everyone as well. Most forum products can implement security to control who may post to and read from your threaded message collections. This security can range from requiring an open registration to obtain permission to access the forum threads to a high-security password-protected user authentication system that no one but your closest friends and the Illuminati can use.

Depending on the purpose, content, and nature of your Web site and its related forums, security may not be an important issue. But if you need to limit or restrict access, make sure you select a product that incorporates the security features you need. If you don't care or don't want to limit your users in any way, which package you select doesn't matter— just don't enable security when it's offered during the installation or configuration process.

Playing God

One of the most important features in any forum product is the forum administrator's ability to manage the messages that visitors post. Without proper administrative privileges, you won't be able to maintain positive, focused discussions, nor to enforce organizational policies (when necessary). At a minimum, a forum package must offer administrative support for message deletion, creation and management of multiple message threads, restriction of membership rights, and some capability to rename forums and headers.

Be persnickety in the area of administrative support, especially if you plan to host forums on a business or professional site. You don't want to be stuck with off-color messages that degrade your organization, or see messages from people who thought it was an addiction recovery discussion, or receive messages from teenagers exploring their new-found infatuation with profanity.

Another useful administrative feature for any forum package is activity and event logging. An event or activity log records everything that goes on in your forums and gives you a way to identify and track abusive users or areas that require maintenance.

Additional genetic traits

The scope of the features, functions, and capabilities in forum products is constantly expanding. Forums on Web sites have just recently emerged as a popular communication tool, and many vendors are scrambling to make their products stand out in a growing crowd of options.

As usual, this kind of vendor competition gives consumers the best range of choices (don't you just love capitalism!). If you're the kind of person who takes an extra spoonful of ice cream toppings, or who likes to grab an extra dinner roll, you may want to look for extra features in your forum products. Be on the lookout for these cool features:

- **Attachments:** This feature enables users to include other file types, such as documents, graphics, or archives, as attachments to forum messages.

- **E-mail notification:** This feature issues a notification message to users via e-mail whenever new messages are added to a forum.

- **Search tools:** These tools enable users to search message bodies, headers, time, and/or author by keyword(s).

- **Sort options:** These options enable users to sort messages by thread, header, date, or author.

- **Spelling:** This feature enables users to spell check messages before posting them.

- **Summary:** This feature displays the first few lines of a message below the header to give readers a preview of its contents.

- **Voting:** When this feature is enabled, each member of the forum gets one vote for an identified issue.

The Contenders

Many, many, many, many (that's too many manys, in fact) Web discussion forum products are available, and more are appearing weekly. Instead of limiting ourselves by discussing just one or two products, we made a list of as many of the products as we could find. If you don't find what you want in this list, take some time and do a little searching on your own. You can go to Search.Com (`http://www.search.com/`) and run queries on `forum` and `chat`. For convenience, our list is in alphabetical order and lists pricing information and what platforms the software supports:

- ✔ Allaire Software's Forums (commercial, $885, Windows 3.*x*, Windows NT):

  `http://www.allaire.com/products/forums/20/`

- ✔ Armidale Software's Yapp (commercial, $500 and up, UNIX):

  `http://armidale.ann-arbor.mi.us/yapp/yapp.html`

- ✔ Databeam's neT.120 Conference Server (commercial, $495, Windows NT, Solaris):

  `http://www.databeam.com/Products/neT.120/`

- ✔ Digital Equipment Corp's AltaVista Forums (commercial, $495, Windows NT, DEC Alpha, Solaris):

  `http://altavista.forum.digital.com/index_lobby.htm`

- ✔ ForeFront Group's RoundTable (commercial, $199 and up, Windows 95, Windows NT):

  `http://www.ffg.com/roundtable/`

- ✔ Frontier Technology's Intranet Genie (commercial, $995 and up, Windows 3.*x*, Windows 95, Windows NT):

  `http://www.frontiertech.com/products/genie.htm`

- ✔ Higgins Consulting's Motet (commercial, $1,000 and up, UNIX):

  `http://www.sonic.net/~foggy/motet/`

- ✔ HomeCom's Post on the Fly Conference (commercial, $495, Windows NT, UNIX):

  `http://www.homecom.com:80/conference/`

- ✔ Infohiway's Big Mouth Lion (commercial, $195 and up, Windows, Macintosh, UNIX with Perl):

  `http://www.infohiway.com/bigmouthlion/`

✔ Lotus/IBM's Domino (Notes) (commercial, $995, Windows 95, Windows NT, DEC Alpha, NetWare, Solaris, UNIX):

```
http://www.internotes.lotus.com/
```

✔ Lundeen & Assoc.'s Web Crossing (commercial, $395 and up, Windows 95, Windows NT, Macintosh, Solaris):

```
http://webx.lundeen.com/
```

✔ Matt Wright's WWWBoard (freeware, requires Perl 4.0.2 or better):

```
http://worldwidemart.com/scripts/wwwboard.shtml
```

✔ Media Machine's TeamWARE Forum (commercial, $60 and up, Windows NT, OS/2, Solaris, UNIX):

```
http://www.forums.com/
```

✔ NCSA's HyperNews (freeware, requires Perl 4.0.2 or better):

```
http://union.ncsa.uiuc.edu/HyperNews/get/hypernews.html
```

✔ NetManage's NT IntraNet Server (commercial, $995, Windows NT):

```
http://www.netmanage.com/products/intranet/index.html
```

✔ Netscape's Collabra Share (commercial, $995, Windows NT):

```
http://home.netscape.com/comprod/announce/dss_coll.html
```

✔ O'Reilly's WebBoard (commercial, $149, Windows 95, Windows NT):

```
http://webboard.ora.com/
```

✔ Oberon Software's Prospero (commercial, $695, Windows 3.*x*, Windows 95, Windows NT):

```
http://www.oberon.com/
```

✔ OnLive's OnLive (commercial, $895, Windows NT, Solaris):

```
http://www.onlive.com/
```

✔ Parallax Microsystems' XA Notes (commercial, pricing information not available, Windows NT, NetWare):

```
http://www.xa.com/parallax/2confer.htm
```

✔ RadNet's WebShare (commercial, $2,195, Windows NT):

```
http://www.radnet.com/
```

✔ Searchlight Software's Spinnaker (commercial, $495, Windows 95, Windows NT):

```
http://www.searchlight.com/spin/spin.htm
```

✔ Spyglass' WebNotes (commercial, pricing information not available, Windows NT):

```
http://www.spyglass.com/products/iap.html
```

✔ Storm Cloud's TALKaway (commercial, $295, Windows 95, Windows NT):

```
http://www.stormcloud.com/ndc2/products/↰
      products.htp#TALKaway
```

✔ TalentSoft's TalentSoft Web+Conference (commercial, $195, Windows NT):

```
http://www.talentsoft.com/
```

✔ UKWeb's Focus (commercial, $495, Solaris, UNIX):

```
http://www.ukweb.com/focus/focus.html
```

✔ University of Wisconsin's NetForum (freeware, requires Perl):

```
http://www.biostat.wisc.edu/nf_home
```

✔ Visualtek Solutions' Rendevous (commercial, $1,000, UNIX):

```
http://rendezvous.visualtek.com/
```

✔ Vocaltec's Internet Conference (commercial, $150, Windows 3.*x*, Windows 95, Windows NT):

```
http://www.vocaltec.com/products/ic/icp.htm
```

✔ Wolter and Weiss's Backtalk (commercial, pricing information not available, Solaris, UNIX):

```
http://izzy.net/~janc/backtalk.html
```

With so many products to choose from, you should surely be able to find something of interest — or even good use — for your own Web site. Forum software makes a powerful and useful addition to any Web site.

Chapter 14

When Push Comes to Shove

*E*vangelists of all sorts, from religion to retail, have one thing in common: They are able to shove their wares into the faces of their victims *ahem* customers. You can use the same idea to distribute the collection of bits you call a Web site out to the masses using a new distribution technology called Push.

Push 101

Push publishing is the automated process of distributing presorted content, such as information, data, documents, or even multimedia, directly to users without requiring them to go looking for it or even to initiate the transfer. In English, content is "pushed" to users instead of users having to "pull" it to themselves. As the information resources on the Internet expand, finding relevant and useful information in a timely manner is becoming increasingly difficult. Even Internet researchers are having to spend more time to find the best information (or at least the best jokes). Push technology attempts to deal with this problem by reducing a user's search time and using *channels* to remove the need to manually filter information.

A channel is a predefined collection of content to which a user can subscribe. When a user subscribes to a channel, the content of that channel is made available to the user. Often, Push products are compared to common broadcast mediums such as TV and radio. The analogy is supposed to communicate the idea that users can tune their computers to a data channel and get instant access to specific, relevant content. However, things don't always work that way in reality. Most Push systems are pull-you-push-me (a cousin of the push-me-pull-you), meaning that the client has to request the information updates for each channel before the Push server initiates the data transfer. Many of the Push solutions attempt to hide the pull side of the equation from the user by automatically polling the Push server periodically for updates, but the pull is still there.

Push systems generally work as follows:

1. A user configures the Push client to tune into specific channels of interest.

2. The Push client requests information updates from the Push server. (This process is often automated and unseen by the user.)

3. The Push server responds with a new update or a no new updates message.

4. The user interacts with the Push client to access the data retrieved from the Push server.

This process is a great idea (too bad we didn't think of it first), but the way it works in real life doesn't quite hold up to the dream. Ideally, Push publishing would force content onto your desktop, requiring you to deal with it by reading it or saving it for future reference (love me or hate me, just don't ignore me). Many intranet-only versions of Push software are moving in this direction, but with the transient nature of clients on the Internet, Push for the general public will not truly take off until dedicated (nonstop) Internet access is the norm.

Pondering Push

You may not fully understand what Push technology is until you interact with it. You can check out plenty of Push systems with a plethora of channels right now. You won't know what you can do with Push until you play around (we call it doing field research) with it. So open your Internet connection, launch your browser, and visit these sites. You'll need to download the client or the plugin, and then subscribe to a few channels. Once you get the feel of what is out there, jump back to this chapter and we'll talk about what you can do with Push.

✔ BackWeb Technologies' BackWeb:

```
http://www.backweb.com/
```

✔ Freeloader's News Topics:

```
http://www.freeloader.com/
```

✔ Intermind's Communicator:

```
http://www.intermind.com/
```

✔ Marimba's Castanet:

```
http://www.marimba.com/
```

✔ Pointcast's PointCast Network:

```
http://www.pointcast.com/
```

Push Prerogatives

The features, functions, and capabilities of Push vary from product to product. As we already mentioned, a discrepancy exists between the Push-only ideal and the pull-push scheme used by all of the Internet-capable Push products. But if you take a minute to think about this discrepancy, it makes a twisted kind of sense. Real Push works only when the client is there all the time waiting for data to be sent from the Push server. If the client is not there, then the server is wasting its time when it pushes content out to the offline client. To avoid this situation, the clients reach out to the servers (which are assumed to be online more consistently than the clients) and request a Push update. Then the server responds to this request by sending out the relevant channel of data.

But what is the channel of data? As the sites listed in the previous section show, a channel can be the entire offerings of a single vendor or data focused on a single issue, such as weather, sports, or the stock market. But channels are more (and sometimes less) than just collections of data, as explained in the following sections.

HTML or proprietary?

Push vendors can offer the content from a Push system to you in one of two general forms: HTML or something else. When the distributed content is derived from Web sites in the first place, it is usually delivered to you in HTML. But many vendors are using proprietary mechanisms to get content to you. Usually, the non-HTML content is pulled from a database or a newsfeed instead of originating on a Web site. For users, the underlying data format is usually not important, but when content is only available in a proprietary format, users are forced to use something other than their Web browsers to access the content.

Hot list or real content?

Getting to the content is the ultimate goal of Push, but the steps you must go through to access that content vary from product to product. Some products provide little more than glorified hot lists. Others support the direct delivery of the full content from text to multimedia. If you went to the sites listed previously, you may have noticed that the amount of data Push offered you ranged from a skimpy URL list to full sensory surround-sound presentations. Although an URL list operates faster and never downloads data you don't want to see, you must access each element to get to the content. The latter type of Push content operates more slowly because your machine downloads everthing. The complete content is immediately available (after it transfers), but lots of not-important-to-me data may be delivered. Using channels to fine-tune the content does help, but only you know what you want to see.

Browser or helper application?

You can view Push content in multiple ways. Browsers and helper applications used to be distinct entities, but no more. Some of the Push software is fully HTML- and modern browser-compatible (meaning that it supports Java, JavaScript, and sometimes frames); nothing more is required to access the content. But other Push systems require plugins or helper applications. Some of these applications integrate into your browser so you don't notice that another application is operating. But too many of them are completely separate from the Web; these applications also are the ones that use proprietary delivery methods.

Push Principles

When thinking about adding Push delivery to your Web site, you need to consider whether most users will meet the requirements to interact with your Push choice. Find out the following information about your users and your Push product:

✔ Which Web browsers are supported?

✔ Are plug-ins or helper applications required?

✔ Which platforms are supported?

✔ What is the size of the Pushed content?

✔ What is the size of the bandwidth pipeline?

You also need to think about the type of Push technology to implement: notification list or full content. Notification lists are little more than an annotated list of hyperlinked URLs. They are a fast and simple way to inform interested visitors of new material added to your Web site. To employ a notification Push system, you must install the authoring and Push server system, distribute the Push client (if required) to all of the users, and create the often proprietary hot list on a regular basis. For the most part, this system is easy to implement and works in many cases. But before you spend your time (and possibly money), answer this question: What does this system offer that an e-mailed notification list or a "What's New" Web page doesn't handle without the additional software? (Answer: Not much.)

Full content systems are great ways for users to download everything to their local machines and peruse the content directly and immediately. This type of Push also requires lots of transfer time, ties up a user's Internet link, and consumes mass quantities of storage space. Not to mention that your server will be burdened when multiple users attempt to download large volumes of content at the same time. Employing a full content Push system can require as little as installing a server and distributing the contents to your users. Often, the system collects and creates the Push content right from your Web site without requiring your intervention. But is Push a service you want to offer? Do you really have content that is worth distributing to users in bulk and loading down your server?

Yes, we are acting as the devil's advocates here. In our opinion, Push is best used in private environments where bandwidth is readily available and the higher capabilities of advanced Push solutions can be used. The next section reveals the fantastic capabilities some Push systems offer to private intranets.

Push in the Private Sector

We are nay-sayers of Push for individuals on the Internet, but when it comes to intranets, we think Push is better than sliced bread (as long as you don't eat it over the keyboard). Real Push systems on an intranet offer some wonderful capabilities, including the following:

- ✔ Virus definition updates distributed system-wide and automatically installed (also used for general patch, upgrade, and new software installation in general)

- ✔ Direct access to raw and processed sales data for marketing and product development departments

- ✔ Internal notification of external events, such as press releases and product shipments

- ✔ Interdepartmental channels used to improve project synergy

- ✔ Handling of employee polling, voting, and/or surveys

- ✔ Distribution of multimedia presentations

- ✔ Scheduling

- ✔ Focused communication with customers

- ✔ Training

- ✔ Basic group collaboration

WOW! And if you didn't say it, we'll say it again for you — WOW! But before you start jumping up and down, you need to remember that many of these features are useless on the open Internet or nearly useless due to the platform and software requirements. But if you ever have the chance to work on an intranet, Push can do some really cool stuff. Check out this list of Push benefits:

- ✔ **Focused content:** Content distribution can be based on user preferences, group memberships, or channel subscriptions.

- ✔ **Reduced search time:** Because content is already filtered for users, they spend less time looking for data.

- ✔ **Improved bandwidth management:** The elimination of random surfing and the intelligent management of content delivery reduces bandwidth usage.

Here is a slightly longer list of drawbacks:

- ✔ **Increased administration:** Adding new components to any system demands more time, attention, and maintenance to sustain satisfactory operation.

- ✔ **Possible proprietary skill training:** No matter what the delivery format is, specialized training may be required to operate the system.

> ✔ **Increased content development difficulty:** With the introduction of new creation techniques and additional authoring tools, content development is more arduous.

> ✔ **Required interval updates:** The core of a Push system is updates; therefore, you must continue to add new content in order for the automated system to detect or create the content update notifications.

Push Particulars

If you want to investigate Push further, stick your nose into one of these great Web sites:

✔ C|Net: Channel Turf:

```
http://www.cnet.com/Content/Reviews/Compare/Push/
```

✔ WebReview: Push Media:

```
http://www.webreview.com/96/12/13/feature/index.html
```

✔ ZDNet: Push Technologies:

```
http://www5.zdnet.com/zdwebcat/content/reports/Push/
```

✔ @dvantage: Digital Distribution: Pushing Content to the Desktop:

```
http://www.atvantage.com/atvhome/leaders/dg022700.htm
```

✔ PCWeek Online: When shove comes to Push:

```
http://www.pcweek.com/business/0210/10Push.html
```

A Plethora of Push Products

Most of these products have servers you can purchase to deploy on your Web site, but usually they are VERY expensive. So, to help you in your exploration of Push, we've divided the systems into two categories: less than $300 and over $300 (actually most of them are $10,000 to $30,000).

The cheap ones

Intermind Communicator is free for non-commercial and non-profit use and works with any MIME-configurable Web server. This product is a notification system. You can find it at the following URL:

```
http://www.intermind.com/
```

Yeah, this product is the only one we found that you can use for free (as long as you don't try to make any money doing so, then it jumps into the take out a loan category).

Take out a loan

One good thing about most of these expensive products is that the clients used to access the pushed content are usually free:

- ✔ Affinicast's Affinicast:

  ```
  http://www.affinicast.com/
  ```

- ✔ AirMedia's AirMedia Live:

  ```
  http://www.airmedia.com/
  ```

- ✔ Astound's WebCast:

  ```
  http://www.ncompasslabs.com/
  ```

- ✔ BackWeb Technologies' BackWeb:

  ```
  http://www.backweb.com/
  ```

- ✔ Caravelle's Transceive:

  ```
  http://www.caravelle.com/
  ```

- ✔ Cognisoft's Intelliserv:

  ```
  http://www.cognisoft.com/product.htm
  ```

- ✔ CompassWare InfoMagnet:

  ```
  http://www.compassware.com/
  ```

- ✔ DataChannel's ChannelManager:

  ```
  http://www.datachannel.com/
  ```

✔ Diffusion's IntraExpress:

```
http://www.diffusion.com/
```

✔ Freeloader's News Topics:

```
http://www.freeloader.com/
```

✔ Firefly's Community:

```
http://www.firefly.net/
```

✔ First Floor's Smart Delivery:

```
http://www.firstfloor.com/
```

✔ Ifusion's ArrIve:

```
http://www.ifusion.com/
```

✔ InCommon's Downtown:

```
http://www.incommon.com/
```

✔ Lanacom's HeadLiner:

```
http://www.lanacom.com/
```

✔ Marimba's Castanet:

```
http://www.marimba.com/
```

✔ NetDelivery's ZipDelivery:

```
http://www.netdelivery.com/
```

✔ Netscape's Push Server:

```
http://home.netscape.com/
```

✔ PointCast I-Server:

```
http://www.pointcast.com/
```

✔ Revnet's GroupMaster:

```
http://www.revnet.com/
```

✔ Sourcecraft's Intellicraft:

```
http://www.sourcecraft.com/
```

- Tumbleweed's Posta:

  `http://www.tumbleweed.com/`

- US Interactive's Digital Bindery:

  `http://www.bindery.com/`

- Wayfarer Communications' Incisa:

  `http://www.wayfarer.com/`

It looks like Push is one technology that will stay out of the hands of the general public for a while, or at least until that big reimbursement check from Uncle Sam comes in! Push may help improve many Web sites, intranets, and methods of retrieving data, but it's obviously not for the small of pocket (these systems can get pretty pricey).

Part IV

Serving Up Your Web

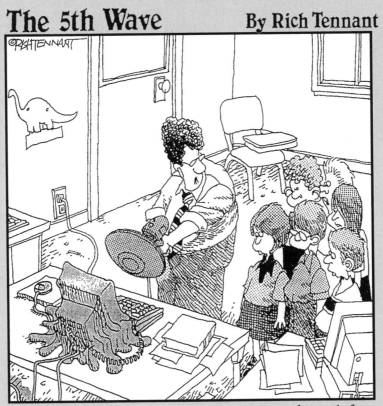

The 5th Wave   By Rich Tennant

"I don't mean to hinder your quest for knowledge, however it's not generally a *good* idea to try to download the entire Internet."

In this part . . .

In Part IV, we advance your Web understanding to the point just beyond initial completion of your site's materials and content — that is, we examine the issues you're likely to encounter once the construction part is done and you prepare to publish your materials for your intended audience. To begin with, we cover the necessary testing and quality control maneuvers you want to undertake before opening your doors to the public in Chapter 15, where you learn about alpha and beta tests and how to solicit (and take advantage of) expert user feedback. In Chapter 16, you learn how to get the word out about your Web site; we teach you how to blow your own horn and make sure everyone who's paying attention knows your stuff is out there. Chapter 17 concludes Part IV and covers the all-important maintenance routine so necessary to keeping your Web site fresh, interesting, and ready to attract new visitors, while retaining old familiar ones.

Chapter 15

Inviting the World onto Your Web

. . . .

In This Chapter

▶ Showing off your work

▶ Staying focused

▶ Maintaining control

▶ Deciding whether to publish or not

▶ Making arrangements with an Internet Service Provider

▶ Doing it yourself

. . . .

*A*fter you add all sorts of amazing and amusing features to your Web documents, you can share your pages with everybody in the known universe (or at least anyone with an Internet connection). This decision made, you must still grapple with interesting issues as you make your pages (and yourself) available to the world.

It's Show Time!

After you decide to publish your Web pages, be prepared to face scrutiny the likes of which you may never have faced before. (Remember, many millions of users will be on the Internet in the not-so-distant future.) This fact reinforces the need to ask for feedback — which we heartily recommend — which in turn means adopting a regular Web maintenance routine to get and keep content current and correct.

Finally, when serving up Web pages, you have a build-versus-buy decision to make. That is, should you hire an Internet Service Provider to house your pages for you, or should you put up your own and invite the world to your Web server?

In this chapter, we tackle all these issues and more, as we investigate how to publish your Web pages. By the time you read the whole thing, you should be ready to do some comparison shopping with your friendly neighborhood Internet Service Providers. You should also be ready to decide whether you or your provider will publish your pages.

Stay Focused on Your Purpose

Before you show your pages to the world, ask yourself again: "What do my Web pages communicate?" Write down a list of objectives and keep them handy. Next, talk to your beta testers and selected members of your target audience about your pages. Ask them what they think your Web pages communicate to them. Write down what they say and *believe it!* They are your target audience.

Compare your list of objectives to your informal audience survey results. If you don't get at least 50 percent overlap, try to figure out what's not working and why. Follow up by asking your testers what they think you should change to meet your objectives. Then make those changes and test again.

Until you get the overlap right, keep testing your pages on your target audience. Don't go public until what you think your pages communicate is what your audience thinks they communicate, too. This advice may seem incredibly obvious, but take our word for it — this step is the most important quality control you can do.

Keep Your Site in Charge

The freewheeling nature of the Web poses a nearly irresistible temptation to turn your site into the crossroads of the world and make it a meeting place for all and sundry. If you intend to make millions of dollars by advertising to millions of visitors, then it may be appropriate to try to lure as many visitors to your Web site as possible.

Otherwise, remember that the best lure for visitors lies in the content that you so laboriously develop. In fact, content is the best way to get visitors to any Web site. Look carefully, and you see that Yahoo! adds value through great organization and presentation of their content, with links to everywhere. They don't just slap several million links in a scrolling list and let users fend for themselves.

If your real objective is to sell software, you need software buyers to visit your Web site, not every stray Cardassian and his grelb (their canine equivalent). And you better not link to sites that take buyers' minds off your products, either.

In other words, the key factor in choosing the links to include on your pages must be *relevance.* Here are some questions to ask before including links to other sites:

✔ Does your targeted visitor understand what the linked site provides?

✔ Can your targeted visitor navigate easily through the linked site?

✔ If visitors leave your site through a link, can they get back easily?

✔ Do the linked sites help you accomplish your primary purpose?

✔ Do all linked sites appeal to your audience for similar reasons?

✔ Do the sites complement your material or detract from it?

✔ Can the sites handle more traffic or are they already overloaded with hits?

✔ Are the sites you link to willing to reciprocate and include pointers to your pages? Don't expect this kind of treatment from Netscape, Microsoft, CERN, or W3, or any other large and important Web site. Your site may appear on search sites (Alta Vista, Excite, Yahoo!) for free, but everyone else's site does, too. However, you should expect colleagues and organizations with which you're affiliated to list your site for free.

✔ Are you willing to show banner ads for other sites if your banner appears on theirs? If so, you may want to join a service such as The Link Exchange:

```
http://www.linkexchange.com
```

The whole idea is to connect your pages with resources that enhance the value of your content and that complement your overall goals and objectives. For example, if you're trying to sell widgets, you probably don't want to include links to competitors' pages (unless your widgets are better and cheaper). On the other hand, you should include links to relevant widget standards and the Institute for Widget Research.

Publish, or Perish the Thought

But hey, don't let these recommendations for the Web production process stop you from publishing your content on the Internet. If you communicate with your customers or colleagues using printed materials, a good way to view the Web is as a print alternative. Just remember that, unlike print, the Web is multidimensional: You don't need to stick only to the two dimensions so familiar to the print-obsessed people in this world.

It's good for business . . .

If your interests are business-related, think of the Web as a means of *corporate communications* — that is, the deliberate design and delivery of messages, in any medium, to create an image and aid the purchase of your products or services.

For you, the Web is another way to disseminate messages. Just be sure to observe the antihype leanings of the Internet crowd, and you'll do just fine. Internet users don't appreciate high-pressure sales tactics. Cross-posting announcements to every newsgroup known to humankind (18,000 and growing) is also a no-no. This cross-posting is called *spamming* in Internet-speak and is universally hated. If you spam, you'll probably find your own e-mail box filled with irate messages and Netizens will try to get your Internet Service Provider (ISP) to cancel your account.

This warning shouldn't dissuade you from mentioning in your favorite newsgroups that you've just published a Web site. You can probably even get away with mentioning it once a month or so. The best way to advertise a Web site to newsgroup readers is to put your URL in the three-line signature at the bottom of every message. If you use the full URL, `http://www.site.com/`, most browsers treat it as a link that newsgroup readers can click and follow directly to your site. This way, every time you post a message, folks see your Web link. Post intelligent messages, and Netizens will be curious about you and your site.

. . . and it's good for pleasure

If yours is a personal page or you're caught in the grip of what some people — not us! — would call a fond obsession, your reasons for Webbing up may be different from those of commercial enterprises. In this case, you still want to make sure that a target audience agrees that you're not sending mixed messages to the World Wide Web. But you can give yourself a great deal more latitude in focus, goals, and objectives.

Back to the content

Whether your focus is completely commercial or purely personal, content determines the effectiveness of your Web site. If your pages read well, include a wealth of easily accessible, interesting information, and are easy to navigate, Netizens will flock to your site. If your pages don't scan, if they're completely weird or totally boring, you'll find your site to be the electronic equivalent of a toxic-waste dump, where not even flies stick around for long.

How do you find out which path you're on? It's simple: Ask your target audience! Most of the comments you receive will be driven by the content, so that feedback should tell you where to spend the bulk of your efforts.

Dealing and Wheeling: Hooking Up with an Internet Service Provider

When you're ready to go public, one option is to simply transport your Web pages en masse to a provider who already offers a Web hosting service. This process is pretty straightforward, but does require planning. It also requires checking basic compatibility issues. Ask yourself — and any Internet Service Provider (ISP) whose Web server you may consider jumping onto — these questions:

- ✔ What kind of *httpd* server do they have? Does it conform to the CERN release, the National Center for Supercomputing Applications (NCSA) release, or neither? Depending on the answer, you need to make script adjustments. Web spaces are not completely portable, so be sure that you're calling the right map-handler and that your image map files are compatible. Be sure that your account has CGI support if you need it for your maps. Be warned that adapting existing Web documents from one environment to another can be time-consuming, tedious, and a downright pain in the kiester!

- ✔ What kind of dependencies lurk within your Web pages? Do you use `<BASE>` tags to set reference URLs? If so, you must change them to reflect their new location. While you're at it, check every link in every page to make sure that all links keep working. The only good link is a working link, and the only known working link is a tested link!

- ✔ How much data resides in your pages? How likely is it that users will download all your pages? Most Internet Service Providers charge a per-megabyte transfer fee for Web access, plus a monthly account fee (and setup fees, as well). The more data you want to share with the world, the more that transfer costs contribute to a build-versus-buy decision.

- ✔ How much demand do you expect for your pages? This question is another way of asking, "How big is your audience?" If you already know the audience, you can probably guess at demand. Knowing the audience size also helps you to guesstimate the amount of traffic you'll get, and its costs to you.

If you decide to work with an Internet Service Provider (ISP), the amount of data transferred from your pages to your users in a month is likely to be a primary cost factor. Some ISP's advertise personal Web hosting for free. Many providers include a personal Web site with between 2 and 5 megabytes of disk space and no charges for transferred data in the cost of an account (usually $19.95 per month, plus tax, for unlimited access). That ISP doesn't expect much traffic to your personal Web site, and disk space is cheap. This approach is the best way to start a moderate Web site. If your site generates more traffic than your ISP is willing to tolerate, you can negotiate for a commercial rate, instead.

Other vendors advertise free commercial Web sites. However, everyone knows: TANSTAAFL (There ain't no such thing as a free lunch). These vendors either rely heavily on revenues from advertisements that you are obligated to place on your site, or they're scamming someone another way, because it's not free for them to run their Web servers. Try one if you're adventurous, but keep your hand on your wallet at all times.

Most vendors that we surveyed reported monthly account fees from $50 to $150, for a commercial account with Web page services. The same vendors assessed charges of two to ten cents per megabyte of data transfer per month. This amount may not sound like much, until you figure that only 20 users a day at 2MB apiece creates charges of $12 to $60 a month; only 100 users a day raises those figures to $60 to $300 for the same period! 100 users per day means 3,000 per month — fairly high traffic for a personal Web site.

Where to draw the line?

If somewhere between 100 and 1,000 users visit your Web site per day, you may find that building a Web site is preferable to buying one. For charges of less than $500 per month, contracting for Web server access with an ISP makes sense. Consider the analysis in Table 15-1.

Table 15-1 Calculating Monthly Charges for Various Usage Profiles

Web Size (MB):	$Cost per MB Transfer:	Users per Day (Average.):	Monthly Account:	Monthly Costs:
2MB	$0.10	50	$50	$354.16
5MB	$0.07	50	$100	$632.29
10MB	$0.05	100	$150	$1,670.83

Assumption: An average of 30.416 days per month is used for calculations (30.416 = 365/12)

By the time you get to the second row in the table, start thinking about installing your own Web server. By the time you reach the third row, your choice is clear (be sure to adjust these averages with your own researched numbers before making any rash decisions).

In fact, the closer your projections are to the high end, the more likely you are to set up your own Web server. Table 15-2 covers the flip side of this coin — figuring the costs of doing it yourself — based on the assumptions covered immediately after the table.

Table 15-2	Average Costs for Web Do-It-Yourselfers			
Monthly Server Costs	*Phone Line*	*Provider Account*	*Staff*	*Monthly Total*
$350.00[1]	$36.00[2]	$80.00[3]	$600.00[4]	$906.00
$350.00	$70.00[5]	$150.00[6]	$600.00	$1,170.00
$500.00[7]	$70.00	$150.00	$750.00[8]	$1,470.00
$500.00	$140.00[9]	$300.00[10]	$750.00	$1,690.00

Assumptions: 1. Pentium P133, 64M RAM, 2 x 1.2G hard drive, and so on (total system cost: $4,000, amortized over 36 months at 10 percent interest; based on equivalent system lease costs)

2. Average monthly cost for dedicated 33.6 Kbps line to provider (telephone costs)

3. Average monthly cost for dedicated 33.6 Kbps line to Internet access provider

4. One-fourth time for system administrator earning approximately $30,000 per year

5. Average monthly cost for ISDN connection through phone company

6. Average monthly cost for dedicated 64K ISDN account with Internet access provider

7. Pentium P200, 64M memory, 4G disk, and so on. (Total system cost: $6,000, amortized over 36 months at 10 percent interest; based on equivalent system lease costs)

8. One-quarter time for system administrator/Web programmer at $36,000 per year

9. Average monthly cost for two ISDN "B" channels from the telephone company

10. Average monthly cost for dedicated 128 Kbps line from ISP for two "B" channels

The quick-and-dirty restatement of Table 15-2 is: If your ISP bill runs more than $900 a month, consider putting up your own server. Remember to adjust these costs (especially the salary for your Web administrator) to match your own numbers, but this example remains a reasonably good rule.

What to work out with your provider

If your analysis puts you on the *buy* side of the decision, you need to find an ISP that can host your Web pages. In addition to the questions mentioned earlier, we suggest that you find out a few more details. Expect your provider to have some questions for you, too.

What else you need to find out

✔ Ask the ISP for references from individuals or organizations that already host their Web sites there. Be sure to check with as many of these as you can. Ask them about the provider's quality of service, responsiveness to problems, percentage of overall system uptime, and user complaints, if any. You need to find out how consistently the provider delivers Internet access, so ask any relevant questions that you can think of. If reference accounts use forms or other input-handling programs, ask them to explain how they install and manage these programs.

✔ Ask the Internet Service Provider to explain their accounting system: "How do you know how many users are visiting your pages each day?" and "How do you calculate data transfer charges?"

✔ Find out how well-known their server is in cyberspace: Use a search engine, such as Lycos or Yahoo!, and look for the Internet Service Provider's URL in other pages. More links is better, in this case!

✔ Ask how long they've been in business and about their growth plans — in other words, how can they accommodate increasing traffic?

✔ Find out how easy it is to run your own CGI scripts or other input-handling programs on their system. Ask for a free trial period, and see how things go. Ask about all the tools and other widgets you may need. For example, ask: "How current is your Perl interpreter? Do you have adequate map-handling software?" Ask about consulting services or other help available to get your forms and back-end services working.

The whole idea is to figure out what your users need from your Web pages and then make sure that you work out all these details with your Internet Service Provider.

What ISPs are going to ask you

From their side of the business, ISPs probably have questions for you. They will ask how URLs appear in your pages, and what services you expect their server to provide. On the other hand, if they're not savvy enough to ask, you'll probably want to answer them anyway, to keep from getting bitten if they ask later on and you don't know the right answers!

✔ You need a new specification for your <BASE> URL definitions. You also need to know what kind of URL references appear in your pages; if the answer's not "Relative links for all pages," you have to walk through your references and figure out how they must change. If you don't know, ask your ISP for help (but be prepared to pay for it).

✔ The Internet Service Provider should ask what kinds of input-handling scripts you want to use on their system and what kinds of languages and services they require. These questions range from queries about programming languages, such as C or Perl, to scripting languages such as the C Shell, to predefined functions for handling image maps.

✔ Finally, the ISP should ask if you need help transferring your Web files (HTML documents, maps, graphics files, scripts and other programs, and so on) to their server. This process could be as simple as setting up special FTP access, to outright hand-holding during the transfer process. *Warning:* The more hand-holding you get, the more you pay!

Your Internet Service Provider's goals are simple: Get your pages up and running on their server as quickly as possible so they can start earning money for user access and data transfer. Their ideal customer is someone like you who has thoroughly researched and tested their pages, who just wants to get all the links and services working.

Webbing It Yourself: What Does That Mean?

Setting up and managing your own Web server is not easy, assuming that you make that decision. Besides the costs involved, ponder other requirements long and hard before hooking a server up to the Internet — especially consider that the server should be up and running 24 hours a day.

Understand the tariffs

Just because we give you some cost estimates to put a server on the Internet doesn't mean that we can determine your actual costs. You must research the options available from your Internet Service Provider and calculate your precise costs.

Considerations vary with location. For example, you may not be able to get an ISDN link to your server, which may require using multiple slow telephone lines or leasing bandwidth directly from a telephone company (for fractional or full T-1 connection). Either option can add to the cost and change your decision to buy rather than build a Web site.

UNIX or no UNIX?

We strongly recommend that you use a UNIX or a Windows NT system for your Web server. UNIX offers the greatest variety of *httpd* implementations and the broadest range of Web-related editors and production tools. UNIX also offers some of the best deals on programming languages and scripting tools to provide back-end, input-handling services.

Windows NT, on the other hand, is capturing a great deal of market share. Microsoft's vision of the Internet compels them to deliver outstanding Web server capabilities on Windows NT. Plus, they include free Web server software with the operating system in NT 4.0.

Although UNIX runs nicely on Intel-based PCs, UNIX expertise is somewhat rare in the PC community, and you may have to import some fairly expensive talent to help deal with a UNIX system. Windows NT expertise is kind of scarce these days, but that's changing rapidly as the system gains more users and proponents.

Try though you might, you can't escape maintenance

If you look carefully at the figures in Table 15-2, you see that the costs for personnel either equal or exceed all the other costs for a Web connection — that is, people costs match or exceed the combined costs of hardware, communication, data transfer, and access. Don't try to skimp on this expense even if you're contracting most of your Web access.

Change is a sure and wearing constant on the Web. If your information goes stale, people will stop visiting your site. You must keep your content current, and you must also keep your site's look in synch with ever-changing Web fashions. Updating takes time and costs money; you're best off if you recognize this necessity and factor it into your planning and budget.

Running a server of your own makes you liable to different forms of obsolescence. To stay current, you need to track versions and patches for the following system elements:

✔ The operating system you're running (DOS and Windows, Windows NT, any of the flavors of UNIX, or the Macintosh OS)

✔ The *httpd* server software and related elements on your server (such as TCP/IP stacks and drivers) that make your Web server run

✔ The programming and scripting languages (such as the various UNIX shells or scripting languages available for many types of servers) that make your input-handling and other services run

✔ The software and hardware that lets the server communicate with the Internet (a modem and an asynchronous communications package or a dedicated router and a full-blown T-1 link to your Internet Service Provider)

Here again, this need to stay current argues strongly for making the care and feeding of a Web server part of someone's official, paid job responsibilities, if not a full-time job. The level of involvement (and expense) depends on how much business or traffic the Internet brings you versus how much it costs you. This balance changes with time; we argue that the scales always tip in favor of more expenditure over time, not less.

For more information on what's required to roll your own Web server, we recommend some online resources:

✔ Apache server site (the number one overall Web server software — runs on UNIX systems)

```
http://www.apache.org/
```

✔ The Microsoft Windows NT 4.0 Web server site (the number two overall Web server software)

```
http://www.microsoft.com/ntserver/
```

✔ Compiled, ready-to-run *httpd* resources:

```
http://hoohoo.ncsa.uiuc.edu/docs/setup/PreCompiled.html
```

✔ Uncompiled, *httpd* source code

```
http://hoohoo.ncsa.uiuc.edu/docs/setup/Compilation.html
```

Are You Ready for Success?

Now, we want you to assume that your Web site is up, either by using an Internet Service Provider or by bringing your own. What happens if you've struck a collective nerve, and your Web site traffic swells to gargantuan levels? Will you be ready to deal with the onslaught, or will it catch you by surprise? If you are surprised, will the bottleneck frustrate your potential users who would gladly access your information, if only they could get to it?

Barring the element of real surprise, we want to suggest that you create a contingency plan to deal with the burden of popularity, should it strike. Be aware that national ISPs (such as PSI, Delphi, ComNet, ANS, and others) offer services that you probably wouldn't want to finance, let alone manage, on your own. Large local ISPs can help here, too.

Even if you don't intend to take advantage of their services immediately, we suggest that you contact them and start building a relationship for possible future business. That way, if your pages become notorious, you can shift them quickly to an environment that can handle thousands of accesses a day (or more). Even if you decide to bring the kind of capacity online to handle this load, you'll be able to handle your users in the interim, while you're getting the equipment and resources running. If you like, you can simply consider this precaution another subcase of the famous maxim, "Always leave yourself a way out!"

The Answer to the Ultimate Question

The central, burning issue of Douglas Adams' five-volume trilogy *The Hitchhiker's Guide to the Galaxy* is the question about ". . . life, the Universe, and everything. . . ." Well, we hate to disappoint you, but if it isn't "42," we don't know the answer any better than you do!

But regarding your Web presence, we hope that we give you the ammunition you need to decide whether to run your own server or to source it out to an ISP. Remember, though, that no decision is final; you can always change your mind. In the meantime, we hope that you're ready to make a decision. If so, now you can tell people that your pages are ready for browsing — onward to Chapter 16.

Chapter 16

If You Build It, Will They Come?

*T*he big day has finally arrived: You've built your pages and tested them thoroughly. Your beta testers are ecstatic, and your survey of the testers shows that your Web site is ready for the world to see. Now, finally, you can go ahead and publish your stuff on the Web.

At this point, your pages should truly be up and running, ready for access. Although you may expect the world to beat a path to your door, let us give you a few recommendations about how to let the world know where your door is and what's behind it. If nobody knows what wonderful Webs you've woven, you can't be surprised if nobody comes to visit. In other words, if you don't blow your own horn, nobody else will blow it for you!

In this chapter, we show you how to get the word out. Pretty soon, you should start to see links to your pages popping up here and there, and a trickle of users should begin to flow in. If they like what they see, links will start popping up everywhere, and the trickle could grow to a torrent. In this chapter, we give you some pointers to make sure that your chances of success are as good as possible.

Announcing Your Web Site to the World

After you're online and ready to provide your valuable information to the public, you want to spread the word about what you have to offer. In keeping with the Web's chaotic nature, no formal registration or announcement process exists, but you can follow a common process for letting the world know that your site is ready for access.

Write a semi-formal announcement

To begin, you need to write a one-page announcement. If you've ever written a press release, this document is similar. It should be brief to the point of terseness and cover the following points:

✔ Indicate who owns the Web site, be it an organization, a person, or some other kind of legal entity. Be sure to include contact information and a contact name to call or e-mail.

✔ Indicate whether the pages are *ready-for-use* or still *under construction*.

✔ Highlight your home page URL so that interested users can find it.

✔ Summarize the content of your pages, emphasizing the value and interest in the materials.

Figure 16-1 shows a sample announcement for a hypothetical cookie company.

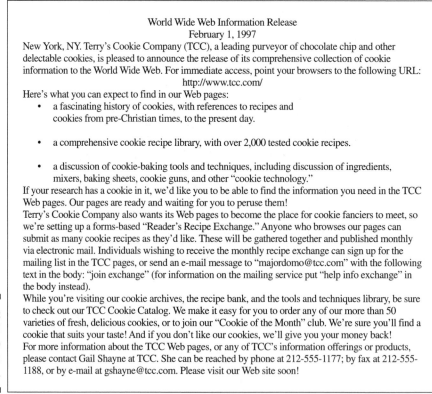

Figure 16-1:
A good
way to
announce a
new site.

World Wide Web Information Release
February 1, 1997

New York, NY. Terry's Cookie Company (TCC), a leading purveyor of chocolate chip and other delectable cookies, is pleased to announce the release of its comprehensive collection of cookie information to the World Wide Web. For immediate access, point your browsers to the following URL:
http://www.tcc.com/

Here's what you can expect to find in our Web pages:

- a fascinating history of cookies, with references to recipes and cookies from pre-Christian times, to the present day.

- a comprehensive cookie recipe library, with over 2,000 tested cookie recipes.

- a discussion of cookie-baking tools and techniques, including discussion of ingredients, mixers, baking sheets, cookie guns, and other "cookie technology."

If your research has a cookie in it, we'd like you to be able to find the information you need in the TCC Web pages. Our pages are ready and waiting for you to peruse them!

Terry's Cookie Company also wants its Web pages to become the place for cookie fanciers to meet, so we're setting up a forms-based "Reader's Recipe Exchange." Anyone who browses our pages can submit as many cookie recipes as they'd like. These will be gathered together and published monthly via electronic mail. Individuals wishing to receive the monthly recipe exchange can sign up for the mailing list in the TCC pages, or send an e-mail message to "majordomo@tcc.com" with the following text in the body: "join exchange" (for information on the mailing service put "help info exchange" in the body instead).

While you're visiting our cookie archives, the recipe bank, and the tools and techniques library, be sure to check out our TCC Cookie Catalog. We make it easy for you to order any of our more than 50 varieties of fresh, delicious cookies, or to join our "Cookie of the Month" club. We're sure you'll find a cookie that suits your taste! And if you don't like our cookies, we'll give you your money back!

For more information about the TCC Web pages, or any of TCC's information offerings or products, please contact Gail Shayne at TCC. She can be reached by phone at 212-555-1177; by fax at 212-555-1188, or by e-mail at gshayne@tcc.com. Please visit our Web site soon!

This announcement follows the model we propose: It identifies itself clearly, highlights the URL, and stresses the content available in the Web pages. It manages to barely suggest some commercial aspirations toward the end of the announcement, after all the important information has already been stated.

Where to direct your announcement

You have many ways to get the word out about your new Web pages, but here are certain bases that you want to be sure to tag:

- Send your non-commercial announcement to this moderated newsgroup, which publicizes new personal Web offerings: `comp.infosystems.www.announce`. Find and read the following posts from the moderator before you post your announcement: *How to Announce in comp.infosystems.www.announce,* and *How comp.infosystems.www.announce Works (FAQ).* They explain everything you need to know about posting your announcement. For our preceding press release, the posting may be "Terry's Cookie Company (`http://www.tcc.com`) delivers cookies, history, and recipes for your delectation."

- Check out Epages' great *FAQ: How to Announce Your Web Site* at: `http://ep.com/faq/webannounce.html`. It tells you everything you need to know about announcing your site and lists loads of URLs where you should place your announcements. It even lists announcement services that will post your announcement to hundreds if not thousands of sites. Some of these services charge a nominal fee, but always remember how much your time is worth to you.

Post the announcement to the following mailing lists for inclusion in various *What's New* and *Destinations* information listings:

- If you are using Netscape's technology and latest innovations, check out the information and fill out the application at `http://www.netscape.com/escapes/dest_program.html` for possible inclusion in Netscape's Destinations listing. Their site gets over one billion hits per year.

- Post your announcement to the `Topics` list in the EINet Galaxy. Consult the *Galaxy Annotation Help* page at `http://galaxy.einet.net/annotate-help.html`

Register your URL with a search engine as follows:

- For mass coverage of a list of search engines, newsgroups, and mailing lists, visit Promote-It!, a compendium of the Internet's best publicity tools at `http://www.iTools.com/promote-it/promote-it.html`. This site contains more ways to publicize your site than you can ever imagine. It's a one-stop-announcement to the whole world!

✔ For Yahoo!, go to `http://add.yahoo.com/fast/add?`

✔ For Webcrawler, go to:
`http://www.webcrawler.com/WebCrawler/SubmitURLS.html`

Also notify these publications:

✔ **Your favorite magazines that are specific to your Web's content:** Look in the magazines for the address of the editor who handles press releases. Frequently you will find an e-mail address to use. Trying these magazines may be better than trying to get your announcement seen in the mountains of computer magazines.

✔ **NetGuide:** This online services magazine covers all the major online information services by category. Submit your announcement via e-mail to `netmail@netguide.cmp.com`. The snail-mail address is: 600 Community Drive, Manhasset, NY, 11030.

✔ **Your local newspaper (if applicable):** Fax or mail your announcement to the Business Editor or the Technology Editor, depending on their positions. This approach helps with local publicity.

✔ **Your local computer magazine (if applicable):** Look for a local news section, column, or reporter who regularly deals with Web issues. This method can help get you more local publicity.

The idea is to dispense your announcement over as many venues as possible. These particular recommendations can reach a large — but potentially disinterested — audience. They may provide some welcome initial exposure, but you want to target publicity more closely to your audience as well. Read on for some more specific advice.

Trolling the Usenet newsgroups

Beyond this basic list, you can find other ways to target your information for more precise delivery to your audience. For Terry's Cookie Company, the following additional Usenet newsgroups look appealing:

✔ `alt.creative.cook`

✔ `alt.creative-cooking`

✔ `alt.food.chocolate`

✔ `ny.forsale`

✔ `rec.food.cooking`

✔ `rec.food.historic`

✔ `rec.food.recipes`

For your own Web pages, you want to peruse the list of newsgroups on Usenet and select those that appear interesting. Before posting anything on a Usenet newsgroup, please locate and read the Frequently Asked Questions list (FAQ) for that newsgroup.

Some newsgroups frown on anything that's the slightest bit commercial, so edit your announcement to eliminate sales-related information for such groups. Others are pretty free-wheeling and laissez-faire. The only way to find out what's what is to read the FAQ, and spend a few days skimming the online traffic before posting anything. When you do post, make it a polite and fact-filled answer to someone's question about your area of expertise. Avoid stating directly that you have a company that sells cookies or whatever. Simply include your Web site's URL in your signature along with your company name — that subtle approach may be enough to interest targeted participants without irritating others.

If you try to fit into the mindset for the newsgroup, you'll be less likely to incite a mail-bombing session or a flamewar. Try to avoid breaking the rules of local netiquette out of ignorance. Think of these precautions as a way of discovering how to communicate with yet another audience for your content!

Niche or industry publications

Find the niche publications related to your Web's specific area of interest and fax them your Web announcement. This effort can very often provide the best publicity you can receive, especially when the audience you're trying hardest to reach has already been targeted by a publication. If you're interested in the subject matter they cover, your announcement will probably come as welcome news to other readers, instead of being just another Web announcement, as it may be for some of the less-focused publications.

The old-fashioned kind of networking

Don't forget that your business and professional contacts form a network of people that you can draw on to get your Web word out. Local professional societies, informal groups, or other congregations of like-minded people can help broadcast your Web location for you, provided you appeal to their interests.

Many of these contacts may also have Web sites or pages of their own. If your interests overlap sufficiently, why not ask them to include a link to your new site in their existing pages? You can even offer to return the favor, provided the relevance works both ways. Inform your colleagues and customers about your Web site. Send your announcement to these individuals or organizations via e-mail or fax, and update your business card to include your home page URL.

Finally, cultivate the gurus, consultants, and other experts in your niche. Many of them have personal Web sites that include links to other sites as well. Again, if their specialty relates to your Web content, encourage them to check out your materials and ask them for feedback. Professional organizations are popping up on the Web. Often these groups include a list of members and a link to their Welcome pages. So join a couple and spread your URL even further.

Unless you know these consultants and colleagues well, boldly asking them to include a link to your pages is probably not a good idea. But if you encourage them to look at your content — perhaps by e-mailing them a copy of your announcement — don't be surprised to find your URL appearing in links on some of their pages.

Stay on the Safe Side of Acceptable Use Policies

Starting in the late 1970s, but most clearly from the mid-1980s and onward, the issue of *acceptable use* of the Internet has been difficult to clarify. On the one hand, having a mix of government, research, academic, and business users on the Internet has always been preferable. On the other hand, certain parts of this network were heavily subsidized by the taxpayers.

In the earliest days, the only organizations using the Internet were those that had something to contribute to its development and deployment or some kind of related effort. Admittedly, the interpretation of *related* was sometimes stretched; the idea soon emerged that the exchange of information was acceptable on the Internet, but that outright commercial activities, such as advertising, billing, or sales-related information, were not. This attitude helped to explain an anti-sales mentality that persisted for years on the Internet, even though the attitude has changed dramatically with the development of online transactions.

The charter of the NSFNET backbone, which in the past acted as the primary coast-to-coast conduit for Internet information, clearly states that its role is to support educational and research activity and to carry only traffic related to those goals. It specifically prohibited the use of the Internet in for-profit activities (consulting for pay, sales or administration of campus stores, sales of tickets to sports events, and so on) or for extensive use for private or personal business. This statement applied to use of the NSFNET backbone only.

Because the NSFNET is no longer providing the backbone for the Internet, these policies are obviously no longer in force. Not that the Internet policy is "anything goes," but you can do almost anything that isn't illegal in the country in which your information originates or where you reside, and even this is under question in the world courts. Therefore, the Net is policed by its own inhabitants, generally in the form of the Internet Service Provider responding to public outcry by canceling the offender's account when a Web site steps over the unwritten line of netiquette. Otherwise, the Internet is subject to the usual policing by local, state, and federal police-type agencies enforcing the laws that apply everywhere.

Here's the bottom line: If you're not sure whether or not your Web's content or operating procedures are acceptable on the local, state, national, international, or galactic level and beyond, ask your lawyer or don't put the content on the Web.

Giving Value Means Getting Value

As we say repeatedly throughout this book, the key to a successful Web presence is quality content. If you provide this to your users and follow our publicity recommendations, your material will ultimately gain the attention it deserves.

As long as users believe that they're getting information, services, ideas, or anything else of genuine value from your Web site, they'll not only use it regularly, but they, too, will help spread the word to other users. This result creates considerable value that comes back to you, in terms of new customers, new sources of valuable information, and new contacts who share similar pursuits and interests.

The Web's law of reciprocal value states that the more value you put into your Web pages, the more you get back from the user community in return, no matter how you measure it!

Making Sure that Your Web Catches the Right Prey

After your pages are published, and the word is out, you can relax and kick back, right? If you believe this, we have options on some real estate on Neptune you may be interested in buying. After publication is when the *real* work begins: You should be encouraging your users to give you feedback at all times, especially about the value and usefulness of your content. Then you should actively work to incorporate their feedback on a regular basis. No matter how good your content is, it can always get better, especially if you respond to user requests and suggestions.

Also, after your pages are published, the maintenance work begins. You need to stay on top of your own content and materials to make sure that you keep things up-to-date. Keep checking your links to other sites and sources. They can change without warning, rendering your potentially priceless link to the Widget Research Institute into the worthless error message `404 Unable to contact server www.wri.com`, which indicates a stale link.

As time goes by, users' tastes in and needs for information change, too. If you stay in close touch with your audience, you can anticipate these changes and keep ahead of them. Otherwise, your Web gets all dusty, strewn with the corpses of information that have long since been sucked dry. Never forget that the Web is an ever-changing, living organism and your site is one of millions of cells that keep that organism alive and growing. Only you can keep your content alive and active on the Web. In the next chapter, we help you stay on top of this maintenance effort with some tips for recognizing and coping with an ever-changing metaverse.

Chapter 17

The More Things Change . . .

*N*ow you can bask in the afterglow of your first grand Web achievement. You've published your pages, you've spread the word, and now your hard labor is beginning to bear fruit — people are actually visiting your site. You deserve a rest, so pack up your picnic basket and take a day off. (One day passes.) Welcome back! We bet that you didn't realize that 95 percent of the life cycle for any information product is spent in maintenance mode.

In fact, what you think that you've just finished is really just getting started. Some people would argue that now is when the fun really begins. You've probably solved the technical problems you've encountered along the way without having to stress yourself too much or stretch your mind too far from its normal configuration.

But now you have to start dealing with the toughest problems of all: people problems and communication problems. We almost guarantee that some of your content won't make sense to some users, that others may disagree with your content (and even be offended by it), and that still others may delight in harping on what you consider to be trivial errors. Don't let negative feedback bring you down. Instead, use it as a reminder that your page can never be perfect and that there's always room for improvement.

In this chapter, we talk about the kinds of problems and feedback you can expect to encounter, and suggest ways to deal with the day-to-day routine of keeping your Web pages and other resources in tip-top shape.

The Two-Dimensional Text Trap

You will want to add more content and (hopefully) more value as you get feedback from users and understand more about the subject matter that drives the content. As pages grow, always remember that participants in your Web site *hate* excessive scrolling around. Keep a constant eye on the number of screens in any given page, especially when making changes. Even though you may be tempted to think of a sequence of screens as the same thing as a sequence of printed pages, the two are not the same.

People are all strongly conditioned by a lifetime of linear printed text, so consider this section a reminder that the *H* in HTML stands for *Hypertext*. This term means that growing pages should be split and hyperlinked to remain readable, usable, and to facilitate users who grow bored with one section of your document and want to jump to the next topic. If you don't make jumping around easy for them, they'll jump ship.

After the number of screens in an HTML document exceeds three, you should plan on adding internal hypertext links to your pages and break them up into chunks of generally no more than 20 lines of text. Judicious use of location anchors (`<A NAME="spot">`) and intra-document links (`<A HREF="#spot">`) make it easy for your users to navigate as the spirit moves them.

Our final word on this topic is that as documents grow in length and complexity, the need for effective structure and navigation grows with them. Don't omit the introduction of these vital elements in some of your pages simply because they started small and grew from there.

Who Says This Stuff Is Stale?

The temptation to rest on one's laurels (old euphemism for your backside) can be nearly irresistible after you overcome the humps of writing, testing, soliciting user feedback, and finally, publicizing your pages. After a "short rest" you can go back through your Web pages and exclaim, "Wow, did I really put those pages out there *last August?* That was six months ago. Boy, this stuff is really out-of-date!" In the fast moving Web world, six-month-old information isn't stale, it's fossilized. The entire look and feel of the Web changes every 12 months or less.

Like leftovers in the refrigerator that have turned into science experiments, stale Web pages can easily become an embarrassment to their owners. The only thing is, the pages can't alert you to their condition by turning funny colors or starting to smell. You have to keep checking them, just to see how they're holding up against the ravages of time.

Check in on your pages regularly, Doctor Web

We suggest that you take on the job of maintaining your Web pages as if it were a real job, rather than something you do in your spare time when the phase of the moon is just right. In other words, make Web site maintenance a part of your scheduled activities. Read over your content at least once a month with an experienced eye toward what has happened in the last month in your area and to see how well your content and links are holding up. We almost always find a stray typo or broken link in our pages whenever we revisit them after a while, and we bet you will, too.

Keep your content current

The real work comes from maintaining your content. If all the information on your "What's New" page is six months old, those pages won't attract too much notice anymore, except maybe from the "The Worst of the Web List." If the stunning new advance in widgetry you spent half your pages on a few months ago has been supplanted by an even more thrilling technological advancement, your coverage is in the morgue. To pick up a newspaper metaphor and mangle it thoroughly, "Yesterday's pages are like yesterday's news; they're only good for lining the bottom of a virtual bird cage!"

Do your links point to nowhere?

In addition to keeping tabs on how current your information is, make sure that your links are all still current and correct. Only one change can make a link useless, but that may be the very link your users need most. Check links weekly either by hand (yuck) or with a trusty link-checker tool that checks them for you. Keep your links in good operating condition, and your users will frequent your site more often.

Another ARGH! is to follow a link only to find an Under-construction icon. A wasted link can really perturb users. Don't fall into this trap: If a link is not ready yet, include the proposed link text but don't link it to anything. Indicate that this soon-to-be link is currently under construction. This technique tells users what you want them to know, without making them follow a link to find out.

Is your HTML passé?

While you're examining your past efforts, check the HTML markup against the standard that browsers support today. If you set up tables in your pages using preformatted text and everybody else is using newfangled, snazzy-looking HTML table markup, your stuff can look pretty lame by comparison. Not that you must keep your Web site on the bleeding edge of the browser feature wars, but you may want to dress up your pages with some of their nice features that most of your users may like. We recommend that you stick with HTML that works with the actually released versions instead of the prerelease or beta versions of browsers (that's the leading but not the bleeding edge).

The whole idea is to keep page content fresh and interesting. If you consider regular site checkups the Web equivalent of cleaning your refrigerator every few months, your Web pages should retain their pristine quality and avoid ending up, as Oscar said, "...very new cheese or very old meat."

If You Ask Them, They'll Tell You

Staying in touch with your users is imperative, especially if you want to keep your Web site fresh. Make sure that you include a form or two on your site, if only to capture more information about your visitors and to solicit feedback on what they liked or didn't like about your site. While you're at it, ask them what else they want to see there.

Always be sure to include an area on your feedback form for open-ended comments, remarks, criticisms, or whatever else your users feel compelled to share with you. The best feedback often comes from completely unexpected quarters and hits you in the least expected places. No matter how well you know a subject or a market, you always have a blind spot somewhere. Open-ended feedback can give your users the opportunity to shed some light on that blind spot and broaden your horizons.

If you treat your pages as an open-ended communications tool with your participants, they'll be more inclined to give you feedback. If you then respond to their feedback, you may even develop an enduring and mutually beneficial relationship with some of them. If so, these sources of quality feedback can become part of the group of movers, shakers, and influencers from whom you always solicit feedback. You may even develop some of your best friends or business contacts through the Web; it happens every day.

Keeping Up with Changes

Feedback creates an impetus to change. Whether it's a dynamite suggestion about a better way to structure one of your pages, a request for coverage of a topic that would complement your information perfectly, or something you saw on somebody else's page that you want to emulate, the net result is more work for you but a better site in the end.

Because suggestions keep coming and good ideas are never in short supply, you may become overwhelmed by change. We suggest that planning for change and handling it in bite-sized chunks may keep you from becoming a victim of the never-ending change syndrome.

We recommend that you keep a list of the ideas that visitors send to your site and fellow Netizens on newsgroups. If a certain suggestion appears frequently, move this idea up in the priority stack to the "Needed" list, which should be the focus of immediate attention. You can set the threshold to move a common response to the "Needed" items list at whatever number seems appropriate. We find that five repeats means that the suggestion really belongs on the "Needed" list. We also learned that our constituents are a fountain of good enhancement suggestions, so we keep a "Cool Ideas" list for future whiz-bang enhancements to our Web site. We want a great site, but we don't want to fall off the bleeding edge.

Assume that you decide to spend every other Tuesday working on your Web pages. During the interim from one of these Web days to the next, you simply collect and prioritize incoming information. You also do your best to monitor changes and developments in your fields of interest and keep another list of suggestions to add to your "What's New" information, possibly culled from the newsgroups and trade magazines that you follow.

On the next Web day, pull out your list, select the two or three elements you have decided to change or add, and formulate a plan of action to implement those changes. By incorporating change into your planned activities and building a process to accommodate it, you can avoid most of the frenzy that last-minute, ill-considered change can cause. If you know that you need to update your "What's New" information every Web day and add whatever new information or page designs that you think are appropriate, this activity becomes just another part of your ongoing relationship with your Web site.

You need to control your involvement with the Web: Don't let it control you! If you wait too long to make needed changes, the job is much more difficult.

Maintenance Is an Attitude, and a Way of Life

Make your Web activities a part of your daily rounds. If working on your Web site is something that you do only when the opportunity presents itself or when crunch time comes, that opportunity will seldom arrive, and when it does, it will be very late. On the other hand, if you make working on your Web site a part of your regular routine, you know exactly what you have to deal with, when, and how long you can stay at it before you have to move on to something else. This approach treats your Web pages as a resource in need of regular maintenance, which is exactly the right attitude.

This approach lets you know when you need to adjust your schedule or — if that flexibility is not possible — when you need to think about acquiring some help. If every Tuesday isn't enough time, you may have to give up cleaning your wastebasket on Wednesday and spend a little more time on your Web-related activities. If you just can't give up this essential task (or delegate it elsewhere, like maybe to the custodial staff), you may have to hire a helper or a part-time consultant to assist you with your Web work.

A wonderful Latin saying is, "Festina lente," which means *hurry slowly.* Its sentiment captures the essence of a good maintenance attitude. Although you shouldn't overdo the time and energy you devote to any of your workday tasks, recognize that regular attention to those tasks can produce the kinds of results you want. If you can't get to those tasks, you quickly learn to prioritize and focus on the ones most in need of attention. If you must hire somebody else to handle some or all of your Web-site maintenance, so be it. Anything less and your Web site will be ancient history before its time.

When Things Change, They Also Break

While you're involved in maintenance and the gradual process of changing your Web pages, remember that even minor changes can introduce unforeseen side effects. In other words, every time you change (or add, or delete) information on your Web pages, you run the risk of causing problems in other parts of your site. You need to test your pages *as if they were brand-new* after every change you make.

Thorough checking means reading (and spell-checking) your content, just to make sure that you haven't introduced another typo for your users to chuckle at. It also means checking and rechecking your links (especially the anchors within documents for link destinations) to make sure that they still connect to the right places.

Always make your changes on a set of copied (production) Web pages on a work computer, rather than on your server. That way, you are free to make as many changes (and mistakes) as necessary. Nobody can see your work until you want them to. We also suggest showing your new versions to a select audience and asking for feedback before switching public access from an old version to the new one. Many a seemingly good idea has blanched in the face of a user-based reality check. Getting the bad news from somebody who knows how good you really are is preferable to hearing from users who are simply nonplussed by your strange pages.

We also keep a section on our server where we duplicate our entire Web site utilizing UNIX symbolic links (known as *shortcuts* if you're using a Windows NT server or *aliases* if you're using a Mac server) to our entire real Web space. When we're changing a page or adding some others, we can test them thoroughly without disturbing the real Web space. If we're changing a file in our test Web, we delete the file's symbolic link. We then make a copy of the file into the test Web, where we do our edits and validations. After it passes our visual inspection and survives the rigors of the HTML validator, we then copy the new file into the real Web space. Lastly, we delete the file from the test Web and replace it with a symbolic link back to the real Web. Voilà! A clean substitution, every time. . . .

Keeping up with change is a real job, so why not treat it like one? If you do, you'll be rewarded with a steady sense of progress in the face of constant changes and course adjustments. As you face these vicissitudes, you may begin to wish for more help from your computer, though. In the next section of the book, we follow up with ways to manage your growing site and how to work with your Web server administrator to make your life a bit easier. But we can't buffer you from the unceasing pace of change on the Web — except to prepare you mentally to face it as a challenge to be overcome.

Part V
Running a Successful Web Site

The 5th Wave
By Rich Tennant

ORIGINAL VAN-GOGH-OF-THE-MONTH CLUB

"SINCE WE BEGAN ON-LINE SHOPPING, I JUST DON'T KNOW WHERE THE MONEY'S GOING."

In this part . . .

This part covers the various topics related to setting up and catering to a Web site. Chapter 18 examines the anatomy of a typical Web site, pointing out noteworthy elements as it goes, and covers the server side of the equation, from hardware to operating system and software. Chapter 19 describes the ins and outs of Web server administration in order to help prepare you to work with a service provider (or to manage your own site, a task you should undertake only with humility and trepidation).

Chapter 20 describes the processes involved in publishing information via the Web and covers what's required to stay on top of the many related activities that entails. Chapter 21 introduces a raft of tools and techniques for managing a Web site, including a number of all-in-one site management solutions, as well as some "best of breed" special-purpose management tools.

In Chapter 22, we describe how to make your site's content available to the broadest possible audience by judicious use of HTML's meta-information tags and by paying attention to some interesting details that may help to guarantee appropriate coverage of your site by the major search engines on the Internet.

Chapter 18

What's Really in Your Web Site?

*Y*ou don't have to build your Web site the way coral polyps build a reef, by adding pieces randomly. You actually have control over what goes where. Even if you're not running your own Web server, you can work closely with your Web service provider to maintain control over what happens to your Web site.

Always remember the difference between the Web server and your Web site. The Web server consists of the computer and software that place your HTML documents on the Internet, thereby enabling users to connect to your site to view your fantastic text, images, and other wonderful stuff.

Your Web site consists of HTML documents, image files, image maps, custom-made CGI programs, Java scripts and applets, and other program files. If your Internet Service Provider (ISP) provides Web server hardware and software, and all you do is upload your files to their site, you're paying to maintain a Web server. This arrangement works well for most individuals and small companies.

If you run your own Web server, may you have the brains of an Einstein, the patience of Job, and the luck of the Irish. It wouldn't hurt to have a UNIX hardware/software technician/programmer chained to the computer, either!

Because this book is named *MORE HTML For Dummies*, not *Web Site and Server Management For Professionals*, Part V discusses only those aspects of Web site publication and management that can help you understand what your Web site contains, as well as how to manage it. After you read this book, you will be able to manage the care and feeding of your Web site documents, as well as intelligently discuss higher-level Web site issues with your Web server administrator and Internet Service Provider. But you will by no means be a full-fledged, free-range, all-powerful Webmaster!

We introduce some of the methods and tools necessary to set up and maintain a Web site, even on your own server, but we don't provide step-by-step instructions on how to set up and run a Web server. If you're far enough along on the HTML learning curve and hard-headed enough to want to run your own Web server, you need to consult more advanced materials than this book.

Know Your Web Server Administrator

Your Web server administrator can be your best friend when you need help with your Web site. Get to know him or her, and your life will be easier. The administrator is the person at your ISP (or in your organization) who's in charge of the care and feeding of the Web server. Frequently, the Web administrator is a network guru who knows everything about the Web server's hardware and software.

A Web server administrator must deal with the layout of the documents that make up the site as they're displayed to a user. Administrators must also handle the organization of the actual computer files that comprise the site; choose the appropriate CGI, Java, or other scripts to use (and decide where they reside); and receive and answer user feedback, among other tasks.

Administrators must also be familiar with user access and error log files and understand their contents. Becoming familiar with terms such as *cgi-bin* and making decisions such as which directory to use in a feedback script are all part of managing a Web site effectively.

Usually, the Web server administrator can help you make better use of the resources available for your Web site, if you ask nicely.

Before you start questioning your Web administrator, you need to know some of the jargon and how the Web server fits into the big picture. Chapter 19 provides a slightly more detailed examination of a typical ISP's Web server. So you may want to read it, too, before calling on an administrator in your network neighborhood.

The knowledge you gain from your Web administrator can give you a better understanding of the platform upon which a Web server runs. The following sections detail a few examples of each major platform type.

Web Server Computer Platforms

Before we start this section, you should know about David Strom's WebCompare site at Iworld. It contains possibly the most extensive information on Web servers in the known universe. The comparison chart lists over 100 Web servers along with prices, versions, operating systems, and links to vendor sites. Comprehensive tables display the best features of each one, and include complete tabular listings of Web server information. If a server is not on WebCompare, it probably isn't significant. Check this site out at:

```
http://webcompare.iworld.com/
```

Because you can easily search this site for the latest and greatest information, we're just going to hit the highlights of the most popular servers in the following sections. According to the most recent (April of 1997) WebCrawler (`http://Webcrawler.com`) survey of the total distribution of HTTP servers: UNIX comprises 84.38 percent; Windows NT constitutes 6.84 percent; Macintosh is 4.64 percent; and Windows makes up 1.92 percent.

UNIX

More servers and related software tools have been available on UNIX for longer than any of the other platforms and operating systems around. UNIX is still one of the two best choices for a large, fast, expensive Web server. On the other hand, you can run LINUX (a fast, cheap clone of UNIX) on either a 486- or Pentium-based PC. Also, A/UX on a comparable Macintosh can handle up to 100 connection requests per minute. Thus, UNIX covers the spectrum from really cheap (and slow) to really fast (and expensive).

Macintosh

The WebSTAR Mac server software on an appropriate Macintosh is probably the easiest solution to setting up your own Web hardware and software. Don't scoff: The latest reports indicate over 4.5 percent of the Web servers on the Internet run on Macs.

Windows NT

Although arguably not as well-suited for heavy multitasking work as UNIX, Windows NT 4.0 does a credible job on a fast PC server for less money than UNIX. If you're comfortable using Windows NT Server 4.0, Windows IIS 3.0 (an *httpd*-compatible Web server) is included with the operating system. The superior performance of Windows NT 4.0 and its great number of available

Web server packages make it the system of choice in the Windows world. To get the best performance from Windows NT 4.0, get a PC with the fastest processor, the most RAM, and the fastest hard disk controller and drives you can afford (in that order).

Web Server Software

The majority of Web sites currently run on UNIX-based servers. Apache, which is free server software, tops the list overall and among UNIX servers. According to the most recent (April of 1997) NetCraft (http://www.netcraft.co.uk/survey) survey of 1,002,612 HTTP servers: 42.79 percent are running Apache; 15.43 percent run Microsoft; 12.16 percent run Netscape; and 7.37 percent run NCSA. Although most of these are UNIX-based freeware, the Microsoft IIS server just surpassed the three combined Netscape servers as the most widely used commercial Web server package. Two caveats apply to this statistic, however:

- After you pay for the Windows NT Server, IIS is free.

- We're not sure, but this survey may also count the Peer Web Services (that ships with Windows NT Workstation) and the Personal Web Server that's distributed with FrontPage under the IIS heading, whereas the Netscape Communications, Commerce, and Enterprise servers all cost real money and indicate real, serious Web sites.

What does this information mean to you? In a nutshell, if you're going to run your own server as more than a toy and you're using UNIX, choose the Apache freeware, or one of the Netscape servers if you're ready to pay for an excellent commercial server with great support. If you're already using (or want to use) Windows NT Server 4.0, IIS is freely available for that platform — you'd be a candidate for a padded cell if you didn't at least try it. You can always switch to one of the Netscape servers for NT if you don't like IIS. And if you're a never-say-die Mac fanatic, go with WebSTAR.

Apache, NCSA, and the rest

UNIX-based Web servers are efficient and fast. Even though Apache, NCSA's *httpd*, and many others are free, they only run under UNIX, which requires an administrator experienced in UNIX setup, configuration, and maintenance. This system can be costly. Sometimes, saving money on software costs more for human resources (always the most expensive kind).

Windows NT

The Microsoft Internet Information Server 3.0 leads the pack here. Hey, it's free and built into the NT 4.0 Server (which isn't free; it starts at a list price of around $795). But Netscape's Commerce, Enterprise, and Communications servers lead the pack of pay-for-what-you-get servers, and their users think that they're worth it, even at $995 and up. Obviously some fallout from the war between Microsoft and Netscape appears in their Web servers — new versions seem to be released every few months.

WebSTAR and MacHTTPD

WebSTAR Mac and MacHTTPD are *the* Macintosh Web servers. Both are outstandingly easy to install and use. If you're a Mac fan and want an instant Web server, you can purchase WebSTAR Mac, take it out of the box, install and configure WebSTAR in a few minutes, and add your Web pages. It doesn't get any easier than that!

How Your Web Site Fits into the Whole Internet

Your Web site consists of the collection of HTML documents, images, AVI files, CGI and Java scripts, Java applets, and the like that you've copied onto your Web server. Web server software makes these documents (and other information) available to the Internet, and thereby to your users, under the aegis of the Hypertext Transfer Protocol (HTTP), the foundation protocol for the Web.

If your Web site includes a large collection of information, it may be the only site on your server. If it's smaller, your site may share that computer with other sites serviced by multihosting Web server software. The same computer may even deliver other Internet services, such FTP, e-mail, and news. Each of these services requires separate server software.

The software that runs on the various computers at the phone company, on the Internet, at your ISP, on a Web server, and at a user's workstation all transmit and receive information for display on a user's screen. All these computers, cables, and telephone lines provide only the pipeline through which digital information must pass. Chapter 19 provides more details about how this process works.

Numerous tools and techniques are available to help you administer a Web site and run and manage a Web server. Chapter 21 explains what you need to know about Web tools and how to locate them.

Inventory Web Server Resources

Before you rush out on the Net and download a Web server package and a bunch of management tools, determine what you have to manage. Inventory the resources on your Web server. Find out everything you can about what elements are there. Answer the following questions: Where's the server located? What does it do? Who can use it? How? When?

Ask your Web server administrator for a list of available back-end service programs. These programs can be CGI scripts, actual C or C++ programs that can be called by your HTML documents, e-mail and related programs, hit or click-through counters (little programs that monitor Web page activity), and more. You can't use them if you don't know about them!

The availability of these programs varies with the type of Web server software in use and with your type of Web account. This goes double if you're paying for a Web account from an ISP—some ISPs don't allow you to run CGI scripts and the like.

Usually, personal accounts that permit Web pages provide only a few bells and whistles. These accounts usually won't give you access to the `cgi-bin` directory for your CGI scripts, but some provide access to the `mailto:` program. You'll probably have to purchase a more expensive business account to gain access to server-side use counters and other, more complex, programs.

Take Stock of Your Web Site

Take inventory of your current Web site. You need to consider a lot of information to assess the overall health and well-being of your site. To help you out, we've provided a comprehensive list of questions to answer:

- How many files are you using? What kind?

- What is your file structure (directories and file names)? What scripts (CGI, JavaScript, VBScript) are you using?

- Where are they located?

- Where do their outputs go?

- How much space do these files consume on the server's hard disk?

✔ How much growth space is available to you on the server?

✔ How much money will it cost to grow, both in terms of file space and user activity?

✔ How much of your time is available for Web administration tasks?

✔ How much time do you currently spend on Web administration tasks?

Answer all these questions in writing before you seriously attempt to expand your Web. With these questions answered, you are better prepared to take advantage of those Web management tools and techniques that are available to ease your burden.

Lotsa docs (it's not a medical convention)

All Web sites contain more documents than you ever thought possible. Just as your desk gathers piles of paper, Web sites gather files. Even a small site may have up to a hundred documents for an administrator to manage and maintain.

Your site inventory can show you what comprises your site, and it will probably surprise you. Plan to keep track of your files with some type of organized system, not just your memory. Remember, not only must you keep track of those files, but you must keep track of their revision dates as well. That way, you can ensure that you always use the appropriate version of a given file.

Graphics galore

No matter how many HTML documents you have on your site, plenty of graphics will always be around. Some are common elements that occur on many pages; others are more unique or specific. Here's the list of graphics-related questions to answer:

✔ What directory structure is used for graphics?

✔ Is a vocabulary of graphical symbols in use?

✔ How big is an average icon? Image? Image map?

Remember that many graphics files are quite large, so a few small graphics will go a long way. Most users still use 14,400 to 33,600 baud modems, and those users don't appreciate encountering 200K images without fair warning. Understanding graphics structure, formats, and usage can greatly enhance your understanding of your Web site.

The supporting cast of applications . . .

Today, any well-equipped Web site includes several back-end service programs, such as databases, e-mail, and peripheral devices. Work closely with your Web server administrator and you, too, can do marvelous things using only standard tools readily available at your site.

Marvelous miscellany

Image maps, map files, indexes, documentation, conversion programs, and all kinds of other interesting things live in Web sites. Look for file names that don't end in HTM or HTML and try to figure out their purpose. Find out how to recognize map files, image maps, graphics, and CGIs, or other programs. Find out what other options are available and figure out how they can enhance your site. You might be surprised, just adding a few bells and whistles can add a lot of value to a site. If you can't do it on your own, ask for help!

"Organized Web Site" Is Not an Oxymoron

At least Web organization is not in the same league as some of the more-often quoted examples of oxymorons. If you take a methodical approach, and write everything down, you'll be pleasantly surprised at how easily you can keep your site under control.

Where does your site live?

What's the URL for your site? If it's something like http://mysite.com, you may be using the same address as the actual Web server. You'll probably be happier in the long run if you name your site http://www.mysite.com and establish that as a domain name. Most folks expect the www part — to let them know it's a Web site, anyway.

Are all your site's URLs relative, or do your pages use absolute URLs or the <BASE> tag? Either approach offers pros and cons. Relative URLs make moving your site easier, but absolute URLs simplify the task of downloading one of your pages, and users remain able to return to your home page by clicking a link in the file.

If you use the `<BASE>` tag, remember to make appropriate changes if you ever move your site. Surrounding this tag with warning comment lines to point it out for future reference (and changes) is also a good idea.

Picture your directory/file structure as a tree

Can't you just see your Web's directory structure up there next to Charlie Brown's kite (in the tree, man, in the tree)? The easiest way to arrange your files and directories is to make use of your file system's capabilities to organize files into branching directories or folders.

Keep your directory structure straightforward. Use obvious, self-descriptive directory names that relate to file categories (for example, `graphics`, `images`, `annual_report`, or `quarterly_earnings`). Be careful to copy the right files into the appropriate directories in the future. Keep an annotated list of files (and subdirectories) within each directory. Make sure that the list contains an explanation of the contents of each file, as well as the date and time it was last revised. If this isn't your cup of tea, read on about FrontPage.

You can't tell the territory without a map

Make a list of the links within each of your HTML documents. Distinguish between local (on-site) and remote (off-site) links. This list provides a map of your site, the way that users view it. It's a valuable tool that can help you understand your site's organization and structure. Some of the better Web management tools automatically display such maps for you, as shown in Figure 18-1 (taken from FrontPage's Explorer).

You can use this kind of management tool or create your own site map on paper. Whatever you use, keep it current!

Understanding all the pieces and parts

Creating a link map is a valuable exercise in understanding the logical components of your Web site. The map helps you distinguish content pages from demo pages, download pages from index or navigation pages, and so on. You should know which of these types of pages you have and where you use them.

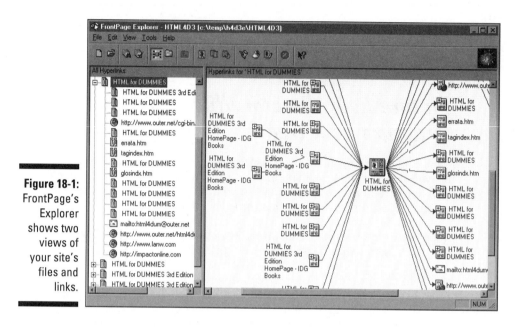

Figure 18-1:
FrontPage's
Explorer
shows two
views of
your site's
files and
links.

If this task seems a bit like creating an outline for a book, you're getting the idea. The more complex your site becomes, the more you need to visualize and understand its components. Then you are better prepared to combine them to create the harmonious collection that your users will call a great Web site.

To make your site better, study those Web sites that you most want to emulate. Examine how they are organized. Look at their source code and figure out how they link among their pages. You don't have to clone their site; just determine their information flow and organization. Then you can create your own site in the same vein, with your own unique text, graphics, and images.

Using remote hyperlinks

Remote links add value to your site only if you select them carefully to amplify your own content and keep them up-to-date. Hyperlinking to a site that provides more detail on a topic than your site covers is appropriate. Jumping into something totally unrelated is not. Just be sure that external links reach out only to useful sites, or those links won't be worth the time they take to maintain.

When you link to another site, you're opening the door for your users to leave. If you want them to stay at your site, provide the information at your site instead of linking to another site.

What's the code situation like?

To use Java applets, Java scripts, CGI scripts or other custom-coded pro-grams, understanding several key points is important, namely:

- ✔ Who controls access to these programs?
- ✔ How can you obtain or create customized versions of code?
- ✔ Who controls test access? Production access?

To get the very best from your site, you must obtain the answers to these questions. You must also address all the other issues inherent in using and maintaining code as a part of a Web site.

If you're a programmer, you should already be familiar with the file permis-sions and other contortions required to manage a large collection of files and programs. If you're not, you need to work closely with your programmer and the Web server administrator to ensure that you have access to (and control over) the code that you need to properly maintain your Web site.

Any image maps in the picture?

Understanding your site's image map type and format requirements is important. Find out what kinds of tools are available to help you construct and maintain image maps. Whether you're in charge of making them or you supervise the person who does, keep in mind that image maps can become quite large and are useful only to users with GUI browsers. If image maps get too big, they take too long to load, and users won't wait for them.

Also, keep in mind that many new users don't understand how to use image maps. They don't know that clicking one section of the picture links them to something related to that section. Using separate images or client-side image maps for hyperlinks gives users a better idea of what's available and where they're headed. Of course, you can insert text hyperlinks after the image map as an alternative. Text doesn't look as nice, but are you trying to win the best image map award or help your users navigate?

Strategic Planning for Your Web Site

After you get your site up and running and start maintaining its content, before you can say "Link Not Found," you'll need to add new content, update your existing materials, and fix your dead links. If you have made reasonable design and layout choices during your Web site's creation, your job will be much easier. If you have a written plan for expanding, updating, and main-taining your site, your job will proceed much more smoothly.

Cliché warning: "If you don't take the time to do the job right the first time, you'll be forced to make time to fix it when you least have the time." Or more concisely, "Fail to plan, and you plan to fail!" The more time you put into designing and organizing your Web site, the bigger the payoff will be when the changes start coming thick and fast.

Biologists say that a baboon can count to three. That's himself, his mate, and their latest offspring. So their number system contains: one, two, three, and one-heck-of-a-lot (the rest of the troop). You'll use a similar system for your Web pages because, before you realize it, you will have one-heck-of-a-lot of pages. You'll probably have many more files than pages, because each page may contain several images and graphics. The only way to keep track of the whole shebang is to use a hierarchical filing system, with carefully planned names and annotation conventions.

This type of system has been widely used for managing computer programming source code libraries on large, multiprogrammer projects. These systems are available on large computers for large documentation projects, such as the construction of an aircraft carrier.

You won't need a system that extensive or costly, but you do need something similar if your site grows to incorporate hundreds or thousands of documents. Later chapters discuss these systems in a bit more detail.

Thinking in terms of functional components, information delivery vehicles, and organizational sets of pages can help you manage your site as a whole, even though it may be constructed of a myriad of small parts. Approach your site in terms of its structures and functions (or systems and subsystems), and you'll be much better equipped to take care of it in the long run.

All in all, the recipe for effective Web site management is two parts knowing what's in your Web, two parts planning, one part using the right tools, three parts organization, and four parts carrying out your plans. Any tool works if you know your Web, make an organized plan, and carry out that plan in an organized way.

The only way to know what will and won't work for your site is to experiment, evaluate, and if desired, implement and maintain. And keep on performing Web maintenance regularly. Keep adding information that your users want. Keep your Web up-to-date, and you'll have the successful Web presence you desire.

Now that you have an inkling of what's in store for you, move on to further details about how you can administer your Web site more easily, and maybe even manage your own Web server. That's the topic we tackle in Chapter 19.

Chapter 19

Web Server Administration — the Easy Way

- -

In This Chapter

▶ Seeing the truth about Web servers and their administration

▶ Getting to know your Web server hosting options

▶ Fitting the Web server into the Internet whole

▶ Surveying Web server management techniques

▶ Following the administrator's information trail

▶ Locating sources for Web administration information

▶ Assessing your Web site's bottom line

- -

*W*hat is Web server administration? Management, supervision, command, and authority are some of the synonyms for administration — therefore, this term must mean caring for, feeding, and controlling a Web server. Remember, a Web *server* includes the hardware and software that runs the Web site, not just your HTML documents. Of course, this is just what you had in mind when you thought it would be a great idea to have your own Web site . . . wasn't it? We don't want to paint too dismal a picture, but think of a Web administrator as a parent who's naïvely expecting one bouncing baby and instead winds up with quintuplets. Ouch!

If your primary goal is to increase your company's profitability by operating your own Web site, you want to minimize the site's (and the server's) administration costs, both in terms of time and money (are these redundant?). In this chapter, we discuss some of the best methods for reaching this plateau of perfection. Along the way, you may also come to appreciate the underlying components — namely, the minimal set of Web server hardware, software, and management tools — to help you work with whomever your Web server administrator happens to be. If we do our jobs well, that won't be you. You'll be educated enough to get someone else to serve the server while you work on accomplishing your primary goal.

If you run your own Web server, security will be entirely up to you. If your site is hosted on somebody else's server, it'll be pretty much up to them — but you'll want to understand how your provider's security setup works, what kinds of access controls are in place, and what potential exposure to sensitive information may be possible. Our advice is that if you're exposing information to the Internet (or public access of any kind) make sure that NO sensitive information is included and that you provide separate, protected access to sensitive materials. The best form of public exposure for sensitive information is no exposure whatsoever. Period!

Web Server Hosting Options

So who can administer your Web server? Maybe a better question is, "Who will host your Web site?" Your options are: a Hosting Service, your ISP (Internet Service Provider), your own organization's LAN server or workstation, or your own computer. In the first two situations, you have access to an experienced person who can help you set up and manage your site. In the third case, your LAN administrator may be of some potential help. In the last case, good luck — remember, we tried to talk you out of it!

Actually, even if you're "doing it yourself," you probably have to go through a local ISP for a link to the Internet, so you may be able to get some help from one of their Web server administrators. The bottom line is that doing it yourself, with only a book or two and some user manuals, isn't recommended for anyone who's purchased this book, unless you're an experienced UNIX/Internet hacker who likes reading our books for our great insight and humor. Anything less is a ticket to Troublesville.

So, we examine these options in a little more detail in the sections that follow. Notice that "do it yourself" isn't just the last element in the sequence but also the last thing we recommend that you do.

Web server hosting services

Numerous companies have responded to the proliferation of the Web by offering to host your Web site or server for only a little bit a month. Many ISPs don't really want to host Web servers, especially when it entails connecting your computer directly to their LAN at their office and giving you access to their premises. Web hosting services come in three flavors:

- ✔ A local company that connects your computer to its LAN
- ✔ A Web server space renter
- ✔ A Web mall operator

No matter what flavor you choose, the organization on the other end of your Web connection provides your Web site's security. Make sure that whoever provides your security cares about it as much as you do.

Local Web server hosts

A local Web server hosting service usually ranges from a small company with an office, at least one T1 digital telephone link, and the appropriate equipment (usually a CSU/DSU, a router, at least one LAN server, and a rack to hold several Web server machines) to a large company with multiple redundant T3s or a fiber-optic link that hosts hundreds of thousands of dollars' worth of Web servers and related equipment.

Most Web hosting companies may maintain all three types of computer platforms, as well as several types of Web server software on their clients' platforms. Therefore, they are well-equipped to handle hardware and software problems and upgrades quickly and efficiently. These companies strive to know what's happening in the Web world and can help you accomplish your primary goal: serving up the best possible Web content.

Such ISPs usually also provide FTP, WAIS, and Gopher servers and may even provide a secure commerce server. They generally don't provide e-mail or news services, owing to the high volume of information involved and the need for more bandwidth and storage space to accommodate this information (and corresponding user demand). E-mail and news services, however, generally come with any standard Internet account.

Web server space renters

Multihomed (that is, more than one home page, so therefore more than one site) Web servers let companies place several Web sites on the same computer. Therefore, if you plan to run a small Web site (with less than 100 modem-attached user connections per day), neither you nor your users are likely to notice much of a difference between a multihomed Web site and one that runs on its own computer. As long as the other Web sites that share the server are small and experience similar usage levels, no one need ever be the wiser.

Many ISPs provide this type of Web service to individuals through a "personal home page," and to businesses via a "virtual Web presence" account. This service usually includes 5MB of disk space for personal service and something like 25MB for businesses. Details vary, but they generally fall within this ballpark.

For such accounts, the level of customer service can vary considerably, as can prices. Some ISPs keep prices low; but after they set up your account, you're basically on your own. They may answer telephone or e-mail questions, but these low-cost ISPs aren't really interested in holding your hand (because they don't charge enough to pay for full-time technical support).

These companies expect you to administer your own Web site while they do their part and keep the server itself running and connected to the Internet.

Local Web server hosting services usually offer sliding price schedules that depend on the level of Web site administration required. If you administer your own site via FTP, the hosting service keeps the server running and connected to the Internet, charging only a minimum monthly fee. If you e-mail the service your files and they make the changes to your site's directory structure and generally maintain the site, you pay more, either by the month or on an hourly basis. But because Web hosting services are primarily concerned with their customers' Web sites, you probably can get much better service from them than you would from a large ISP.

Web malls and turnkey Web services

Web malls are services that can host many small sites — like yours — simultaneously on their own multihomed Web servers. In addition, their services generally include assistance with setting up a Web site, obtaining a domain name, and listing that name in their *Mall Directory*. Besides offering you more exposure, mall operators often provide secure order taking and credit card processing services if you want to sell directly to your users. In other words, it's one-stop shopping for small-scale content providers, as well as for customers who visit such "virtual establishments."

Web malls also advertise their existence — and yours — throughout the WWW to draw more visitors. Of course, they want to host popular sites so that they can induce advertisers to pay for mentions on their directory pages. Likewise, they'd like to justify charging more for hosting your Web site, because of the large number of potential customers that visit their mall and see your listing. This is a standard retail store approach and is priced similarly. Malls offer more services and may be more expensive than the other Web hosting companies or ISPs we've discussed, but they may be just what an online retail marketing operation needs.

Along with Web malls, a new service organization has arrived to handle your company's Web site needs, no matter how large. Smart Technologies, Inc. (http://www.smartdna.com) provides turnkey Web sites primarily to the Fortune 500 companies. Smart Technology's staff works closely with your marketing, sales, public relations, and other appropriate departments to ensure that your company's goals are realized on the Web site that Smart Technologies sets up and operates for you (on their equipment at their offices). True, Smart Technologies services are expensive, but you get the best professional Web development, administration, and maintenance that money can buy. This option is massive overkill for personal Web sites, but we mention it to cover options for those who play the Web on a larger scale.

When situating your Web site decision, the best bet is to check with administrators who use such services and learn from their experiences before deciding anything. E-mail them and ask for their impressions and experiences. You'll be amazed at how open many of them are. Check these newsgroups: `comp.infosystems.www.servers.mac`, `comp.infosystems.www.servers.ms-windows`, `comp.infosystems.www.servers.unix`, and `comp.infosystems.www.servers.misc`. These newsgroups also provide up-to-the-minute information on who's hot and who's not.

Your friendly neighborhood ISP

Start your search for a home for your site at your current ISP (assuming that you're happy with their service and pricing, that is). Check their Web site and other ISPs' Web sites for pricing and service options. Competition is intense and pricing appears rather reasonable for those ISPs that offer multihomed Web sites. Don't be surprised if you find that many ISPs aren't interested in situating Web server hardware in their offices, attached to their LANs.

Prices for this kind of service, when available, are generally high, unless the ISP has a separate subnet linked to its Internet connection, specifically for hosting Web servers. In that case, the ISP is running a Web hosting service, similar to what we've described previously.

Remember, these operations provide the security for your Web site. Are they ready for prime time? Are you? Is this starting to sound familiar?

Your organization's LAN

If you work for a company or are in an organization that operates its own local area network (LAN), someone may have asked you to set up a Web site at your own location. In this case, you need to work with your LAN administrator to determine which machine should be the Web server. If your organization uses UNIX-based computers, the LAN is probably already running Transmission Control Protocol/Internet Protocol (TCP/IP), which is the primary protocol used on the Internet. Because TCP/IP is already part of UNIX, it's no surprise that most Web servers run on UNIX.

If your LAN is Macintosh- or Windows NT-based, not to worry. Both of these operating systems also use TCP/IP. In fact, Windows NT 4.0 Server includes IIS Web Server software, so you don't need anything but your HTML documents and a telephone connection to the Internet to publish a Web site.

Regardless of which computer platforms you use in your organization, your LAN administrator can set up and run a Web server. Of course, you must address numerous other concerns when running a Web server on your LAN, especially if the server is available to the Internet. Your LAN administrator will have far fewer worries if you plan to use the Web server only within your organization.

Work closely with your LAN administrator when planning to deploy your Web server (or Web site). In case your LAN administrator is not a Web server expert, you can find several good references listed at the end of this chapter. These references cover the setup and operation of Web server hardware and software; chances are that both you and your administrator will want to consult one or more of these tomes and other resources.

Security for your Web site is your organization's problem now. Doesn't that make you feel more inclined to restrict access purely to internal use?

You!?

If we haven't dissuaded you from setting up and running your own Web server, you need every bit of knowledge you can gain from this book and from *at least one* (or more) of the references listed at the end of this chapter. You probably need to get your Internet feed from an ISP, which can assist you in setting up your hardware and software (especially if you're willing to pay for some help).

However, you must arrange for the phone line from your local telephone service provider, even though you're connected to your ISP's system. Therefore, you have to deal with TPC (The Phone Company). If you're in a residential area and are seeking to get an ISDN line installed, you may have to pay as much as $500 for installation and wait up to several weeks for the company to get a magical "round tuit." If you want a 56K leased line, you may have to wait longer (or forever, if it's in a residential area without business services available). If you're in a business district or building, you may be able to get faster service, but don't count on it. There's quite a rush for fast Internet connections, and TPC isn't always up to the task of delivering quickly. If that's the case, look around for an ISP or telecom specialist to handle the job for you, or at least help with the task!

This bit of information about obtaining phone lines should make you think seriously about availing yourself of a Web hosting service or ISP, unless your organization already has excess telephone service installed (or at least, readily available).

But wait! Just one more thing . . . maybe two: your domain name (and its associated Web server name). You have to order your own domain name instead of instructing your ISP or Web hosting service to obtain one for you.

Of course, you want users to find you at `http://www.yourdomain.com` rather than at `http://www.yourisp.net/~yourname.html`. Just to register for the first two years costs $100, and it's $50 per year thereafter. Filling out the form isn't too difficult, but sending it to the InterNIC (the Internet name authority that handles nonmilitary domain names) is sometimes tricky, as we discuss later in this chapter.

And finally, what about you? You may have been one of those who ran a BBS back in the '80s (or would have, if you'd been into computers then). Web sites are the BBSes of the '90s. You obviously enjoy a challenge and the freedom to do things yourself, your own way. All we can do is wish you "Good luck!" But please, read on. . . .

You, you, you provide the security for your Web site.

How the Web Server Fits into the Internet

Chapter 18 provides a brief look at Web servers, which we expand on in this chapter to just shy of the point where your mind rebels and you start thinking of the sunset over the waves along the seven-mile beach just outside of Georgetown, Grand Cayman (oops, we're doing it already). At least, that's the plan.

Before you start calling Web hosting companies or ISPs, you may find it helpful to understand where and how the Web server fits into the overall picture of the Internet, both from a hardware and a software viewpoint.

The hardware: computer and telephone equipment

Picture your telephone system and the equipment you can see, namely your own phone and the wire that goes into the wall. Now, picture a computer system with an external modem for connecting to the Internet (see Figure 19-1).

The telephone wire comes out of the wall plugs into your external modem, which in turn plugs into the serial port on your computer, which is part of the computer's hardware system controlled by its Basic Input Output System (BIOS) and the computer's operating system. The modem changes the analog telephone signals into digital signals for the serial port. Next, the serial port sends them to the computer's CPU for processing. Of course, this is simplified, but this is the most useful level for you to grasp, okay?

Figure 19-1:
Here's a typical phone line/ modem/ computer configuration.

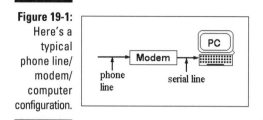

Picture the following: A T1 line from the phone company goes into a Channel Service Unit/Data Service Unit (CSU/DSU), which in turn connects through a wire to a router, which connects to the LAN through a hub or some other kind of connection. Finally, this connects to your Web server, which is attached to the LAN (see Figure 19-2).

Figure 19-2:
This is a generalized Internet hardware configuration.

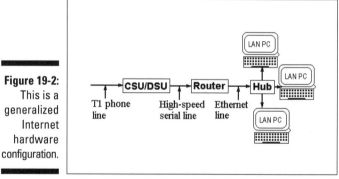

In a way, digital or networked Internet communications are similar to a modem system: Telephone signals arrive over the T1 line, albeit in digital form because that's the way T1 signals are transmitted. The CSU/DSU converts these incoming signals to the proper format for the router. The router controls the flow of Internet information between the CSU/DSU and your LAN, using TCP/IP. The router also converts a high-speed serial data stream from the CSU/DSU into the Ethernet (or other networking) formats used on your LAN. After the signals are in the proper format, your LAN can forward them to the appropriate IP address (that's the *IP* from TCP/IP). Your Web server answers to a specific IP address where all its Web-related packets are delivered.

If that seems logical to you — it is. Pat yourself on the back; you're catching on quite nicely. In case you're wondering, all of this hardware works in reverse when the information flows out from your Web server to the user. Isn't that clever?

Web server software and (briefly) how it works

The telephone wiring and computer equipment provide only the pipeline through which digital information may pass. The software in the various computers at the phone company, on the Internet, at your ISP, in the Web server, and in the user's computer is what makes information flow. Incidentally, the software is also what displays that information in a recognizable form. We hope you get the idea that the software is important stuff. We don't want to make your eyes glaze over as we recount all the gory details of the Internet software involved in handling WWW-related transmissions. You really only need to know just a smidgen about how various pieces of software — including the actual Web server — work. Therefore, brace yourself for incoming smidgens!

The basics

Each Internet service is handled by software components, be it FTP, e-mail, news, gopher, or the WWW. WWW software is commonly called *Web server software.* Actually, the software also can be called *httpd* (an acronym for Hypertext Transfer Protocol Daemon, a common name for this software in the UNIX world) or something similar. This acronym alludes to Web servers' ubiquitous use of HTTP (Hypertext Transfer Protocol) for communications between Web browsers and servers. HTTP is an application-level protocol that belongs to the TCP/IP family, or suite, of protocols. Because HTTP provides the foundation for all things Internet, including the Web, it's where we pitch the foundation for this discussion, in the very next section.

TCP/IP protocols

The TCP/IP suite includes the intertwined, low-level protocols upon which the Internet depends for its communications. TCP/IP helps to keep each piece of data in its the proper sequence and ensures that no errors have crept into the data that gets delivered to its final destination. Internally, TCP/IP uses specific arrangements of groups of 8-bit numbers to represent whatever information you want to convey. As long as all the software on the Internet uses TCP/IP, that information should be passed along to its proper destination, free of errors — at least in theory. This depends on a complex combination of factors, the most important parts of which we explain next.

IP addresses

TCP/IP requires each computer to have its own unique IP address. An IP address is a 32-bit number, usually represented by four 8-bit numbers, called *octets,* separated by periods (called *dots* in Internetspeak). A typical IP address looks like this: 192.15.2.244. As the Internet grows and additional IP addresses are assigned, a new numbering scheme will ultimately replace the current one to make more addresses available for the ever-burgeoning Internet community.

This new system is being designed to be compatible with the existing addressing scheme, but that doesn't prevent it from sowing consternation among those concerned with keeping the Internet working. All we can say is "Don't worry; be happy," because mere mortal users can't do much about addressing, anyway.

Domain names

If you were forced to remember 124.35.223.4 rather than yourdomain.com for every domain you used, you would either be pretty irritated or suddenly less able to remember as many phone numbers. For this reason, domain names function as more-memorable aliases for the actual numeric addresses to which they correspond.

Domain names reside in the Internet Domain Name System (DNS) under the auspices of the Registration Services maintained by the Internet's Network Information Center (InterNIC). The InterNIC's URL is http://ds.internic.net/rs-internic.html. If you want to find out whether a domain name is available for your use, type the name into the location field in your browser and attempt to link to it. If you succeed, it's already taken. Actually, a more effective approach is to search the InterNIC's DNS database to find out if the domain name you want is already registered.

Although you can register your own domain name, you need to have a Web server up and running when you do. Alternatively, if you avail yourself of a Web hosting service, that service usually registers your domain name for you, for a small fee. The InterNIC invoices you directly for the $100.00 name registration fee (good for two years from date of issue). Your ISP or Web hosting service invoices you for whatever additional charges may apply.

Domain names can be *aliased* in your Web server. Instead of assigning the actual server's domain name (domainxyz.com) to the Web server, most Web administrators create an alias for the corresponding Web server that reads like this:

```
www.domainxyz.com.
```

A *www* alias is common for Web sites; this alias also allows you to move your Web site to another physical Web server, as long as you inform the person who runs your local DNS database about this change so that he or she can reassign it to the new address. Remember, each computer has a unique IP address; your Web server software must reflect this location. Thus, you can move your domain name, but usually not your IP address.

URLs

Uniform Resource Locators provide an unambiguous method to tell a Web program where to find any particular item of information. Usually, an URL identifies that item's Internet location. In common Web parlance, an URL defines a Web page address. A typical URL looks like this:

```
http://www.domain.org:80/dir1/dir2/filename.extension
```

Although the Web accommodates a variety of protocols, most URLs begin with `http:` to tell the browser and server that the HTTP protocol is to be used. The next portion, `//www.domain.org`, represents the host name where the item resides. Sometimes a port number is given after the host name, as in `:80`. Frequently, the host name is followed by a path to a specific directory or file, as in `/dir1/dir2/filename.extension`. If the path indicates a directory, it should end with a slash, as in `/directoryname/`.

Passing information into and out of the HTTP server

When users click a bookmark, the browser interprets this action as an instruction to fetch the URL by using the HTTP protocol. At this point, the browser connects to the HTTP server that the URL indicates, sends a request for the specific location on the server, receives a reply from the server, and finally displays the contents of the reply on the screen. The key elements of this exchange are the *request* phase and the *response* phase.

The most common *request* methods are:

✔ **GET:** Returns the specified document's contents

✔ **HEAD:** Returns the specified document's header information

✔ **POST:** Treats the document as a script and passes information to it

During the *response* phase, the Web server sends various codes to the browser followed by the requested data, if it's available and no problems are encountered. Details of these transactions are useful primarily to script writers and we include them here just to give you an idea of what transpires when you click a link. Got that? *Wake up*, please. . . .

If you remember even a little of this, you're way ahead of most folks who want to set up their own Web sites. Your Web server administrator also will appreciate your ability to discuss your server needs more eruditely.

The Savvy Webmaster's Management Techniques

By careful design and planning, you can avoid the biggest headaches that managing a Web site can sometimes cause. If you take the time to plan its overall structure — that is, to lay out the arrangement of pages within the site, to design its file structures and file handling system logically, and to plan for the inevitable changes that you'll need to make — you may not need that giant bottle of aspirin at all. If you plan your site well, you also have more time to spend on your primary goal: to make your Web site a boost to your organization and its bottom line.

Among other things, good Web site planning means maintaining strict separation between publicly accessible materials and any kind of sensitive data that you may want to share with a restricted audience. Most of the organizations we polled operate a separate, highly-secure Web and/or FTP server for sensitive data, completely detached from their public Internet sites.

Laying out your Web space

If you're planning a Web site of more than 30 documents, which we've arbitrarily set as the dividing line between a small- and medium-sized Web site, you probably need to create a sketch of the links between each document or use a product similar to FrontPage to keep track of your documents. Even if you can mentally picture the links between 30 or more pages, sketching them on paper can help you remember what you were thinking when you're ready to expand your Web a few months down the line. Sketching your Web site's links also helps anyone else in your organization who needs to understand its structure. So, whatever structure you choose, commit it to paper or a Web management program.

Designing and handling the file system

Whether you're operating your own Web server or renting space on a multi-homed system, you need to plan where your files reside and how to revise or replace them when the time comes. This may not be any more complicated than what you already do on your own computer if your Web site runs on a similar operating system. But if your Web site is on a UNIX server and you're an inveterate Macintosh or Windows user, you either need to learn a few UNIX commands and how to access the server via Telnet, or you need to make arrangements with the server's administrator to set up the directory structure for you. In either case, you must determine where your files will reside, especially in terms of how they fit into the target server's directory structure. This determination is crucial because each link that points to a local file must contain the proper URL.

As with your HTML document link layout, sketch the file structure on paper. Plan to place files in directories and subdirectories that will remain stable over time so that you won't have to change links in every file just to move a directory. Of special importance is the Web server's *root directory* and the root directory for your Web site. On many systems these directories are called the *server root* and *document root,* respectively. The server root contains the Web server software's executable files. The *document root* contains the files and subdirectories for files that are available to your Web site's visitors.

On UNIX and other secure network systems, file ownership and directory and file access permissions can be a big issue. Placing files in the appropriate directories can simplify the job of assigning and maintaining permissions. If your Web site resides on a Windows NT, Windows 95, or Macintosh system, you need to check security options with the server's administrator.

Complete Web administration and maintenance systems, such as FrontPage, have finally become widely available. These systems should greatly simplify your task of keeping track of your Web documents. Check them out in Chapter 21.

Working with log files

Web server log files can be among your most useful administration tools. Most Web servers keep *access* and *error* logs and allow you to specify which logs to keep active. Some create new access and error logs each day. Others just keep adding information to the same files until they fill up your hard disk or until you archive them and start over. Of course, managing log files on at least a weekly basis is a good idea if you receive numerous hits per day or if you receive feedback that your site is misbehaving.

You need to check the error file to see whether it can help you determine whether the problem is local to your site or is being caused by something else. You may even want to put your site's usage statistics in an HTML document for display at your site. Whatever you do, you'll be a better administrator if you set up a regular procedure to summarize and archive your site's log files. Who knows, you may even learn something.

Some newer Web servers contain tools for log file management and interpretation. You'll soon find that without the help of a summarizing tool, obtaining the information you want from the vast amounts of undifferentiated data in a 5MB log file can be an exercise in frustration. Some commercial Web server software companies have therefore added log file manipulation features to their servers. Macintosh and Windows NT/95-based servers use graphs and other graphical displays for selected mathematical summaries in upcoming releases (you may find these tools available as you read this book, given the headlong rush to provide new features). To help you deal with the important stuff in log files while ignoring the dross, Chapter 21 covers log file analysis tools in more detail.

Administration and monitoring tools

As we discuss in the previous section, an increasing number of commercial Web server vendors have added sophisticated, easier-to-use Web administration and monitoring tools to their offerings. The best of these seem to run on Windows NT or Windows 95 and the Macintosh. They seem to think that UNIX hackers can handle such tasks for themselves, but that Windows and Mac users are generally less experienced and therefore willing to pay for better integrated, simpler administration tools.

Boy, are they ever right about the latter! This is especially true in organizations where the Windows or Mac guru (probably you) draws the short straw and gets saddled with putting an organization's Web site up on the Internet and making it available to the public. All too often, the job must be finished yesterday because management fears being labeled as *way* behind the times without a Web site of its own. Because you're probably either a Macintosh or Windows person, you may opt for a Web server based on a familiar platform, especially if "they" insist that you run the Web server in-house.

If "they" allow you to arrange a service to host the Web site, that hosting company's service administrator primarily determines your site's administration and monitoring tools. This is good because that server administrator can help your organization's Web site administrator (you're everywhere, aren't you?) figure out which tools to use and perhaps even provide some instruction or guidance on how to use them.

Even if you do run your own server, you probably need to obtain your Internet connection from an ISP or hosting service. Chances are good that your ISP employs someone who can assist you in learning about Web management tools. If you're a rugged individualist or simply don't like asking for help, some of the commercial Web server tools are already quite useful. The descriptions in Chapter 21 give you a pretty good idea about what kinds of tools you can expect from several of the Windows NT/95 packages.

For More about Your Web Options . . .

WebMaster Magazine On-line provides a wealth of information for Webmasters-to-be and for novice and professional Webmasters. Their WebMaster's Notebook section on Tools and Links, at the `wm_notebook.html` URL that follows, is a great list of links to virtually everything you could ever want in the way of Web-oriented information. And if this isn't enough, you can always search Yahoo! or your favorite search site by using the search strings `"HTTP"` and `"server"` and then following the thousands of resulting links.

```
http://www.cio.com/WebMaster/
http://www.cio.com/WebMaster/wm_notebook.html
```

The Web Servers Comparison chart at the following URL contains every Web server known to man, with a comparison chart of specifications for each one and links to each server's home Web site for further information. This site is a fantastic resource if you're really interested in the details of any specific Web server package.

```
http://webcompare.iworld.com/
```

Okay, now it's time to beat that dead whatever-it-is one more time: If you're going to set up and run your own Web server, a good book (besides this one) can help minimize the headache factor. We humbly suggest *Building a Windows NT Web Server* (Indianapolis: IDG Books Worldwide, 1996) by Ed Tittel, Mary Madden, and David B. Smith.

Weighing Costs Against Other Considerations

The cost of running your own Web server is much more than the sum of the costs of the individual parts of the server, plus the cost for the time it takes to administer it. You must also include the costs of the space to house the equipment, the electricity required to run the equipment, the extra heating and cooling needed, and the maintenance, repairs, and replacement of broken or worn-out equipment. That's a lot of costs.

In addition to the time you spend working on HTML documents for your Web site and babying the Web server hardware and software, you'll spend time talking with various people who have trouble connecting to your server or who have problems accessing your Web documents. This looks, smells, and sounds like customer support, therefore it must actually *be* that dreaded job. After all, you *are* the Web Administrator.

And yes, middle-of-the-night power outages, hard disk crashes, network blowups, and phone system blackouts will always occur. Now do you see why we keep pushing the idea of paying someone else to host your Web site while you concentrate on preparing its contents and keeping it current?

What's your bottom line?

Before you purchase any equipment, put together a Web site development and management plan that includes phases and cost estimates for Web server hardware, software, procurement, setup, configuration, and maintenance; for telephone connection design, and acquisition; and for Web site design, setup, and maintenance. From this collection of cost estimates and tasks, you can predict the amount of time you need to get your Web site up and running.

You also get a good handle on the associated costs, both in-person hours and out-of-pocket expenses. Prices for computer hardware change almost daily, so check out the Web sites of the Web server manufacturers or call your tried and trusted local computer retailer for the current prices on the parts you think you want.

Home-grown versus store-bought Web sites

Unless you've already made the decision (or it's been made for you), you can benefit from building separate plans for handling your own Web server versus paying a service to host it for you. The bottom line is to make sure that you know your reasons for taking your particular path to Web site delivery (do-it-yourself or through a third party) and to predict the effects your choice will have on your own bottom line. A better understanding of the process of publishing information on a Web site, which we examine in the next chapter, can help you figure all this out.

Chapter 20

Managing the Web Publication Process

● ●

In This Chapter

▶ Deciding what should be in your Web site

▶ Planning for your Web site's future

▶ Updating your Web site

▶ Creating documents for multiple uses

▶ Working as a team to produce your Web site

▶ Converting existing documents to HTML

▶ Reviewing good HTML style

● ●

*P*ublishing on the Web is like raising a child. The act of creation is enjoyable, but developing it, bringing it into the world, and nurturing it to maturity can become tedious. Also, if you don't care for it properly, you'll watch it deteriorate and drift into oblivion — you know, just down the coast from incognito!

The act of publishing information on the World Wide Web is more than simply hacking together a few HTML documents and putting them on a Web server. For a truly successful Web site, you must design to accommodate the myriad of changes that will be necessary to keep it fresh and alive.

Nothing kills a Web site's Net appeal quicker than old material or slow deposition of time-sensitive material. You must be keenly aware of your user's needs and desires concerning your site and its content. If you don't plan your site so you can easily update content as often as users demand, you'll burn out long before users get tired of your material. Therefore, managing the publication process is perhaps the most important aspect of long-term success for any Web site.

What Should Be Hanging in Your Web?

Your Web site should make you happy, or at least make your employer happy so he or she doesn't bother you, which, in turn, makes you happy (or, at least, not unhappy). You can accomplish this goal most easily by providing your users with the freshness, type, and quantity of content that makes them happy. Good content also keeps them coming back for more, which makes you provide even more, and so on. The idea is to give the customers what they want, when they want it, if not sooner!

Remember that no matter what anyone says, your users want everything immediately and for free. Your only chance of survival is to provide them with an in-depth, up-to-the-minute look at your specific eddy in the information ocean.

Keep just one crucial concept in mind at all times: While users are accessing your Web site, you have their undivided attention. At that time, you can provide as much detail on your service or product as they can assimilate (or download). Unless your real goal is to get people to call you on the phone, put everything users could possibly want to know about your product(s) or service(s) in your Web site. Then their self-service experience can be completely satisfying, without requiring you to get involved.

Project the amount of time that you and your staff must spend to keep your site's information up-to-date and alive, while allowing time to add new areas of coverage. If you're starting a Web site for a magazine, start with the basics that set the magazine apart from the rest and keep the site simple. Plan to expand it as the magazine's readership increases its usage of the Web site.

If your Web site is primarily a source for internal company information, you can start with a few of the company programs that require the most time-consuming, employee contact (do health care and 401K ring any bells?), and then spread out into more static programs. Plan to put your employee newsletter on the site if you can get someone else to prepare the text for you. Or use one of the word-processing format-to-HTML conversion programs that we discuss later in this chapter.

Remember, you can always expand your Web as users demand more. Keep it small at first. Do the job right from the start. Expand only when you can keep the quality up, along with any increases in quantity. If you overdo it, you may have trouble garnering attention and respect from users when you're finally ready for prime time.

Planning for Now and the Future

Considering all the words of wisdom in the preceding section, how should you plan your Web publishing process? That task is easy: Plan it just like any other publication process, except that you don't have to deal with typesetters, service bureaus, or printers.

By *publication process,* we mean the process from an idea's conception to making that idea available on your Web site. This process includes: the design of your Web site's format and its layout (both the visible layout and the underlying Web server directory structure), content creation (text and graphics), editing the text, laying out each page's text and graphics, HTML coding and document linking, and, finally, uploading your documents to a prefabricated directory structure on the Web server.

If your Web site is meant to be a Web equivalent of an "explore the endless caves" game, by all means, link your Web documents to each other randomly, so nobody can conceptualize its structure. But if you want to make your site easy to navigate, use a standard hierarchical tree or a folder structure metaphor. Sure, both of these metaphors are used everywhere, but for good reason — namely, everybody can relate to them. You can also easily add more limbs and leaves to a hierarchy for new products or services.

This organization works equally well for onscreen layout and for a server's directory and file structure. To make the task easy on yourself, you may as well make both structures similar. That way, you can visualize files residing on the hard disk in the same location as the Web pages in the document hierarchy. This structure also helps others who work with you (or after you) upgrade or change the content of those Web pages.

This approach works all the way from the top to the bottom of your Web, with one notable exception — namely, shared graphical images. You don't want to make multiple copies of a blue dot image file and put a copy in each subdirectory with every HTML document that references it. Instead, create a common graphics subdirectory, and keep only one copy of each shared graphic. Place this subdirectory immediately beneath the main Web root, use the Web root directory as your <BASE> or primary point of reference, and use relative URLs for each graphic. You can move your site more easily than if you use absolute URLs for graphics.

If you're careful, you can cross-link a few pages to each other when the content so dictates without turning your site into an incomprehensible bowl of spaghetti. You can also differentiate major limbs of your document tree with unique backgrounds or colors to give users an immediate cue to their position within your structure. Plan to do this and your users will love you.

If your site deals with large amounts of data that changes periodically, keep the data in another location rather than in the "leaves" of your directory structure. Perhaps data files could reside on a separate hard disk, or even another workstation on the network. This location may be preferable, if you want to facilitate changeovers after completing an update.

You probably won't want to take your Web server offline to make updates. Therefore, plan for a seamless transition by switching from one copy of the data to another (perhaps by reassigning symbolic links) or by replacing files in a preplanned order.

The quickest and safest method for making a switch is to keep separate subdirectories that contain your old and new data files side-by-side on the same hard disk. If you use different names for the subdirectories but identical names for the data files, all you need to do is change a few pointers.

Assume that your Web server accesses a directory named WEBDATA under normal operating conditions, because that name is used in all your URLs. Further assume that you make updates and changes to your files on other computers on the network and put the updated files in the NEWDATA directory on the same level as WEBDATA. When you're ready for the changeover, rename WEBDATA to OLDDATA, and then rename NEWDATA to WEBDATA. See: The process is really quick and painless if you plan ahead!

Try this in the wrong order and you'll wind up with plenty of nothing (such as two copies of the wrong version of material, with the original completely lost). Therefore, be sure that you have a backup copy of both old and new materials somewhere else in case you make a mistake. That way, you can get back where you started (to the old materials) or move on to the updated materials (the new stuff) no matter what happens. And believe us, "no matter what" happens much more often than you may think.

Planning for Regular Updates

When you're designing your Web layout, if your content deals with time-sensitive material (for example, newsletters, press releases, or other event-driven or periodical publications), you need to plan appropriate space on your home page. Sometimes, reserving some space on your second-level pages for hot and new items is also a good idea.

But familiarity breeds contempt, even on the Web. If you always place a little Hot icon next to second-line headings, users will learn to ignore it just like they ignore roadkill on the highway. Shake up things regularly: Prepare and use different icons; rearrange your layout from time to time; keep the design visually interesting by changing element placement.

If you use Java applets for animation and make these elements appropriate to your site's information content, you can jazz up your Web site. Remember, you're not only trying to attract new users, you're trying to convert them into regulars who'll come back for more.

So, how do you plan for frequent updates? Determine how often to process updates, based on your users' desires, your own time, and the availability of new information. Provide regular, on-time updates so that your users can expect and receive updated information when promised. In other words, reliability is paramount. How do you react when your morning newspaper is late? How do you react when your morning newspaper doesn't arrive at all? It's not quite as bad as getting up in the morning and finding you're out of coffee, but almost. . . .

Planning for less frequent updates is better than trying to update more often and failing to deliver on time. But if your information changes daily and you can't provide changes to your users on the same basis, you may want to rethink your Web objectives. In fact, you may be occupying the wrong niche! Detailed time-management coupled with automated information processing may be exactly what you need to convert and transmit your information to your Web site on a timely basis.

Prepare a project schedule for yourself and your staff, preferably using computerized project management or scheduling programs. Prepare a schedule even if you are the only staff member. This approach helps determine your limitations by forcing you to list all tasks necessary to produce an update, and then to link them in a critical path with the time required to complete each one.

If you follow this approach, you can see immediately how much information you can update and how often. If you haven't used a project management program, now's a great time to start. Search for one via the Internet; use the search words "project management software" at your favorite search site or on a shareware site, and you can find options in all price ranges.

Designing Documents for Multiple Uses

You can save yourself a great deal of time if you design your original documents for multiple uses (in hip buzzword terms, this concept is known as "repurposing," which sounds to us like something you do to an aquatic mammal. . .twice!). In other words, use your information online as well as in printed form. Depending on the type of information involved, *multiple uses* may also mean deploying your content in video, audio, multimedia, and online multimedia forms, as well.

Fortunately, numerous options to convert existing content (or to use it directly) are available. Complex word processor-based documents containing tables and figures can automagically appear in your Web site. You can convert these documents into HTML by using any of several programs we discuss later in this chapter, or you can use a portable document format (assuming that your users have the right plugins or helper applications available to view these files in their browsers).

Programs to allow computers to accept video and audio input from almost any source and digitize it into acceptable Web document formats are also available. This process is the technical end of the operation and in many ways, the easiest to accomplish. You must design the layout and presentation of your information to make its design compatible with multiple formats before you can convert the information to HTML — or any other formats, for that matter — to reach your users effectively, whether online or off.

Although this technology is available in many browsers or in the form of software add-ons, few Web surfers have fast enough Internet connections to download large multimedia clips quickly. For that reason, many users won't take the time to mess with multimedia. But because most leading-edge browsers can handle Java applets, using a few small animated graphics can be a nice touch. Go easy on the multimedia content, and you'll probably benefit more users than if you concentrate on those who have the links and the equipment to appreciate massive multimedia maneuvers.

Likewise, only a few Web users have audio systems in their machines. Sadly, many of those who do have audio work in locations (such as offices) where they can't appreciate a talking Web site. Of course, sites exist that do allow users to preview audio CDs or listen to radio shows on the Internet. By and large, these are specialty sites that make excellent use of appropriate technology and feed only small, selected audiences — but with some new developments, this situation could change very quickly.

If your site is geared toward a specialty niche that justifies one or more of these technologies, by all means, plan to use them. But the emphasis is on the word *plan*. You must research your audience to understand the need for this content, in addition to delivering more conventional content in standard text and graphics format.

Working with Creation and Production Staff

If you're not solely responsible for your Web site, you must adjust to working with your creation and production staff to take advantage of the Web's special capabilities and requirements. If you're in charge of getting your organization's Web site up and running from existing information, your task will be easier if you can get the people who originally created and produced the information to convert it for Web use. Maybe they understand the Web, and maybe they don't. You may need to determine which members of the staff you can expect to know something about the Web, and how their creations can be made to work well on the Web.

Enlisting staff support and assistance

Enlist the assistance of your supervisor and the supervisor of the creation and production staff to make sure that you build your Web team so everyone feels involved. Nothing makes your job more difficult than failing to get the support of the appropriate people in the creation and production departments. Mess this step up, and you'll find yourself converting every bit of information by yourself or with minimal, grudging assistance. If you can show the information creation folks how well their graphics and nicely formatted text appears on the Web — and how easy it is for them to create and produce this content — they'll be more likely to help out. Otherwise, they will just resent you for adding extra work to their already busy schedules.

Help the staff members find, acquire, and use the tools they need to create or convert the information to the required Web formats. Help them understand that if they're still thinking in paper-based terms, they're not prepared to deal with the information age.

Although mastering the transition from paper to a digital landscape may paint a bleak picture for the creation and production staff, you'll generally find that they are way ahead of you in their own areas of expertise and are anxious to produce their magic for the Web. In this case, as the Web site administrator, you'll be their hero for involving them in the process. Work closely with them when you're planning and scheduling your Web projects. Keep them abreast of the latest information, and they'll happily work with you to make your site successful.

Integrating the Web into the overall process

Remember that in most circumstances, a Web site is only a small part of the big picture in your organization's world presence. Although the site is your highest job priority because you're the Web administrator, it's really only a piece of the puzzle. The company's Web presence may become a rather large piece of the puzzle in the near future if you do your job well, which may result in your gaining more than a pat on the back for a job well done. However, if you act as if "your" Web site is a divine gift that's going to make your company another Micro-whatever or Global Motors, you'll find yourself all alone with your HTML.

Strive to integrate the processes of creation and upkeep of the Web site smoothly into your organization's overall public relations, marketing, advertising, and sales process. To these departments, a Web site is simply another way to put your organization's information in front of potential customers, clients, users, or whoever — similar to the television, radio, and printed distribution of your information. So find the similarities and help everyone, including yourself, understand that creating and producing information for a Web site isn't going to be much of an additional burden.

Conversion Is a Real Time-Saver

Converting current information into Web-ready format can save tremendous amounts of time. Otherwise, you must recreate information from scratch. ("Scratch" is a blank word processor screen labeled `Untitled.doc`.) This process is also known as "death by boring repetition" if you have to insert HTML code manually into numerous, long text documents. Fortunately, you've waited long enough that several enterprising companies have begun to market good conversion programs for most popular word-processing and page-formatting tools. More about these programs after you see what you'll be missing by not converting information manually.

Doing conversion manually

Having manually converted numerous word processor documents into HTML documents ourselves, we know what we're missing . . .and we don't miss it one little bit. You've created HTML documents, so you know at least a little about what we mean. To see the difference, just view a page of text in your browser, and then view the document source. In most popular browsers (for example, Netscape Navigator and Internet Explorer), HTML tags are a different color from the actual text, and links are yet another color. This difference lets you see how much HTML code must be added to even a basic text file for use on a Web site. Yuck!

The more complex your style sheet, the more work that's required to duplicate it on the Web. It's click, drag, click, drag, drop, click, click, and so on with your HTML editor, provided that it handles your big file in the first place. You also have to convert images to either `GIF` or `JPEG`, and turn word processor tables into HTML tables. Of course, you must do this perfectly or you end up with the last half of your 10-page text document formatted in bold, italic, heading 1 font, or worse.

Although currently available conversion programs are good, they're not perfect, as the next section shows.

The power (and limitations) of automated conversion

The good news is: Conversion tools really do work. They do a good job of converting the styles, formatting, tables, and images in existing files to Web server/browser-compatible files. The bad news is: You still must provide appropriate style, formatting, and layout in your original file, or the Web document the conversion produces won't look good onscreen. Also, conversion tools can't perform complex layouts such as frames or produce outside links without significant effort on your part. You still need to understand the basics of Web layout and HTML to produce high-quality HTML documents and an outstanding Web site.

As we state many times, the layout and flow, both within and between your Web documents, are extremely important to making yours a successful Web site. Conversion programs can't help with these design issues.

After you've designed your Web site using a layout appropriate for your information content and users' needs, you may be able to make use of conversion programs to convert existing text documents for use on parts of your Web. You still have to make adjustments to each document unless these documents are highly standardized and never change. If your site presents large amounts of frequently changing text, using a conversion program is a great time saver. Download a trial version to see whether this type of program is worth using for your situation.

Seeking tools

Finding HTML converters is too easy. Use Yahoo! (or your favorite search engine) with the search words `HTML converters`, and you get listings for every type of converter you can ever imagine, and then some.

Or you can go directly to the following URLs at the World Wide Web Consortium site, which contains a comprehensive listing of converters:

```
http://www.w3.org/hypertext/WWW/Tools/Filters.html
```

```
http://www.w3.org/hypertext/WWW/Tools
            /Word_proc_filters.html
```

We discuss a few of the more prominent converters for the major computer platforms and information creation tools in the following sections.

Cyberleaf

Cyberleaf, from Interleaf, converts text, graphics, and tables from Word, RTF, WordPerfect, Interleaf, and FrameMaker formats to HTML and GIF. Cyberleaf has versions available for several species of UNIX, Windows NT, and Windows 95. In addition to providing comprehensive conversion capabilities, Cyberleaf contains the following Web document management features:

✔ Interactively refines and saves parameters used to convert documents, reapplies defined styles and hyperlinks to your updated Web site, and identifies broken links that require manual intervention

✔ Facilitates browsing by allowing long documents to be outlined based on selected style names, such as chapter or section, which creates a table of contents for your Web site

✔ Automatically inserts hyperlinks between document outline elements and their corresponding sections in the HTML output file

✔ Includes a Post Web function that automatically copies completed Web documents to your Web server on demand

For more information on Cyberleaf, visit the following URL:

```
http://www.ileaf.com/ip.html
```

HTML Transit

HTML Transit for Windows NT, Windows 95, and InfoAccess 3.x uses a template approach to specify how each element in a source document is treated in a Web publication. The HTML Transit template stores everything about an electronic publication, including which input files to translate, which output files to generate, text and graphic treatments, and dynamic link behaviors. To update a Web site in Transit, revise your source files, reload the template, and click Translate Publication. HTML Transit may be the most comprehensive of the available conversion programs.

As you can see in Figure 20-1, HTML Transit allows you to add both your favorite HTML editor and Web browser using the lower-right two buttons shown in the figure. This program is a bit cumbersome to use because it uses a powerful template method, and it doesn't do forms, but if you're administering a large, frequently changing Web site or multiple sites, it may well be worth the $495 list price.

HTML Transit includes a raft of features and formats, as the following lists indicate:

Supported input formats

✔ ASCII text, RTF, Microsoft Word, WordPerfect, Lotus AmiPro, FrameMaker, Interleaf

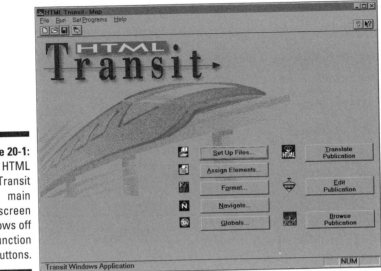

Figure 20-1:
The HTML
Transit
main
screen
shows off
its function
buttons.

Supported graphic formats

✔ BMP, CDR, CGM, DIB, DRW, DXF, GEM, GIF, HPGL, JPEG, MSP, PCC, PCX, PIC, TIFF, WMF, WPG

Supported output formats

✔ HTML DTDs (draft specification)

✔ Netscape Navigator extensions

✔ Microsoft Internet Explorer extensions

✔ Graphics as GIF or JPEG

File controls

✔ Single or multiple source files

✔ Selectable segmentation into smaller, linked files

Automated translation

✔ Automatic generation of HTML tags for body, table of contents, and index

✔ Source document style name recognition

✔ Source document attribute/pattern recognition

✔ Automatic graphics conversion to GIF or JPEG formats

✔ Graphics as full-size or choice of six linked thumbnail sizes

Publication formatting

- Character, paragraph, lists
- Graphical separators and icons
- Background colors and patterns
- Independent formatting for body, table of contents, and index

Navigation buttons

- TOC, index, next page, previous page, next item, previous item, specified HTML file (home page, help, and so on)
- Automatic insertion
- Control over placement
- Address/signature e-mail links

You can download a 30-day trial version of HTML Transit from the InfoAccess Web site.

```
http://www.infoaccess.com/
```

Web Publisher

Web Publisher 1.1 from SkiSoft converts Microsoft Word, WordPerfect, Lotus AmiPro, RTF, and FrameMaker format files into complete HTML documents. This conversion program works with Windows NT, Windows 95, and Windows 3.1, as Figure 20-2 suggests.

The list price of the standard version of Web Publisher is $495, and the Professional version, which includes the Long Document Utility, is $990 for a single PC. The Long Document Utility splits long HTML files into multiple documents and links them to another HTML file that contains a table of contents. Web Publisher automatically performs the following tasks:

- Converts images into GIF files
- Builds Netscape 1.1 tables
- Builds tables of contents with links to headings
- Interprets style information to build corresponding headings
- Converts numbered and bulleted lists
- Places signatures, mail-to URLs, and images in your documents
- Converts multiple documents in a single pass using templates
- Creates headings and navigation buttons

Figure 20-2:
The Web
Publisher
main
screen
displays its
function
buttons.

You can download a trial version of Web Publisher from the SkiSoft Web site, but you must e-mail SkiSoft to obtain an activation code before it will run.

`http://www.skisoft.com/`

WebWorks

WebWorks Publisher from Quadralay converts FrameMaker files to HTML on Windows, Macintosh, and several UNIX platforms. This program converts among graphics, tables, lists, ISO Latin 1, Greek, and equation formats. WebWorks Publisher also supports RTF, Word, WordPerfect, and Interleaf format conversions by using FrameMaker's file import.

WebWorks contains advanced graphic generation controls to:

- ✔ Generate transparent `GIF` files
- ✔ Generate graphics for viewing inline, external, or both
- ✔ Create graphic thumbnails
- ✔ Scale or rotate output graphics
- ✔ Adjust colors

For more information on WebWorks, visit Quadralay's Web site:

`http://www.quadralay.com/Company/products.html`

What should you remember about HTML converters?

When all is said and done, both HTML Transit and Web Publisher are good at what they are designed to do — convert your existing files into working HTML documents. You still need to know enough about HTML to design and lay out a Web page properly, but they help by automatically performing many tedious, repetitive tasks.

No conversion program magically converts existing text, graphics, or data files into fantastic-looking, state-of-the-art Web pages, much less a complete Web site. One way or another, you must determine which documents to link and in what order, lay out the frames or other goodies in your Web site, size and place graphics and Java applets, and so on. Some of the conversion programs' templates may assist you with some of these actions, but you must still picture the site in your own mind and use a conversion program's template maker — or manually edit HTML code — to get your ideas across to a Web browser, as well as clean up the code until everything is in tip-top shape. You remain the key, no matter what tools you use to help you perform your job more efficiently.

Déjà Vu — Elements of Page and Site Design

Yeah, yeah, you already know everything you need to know about Web page and site design, right? Do you know that the only way to get a framitz to link to a gazingleforkee across a 128K ISDN line is to use a skyhook with a frimmer? You do? Well then, you're one up on us!

The next section is more than a review of how to build HTML documents and create a Web site; we hope that it tells you what to watch for from the viewpoint of a Web site administrator. You need to stop thinking about the content and layout of your Web pages and site and add these dimensions: user interest, information flow, update cycling, and file management, just to name a few. Step back from the text and GIFs, and look at your site from a user's point of view. Don't just look at the pages in your browser. Think about why users are interested in visiting your site in the first place. Think about what deep psychological needs your site can fulfill. Think about what keeps users coming back for more. You want your site to be irresistible and addictive, but legal.

This is a tall order for a site that provides daily updates for the dilithium futures market on Ragnar III. But you can do more than simply dump loads of data into tabular form on several nearly identically formatted Web pages and slap them onto a default background. Use your imagination to create at least some variety that a user's eye and brain can grasp. Maybe you could put a new icon on each page every day. Maybe you could put a small box with a daily message on the home page. Whatever you do will be appreciated by the users if you do it tastefully, and don't let it interfere with the real reason they visit your site, whatever that may be. (You'd better know the reason, or your site could become a ghost town overnight.) Always give 'em what they want and a bit more — and do it with a smile.

Give all pages a title

Every HTML document, not just the first page in your site, should have a title. Not only is it displayed in a browser's title bar, but it's also used in Web searches (Yahoo!, AltaVista, WebCrawler, and so on) to index and list your pages. And, of course, you want as many of them to be listed as possible. Therefore, take the time to be creative and thorough when creating a document's title. If you performed a search on chocolate and came up with two sites: "Fred's magical choco-universe" and "Untitled," which would you choose?

Make the most of text and hypertext links

Text is the primary element in most HTML documents. Although a picture in the right place may be worth a thousand words, it's a rare HTML document that doesn't include some text. Making maximum use of that text is up to you. Remember that you can enhance the actual content of your text in many ways: layout, white space, different font colors, and links to related pieces of text.

If you're not good at page layout, get help from someone who is to ensure that the text is easy to read and pleasing to a user's eyes. Nothing turns surfers off quicker than being forced to scroll through screen after screen of tightly packed text to find the information they want.

Use tables of contents or icon-based navigation bars with hypertext links to provide ready access to the sections within your text documents. Internal links to named locations in documents not only provide users quick access to the section they want, but can also help other sites easily address locations on your pages other than at the head of a document. Remember that internal links are referenced by text names, which must be unique within all the full set of anchor names defined for each document.

Use graphics for maximum effect

First impressions are critically important to entice a surfer deeper into your Web. Use your most unique, eye-catching images on the front page. Remember, if an image takes forever to load, surfers click to another site before the images finish loading. Small, quickly loaded images are optimal. Save your bigger masterpieces for internal pages, where you can provide a thumbnail and give the user the option of loading the larger version. A few more tips for using graphics follow:

- ✔ Use graphics only when they add value to a page. Don't toss in a few small, annoying graphics just because you like them. Make sure that they perform functions that users will appreciate.

- ✔ Keep your graphics fresh. Even a corporate logo gets stale with time. Look at the various logos of numerous megacorporations over the past century, and you see that they update them as times change. Well, times change very rapidly on the Web, so make sure that your logo represents the message you want to communicate to users. The idea that an organization is cutting-edge can really be emphasized by using improved images and techniques on its Web pages.

- ✔ Use Java applets to animate your images for Java-enabled browsers.

- ✔ Make sure that GIFs have transparent backgrounds and are interleaved.

- ✔ Compress JPEGs as much as possible for quick display, while still keeping the resolution acceptable.

- ✔ Keep graphical elements to a reasonable number per page. If you must use numerous graphical elements on a page, keep them small to minimize transfer time.

The temptation to stick in another image can be strong. Resist the urge. Ask yourself: "What does this add to my document that my users will find irresistible?" Don't fool yourself with your own answer, either. Ask someone else's opinion.

Think in 24-D

Although hypertext is new and exciting, the legacy of thousands of years of linear text is hard to overcome. In other words, even though you can do incredible things with linking and hypermedia, your users may not be able to follow your path unless you make it as obvious as the yellow brick road. Linking adds a third dimension to the Web, but use it wisely and always, always give your users an easy way out to somewhere they will instantly recognize.

Stringing pages together, the book way

If part of your information is a report, it probably should be read linearly. Therefore, you can present it as a single Web document (if it's no more than five screens long) or split it into several HTML documents linked by navigation buttons (next, previous, top, bottom, start, end) at the bottom of each document. Make liberal use of links to other documents, to a glossary, or cross-references to other parts of your document, where they are appropriate. Just because your primary format is linear doesn't mean that you must force your users to move linearly. Let 'em jump around if they know where they're going, but always make getting back easy for them.

Hierarchies are natural

A hierarchical approach to Web document links is universally understood. Because a branched or hierarchical structure is one of the most basic structures in nature, improving on this type of structure without adding complexity is difficult. Unless your intended audience is especially good at mental gymnastics or your site is designed as a puzzle, stick to the basic structure shown in Figure 20-3. Both you and your users will be much happier.

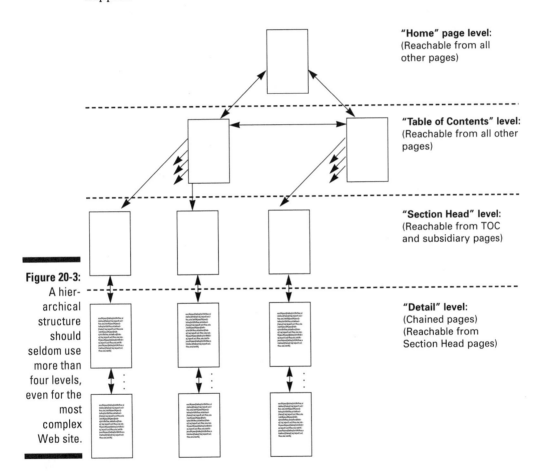

"Home" page level:
(Reachable from all other pages)

"Table of Contents" level:
(Reachable from all other pages)

"Section Head" level:
(Reachable from TOC and subsidiary pages)

Figure 20-3:
A hier-
archical
structure
should
seldom use
more than
four levels,
even for the
most
complex
Web site.

"Detail" level:
(Chained pages)
(Reachable from Section Head pages)

Multiple tracks for multiple audiences

Building a Web that includes several levels of material to meet the needs of different levels of users within your general audience is somewhat time-consuming but may pay off in the long run. Linking your Web's home page with a tutorial, a technical overview, and the detailed reference materials that comprise the bulk of your information is easy. Using this approach, you can design a home page that points beginners at a track that starts them with a tutorial and then leads them through an overview, before assaulting them with the down-and-dirty details of your real content.

This kind of organization, depicted in Figure 20-4, lets you show experienced readers how to access in-depth content directly, bypassing introductory and explanatory materials built for novices. Although HTML itself has no limits on the kinds of hierarchies you can build, your readers' ability to handle added complexity may be limited. For everyone's sake, we suggest keeping the hierarchy as tight and shallow as possible.

This organization combines elements of both a linear and a hierarchical structure in its actual page linkages. The tutorial is typically linear, whereas the reference materials are usually consulted by topic and are best structured in a hierarchy.

Extending your Web, a comment at a time

If you really want to encourage feedback, use a CGI script to solicit input from users and append their comments to the end of one of your pages. This approach creates an open-ended document that grows like a colony of coral or some other organic life form. You can also use this approach to create neverending stories or other serial creations on the Web. If you have the hard disk space — and know how to program the underlying CGI scripts — feel free to explore this approach.

For an example of a living, ongoing document, consult this URL:

```
http://bug.village.virginia.edu/
```

WAXWeb is a hypermedia implementation of a feature-length independent film, *WAX or the Discovery of Television Among the Bees* (David Blair, 85 minutes, 1991). WAXWeb is a hypermedia database available on the Internet with an authoring interface that lets users collaborate in adding to its story. WAXWeb includes thousands of individual elements, including text, music, motion videos, and video motion picture clips.

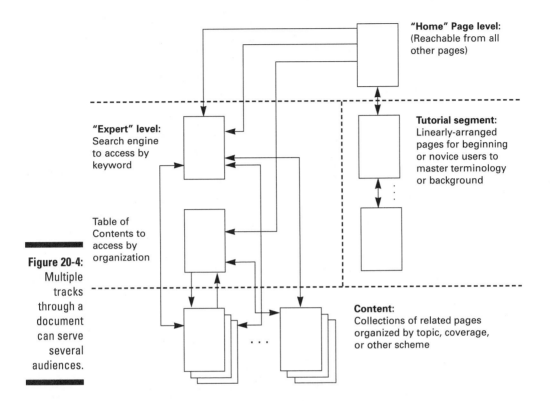

"Home" Page level:
(Reachable from all
other pages)

Tutorial segment:
Linearly-arranged
pages for beginning
or novice users to
master terminology
or background

"Expert" level:
Search engine
to access by
keyword

Table of
Contents to
access by
organization

Figure 20-4:
Multiple
tracks
through a
document
can serve
several
audiences.

Content:
Collections of related pages
organized by topic, coverage,
or other scheme

The essence of managing Web publishing is to implement a process that
provides users with fresh, attractive, and timely content. You must manage a
process that gathers information, creates HTML documents, and introduces
those documents into your Web site quickly enough to be acceptable to
your users, your employer, and yourself. To accomplish this feat, you must
carefully plan and execute your processs and work closely with the Web
administrator to ensure that all your hard work is available to your users.
We discuss numerous tools to assist you in your tasks in this chapter, and
even more appear in the next chapter, along with further techniques to help
you make your site a smashing success.

Chapter 21

Web Site Management Tools and Techniques

- -

In This Chapter

▶ Working with a myriad of documents

▶ Evaluating alternative management tools

▶ Seeking specialized tools

▶ Managing by routine

- -

*W*hatever you put into your Web — text, graphics, CGI scripts, forms, or something truly exotic — must be logically arranged so that you can be sure that you're using the proper version of each element. Constantly monitor your Web's security and frequently inspect your links for freshness and validity. Check your HTML documents for proper syntax to ensure that they'll work flawlessly with your users' browsers. Read all user feedback; then write and file your responses. And most important of all, periodically update your site's content to keep your users happy.

All the work involved in managing your site is up to you and your site management team (if you're lucky enough to have one). Without the proper techniques, good rapport with your Web server administrator, and a few handy tools to help you administer your Web site, you and your Web site may be more than a day late and a dollar short!

This chapter covers site management techniques instead of specific tools, because these tools vary widely and often depend on the Web server software in use. Also, the trend is toward more comprehensive Web site management systems for Windows 95, Windows NT, and Macintosh platforms. In this new wave of Web servers, each system contains a built-in set of management tools and, often, content creation and management tools as well. Nevertheless, you can find plenty of stand-alone Web management tools for all the popular platforms. We include suggestions later in this chapter.

Managing Multitudes of Documents

Your Web site consists primarily of HTML documents that contain the content — your Web site's reason for existence. Whether you have a single personal home page or minister to a Web site with hundreds of pages of content, you must keep track of the documents. The human mind is a wonderful biological computer capable of remembering seemingly countless bits of information. However, you still can't remember where you left your reading glasses or when you last changed the oil in your car. Why, then, should you expect to remember when you last revised one of your Web documents or where you left the document on your hard disk drive?

If you arrange your Web-related disk files logically and label them properly, you won't have to remember details about any specific document. If you follow our suggestions to the letter and keep a *change log* for your site, you only need to remember the name of the *change log* file. If you can't remember where the *change log* resides, you can always use a File Find utility (provided you can remember the *change log*'s file name).

How big is your Web?

We thought long and hard, and then we threw a few darts at the board, to determine approximate sizes for Web site categories. We consider that a small site includes 30 or fewer documents, a medium site contains from 30 to 100 documents, and a large site consists of more than 100 documents. A document can be any file — whether it's an HTML document, image file, CGI script, Java applet, or whatever — that resides in the Web site's directories on your Web server.

Because this is a *...For Dummies* book, we concentrate on small- and medium-sized sites. However, the techniques in this book work for all but the largest sites (those with thousands of documents or more), and even these monster sites use fundamentally the same approaches that we suggest. Only the tools change drastically: Monster sites use networked document management systems (costing tens of thousands of dollars) to handle the hundreds of thousands of documents they process every month. You, on the other hand, want to keep your Web site fresh and alive without spending all your time (and money) on its care and feeding.

Organize to untangle your Web

Organize! Organize! Organization is the key to minimizing Web administration time. Think of organization as the *Vulcan approach*, that is, always logical and precisely arranged. Even though you easily remember over 100 separate names for people that you know, you probably can't remember 100 disk file names, nor should you try.

Try this simple file management system. Group files by common characteristics, name them with similar, sequential names, and place those files in hierarchical subdirectories. Thirty documents aren't difficult to manage if you separate them into seven subdirectories. Look over the following directory structure with suggested (and frequently used) directory names:

- ✔ INDEX.HTML: The primary directory where your Web's home page can reside
- ✔ GRAPHICS: A subdirectory for somewhat fixed graphics files, such as navigation buttons, logos, and backgrounds
- ✔ ABOUTUS: A subdirectory for your organization's information
- ✔ CONTENT1 **and** CONTENT2: Two subdirectories for your Web pages' contents
- ✔ IMAGE1 **and** IMAGE2: Subdirectories of CONTENT1 and CONTENT2, respectively, for unique images pertaining to the content in that directory

Figure 21-1 shows how this directory structure may look on your hard disk drive.

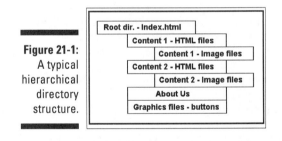

Figure 21-1:
A typical hierarchical directory structure.

Even if your site has 100 files, you probably need no more than 15 subdirectories. Adding four more CONTENT subdirectories, each with its own IMAGE subdirectory, increases the total number to 15. These additions give you six content subdirectories where you can put 10 files each and six image subdirectories with six files each for a total of 96 content-related files. This number of files equates to quite a bit of information (probably 5MB to 10MB, depending on your specific information).

You can keep track of this type of arrangement easily. Even if you update your content daily, you can proceed in an orderly fashion through your directory structure.

Keep adequate working and backup copies of your Web site's directory structure and files. On your own computer's hard disk drive, make two copies of the directories and files that reside on the Web server. One of the two copies contains working files; the other contains the most recent copy of each file from your site. (The latter is the copy that you upload to your Web server when you update your Web site.) In addition to these two copies, make another backup copy of the directory structure and files on another computer, your LAN server, or some other means of directory/file backup.

Document management systems

You may have heard or read about electronic document management systems that enable storage of computer files in a database just like those files' paper equivalents can be placed in a filing cabinet. Some document management systems even manage images and help you attach keywords to the image files before storing the files in a database. In turn, these keywords help you search for the images.

This concept looks great on paper, and many document management systems cost less that $500. The best products support full-text and customizable keyword indexes that use fuzzy-logic, Boolean, and template-based searching. They also include OCR-based, full-text indexing that you can use if you have a scanner and your information isn't available in electronic form. (You live in the middle of the Sahara desert maybe?)

So why don't you rush right out and buy a document management system? The following ideas and examples may help you decide if you need to purchase this system:

✔ If you handle numerous paper documents each day, a document management system may help you. One useful feature of these systems is their capacity to scan and store document images and make these images quickly available for viewing by searching a database. For example, a claims adjuster for a small insurance company could use this feature to check policies, signatures, and payment records.

Combine the output from a document management system with an HTML conversion program for text with an image converter for images, and you can automatically create Web pages from the documents stored in the management system.

✔ If the primary thrust of your Web site is to provide readers with a searchable database of electronically available data, you can definitely benefit from any of several available software systems. If you're going to charge for your service, you may be interested in the Basis Document Manager system from Information Dimensions, Inc.

The Basis Document Manager is an integrated server component built on BasisPlus, a proprietary, text-oriented extended-relational database. This software provides document management library services, full text retrieval, document control, document delivery, security, and authentication. The Basis Document Manager is integrated with Netscape's Communications Web Server and Commerce Web Server software and is scalable from small implementations up to thousands of users. Starting at $7,500, the Basis Document Manager provides a relatively low-cost tool for posting corporate information on the Web.

✔ If you're running a one-person Web administration department on a limited budget and you process several — but not hundreds — of pieces of information a day, your needs are pretty modest. You can concentrate on a simple, straightforward system to receive, process, store, and place your incoming information on your Web site. You don't need to bring in the heavy artillery.

We hope you get the picture. If you don't think that an electronic document management system is for you, don't despair — other Web management alternatives may better suit your needs, time, and budget. We discuss some of these alternatives in the next section.

Examining the Alternatives

Commercially available Web management tools haven't proliferated as rapidly as Web browsers and servers. The reason for this situation may be that most Web servers are UNIX-based, and the UNIX crowd creates its own utilities (which only they are able to use). Do you get the idea that Web management has been a somewhat programmer-oriented culture until recently? With the unveiling of several Windows 95-, Windows NT-, and Macintosh-based Web servers, the game has opened up considerably.

Of course, Windows and Mac users don't use command-line utilities — at least, not like UNIX folks do — because their outlook on life is GUI-based. You can't just kludge together a GUI-based Web management tool the same way that UNIX users created tools in the past. As a result, only a few shareware tools for Windows or Mac Web administrators are available. We discuss the more promising tools briefly in the following sections to give you some ideas about where to start your quest for a perfect tool set.

Augment these discussions by checking your favorite search engine sites and checking out the outstanding compendium of information and links at:

```
http://webreference.com/
```

Web site managers

A new class of tool is emerging to help Web administrators manage sites. Some tools consist of a collection of utilities, and some take an all-in-one system approach. We discuss examples of each kind in the following sections.

SITEMAN

SITEMAN is a set of utilities that checks internal references, lists all files that contain a call or a link to a file, and identifies *orphan* files (those files not hyperlinked to any other files in the directory). These utilities run under Windows NT, Windows 95, and Windows 3.*x* and present the user with the following processes that help with managing a Web site's files:

- ✔ **File integrity check:** The file integrity check reviews each internal link from each file to ensure that the link connects to another file in the directory. The routine does not check external, extra-directory, and same-page links. The resulting output lists all links not connected to a valid file and all files that are referenced but do not exist in their indicated directories.

- ✔ **Reference list:** For each file or set of files selected, the reference list routine lists all references to other files found in `<A HREF="...">..</A>`, `<IMG .. SRC="..">`, or `<BODY...BACKGROUND="...">` tags. The resulting list contains all these references, including those that are not tested by the file integrity check.

- ✔ **Global file name change:** Global file name change is available in SITEMAN 2. By using this function, you can select a file, modify its name, and make all references to that file (in all HTML files in the site) change automatically to the new name.

- ✔ **Individual file name linkages:** The individual file name linkage function lists all files in the site that link to the file you select. Use this function to find file dependencies within your site.

- ✔ **Orphan file search:** This routine lists orphan files, that is, those files in a selected directory that aren't connected by links to any other files in the directory.

Find more information about SITEMAN at the following URL:

```
http://www.morning.asn.au/siteman/index.html
```

LivePAGE

LivePAGE offers a collection of Web management tools for Windows NT, Windows 95, and Windows 3.*x.* The LivePAGE products include:

- ✔ **LivePAGE Web Organizer:** Manages small intranets (prototyping system, single user)

- ✔ **LivePAGE HTML Edition:** Manages large intranets (multi-user, uses database)

- ✔ **LivePAGE dbConnect:** Accesses databases in real-time

- ✔ **LivePAGE CD Publisher and Web Publisher:** Publishes to multiple media from a single source

- ✔ **LivePAGE SGML Edition:** Extends HTML Edition to support full SGML

The LivePAGE Web Organizer performs the following tasks:

- ✔ Manages your Web site as a single document

- ✔ Publishes your site document for the Web at the press of a button

- ✔ Resolves links

- ✔ Generates navigation buttons and dynamic tables of contents automatically

- ✔ Ensures valid HTML syntax

- ✔ Works with existing HTML editors

- ✔ Requires no special Web Server software

Inforium provides an overview of its LivePAGE products at:

```
http://www.livepage.com/
```

SiteMill

Adobe Systems offers SiteMill for Macintosh and Power Macintosh. SiteMill includes the functionality of Adobe's outstanding PageMill software, which you can use to create HTML documents. SiteMill includes WYSIWYG Web page editing, integrated image manipulation, and format conversion. SiteMill provides the following:

- ✔ **Link management:** Adobe SiteMill lets you easily maintain correct links for your entire Web site including links to external sites, because SiteMill automatically repairs links that break when you rename pages or files or change the location of files (move them into subfolders, for example). The program displays a view of your Web site that shows your page structure along with pop-up menus of the links to and from each file.

✔ **One-step error correction:** SiteMill finds and summarizes any errors present in your Web site. You can then correct them with a simple, one-step, drag-and-drop procedure. From then on, under the watchful eye of SiteMill, your site remains error-free. Also, Adobe SiteMill can read existing Web sites and automatically find and summarize the errors present in them, too.

✔ **Creating new links:** The SiteMill software integrates the *Site view* (the display of your Web site's structure and resources) and the *Page Editing view* (the layout of your Web page document), enabling you to create new links by simply dragging a file or an image icon from the Site view into the Page view. You don't have to know about the uniform resource locator (URL) link addressing scheme or the page path name syntax, and you don't have to type any file names. SiteMill automatically creates the correct links.

SiteMill performs the following tasks:

✔ Shows all resources, page titles, and folders in the Site view

✔ Shows warnings for unreachable or unused resources

✔ Automatically fixes all links throughout the site when files or folders are renamed, moved between folders, or deleted

✔ Enables link creation by simply dropping a resource from the Site view into a page

✔ Shows all bad links and allows one-step correction from the Error view

✔ Shows all references to external Web sites and allows easy global renaming of files through the External References view

Additional information on SiteMill is available at:

```
http://www.adobe.com/prodindex/sitemill/main.html
```

FrontPage

By purchasing Vermeer Technologies in 1995, Microsoft acquired FrontPage, perhaps the top all-in-one system Web management system available today. If Microsoft continues to develop FrontPage and open it up for use with other Web servers, FrontPage could become a major player in the Web management game. The system already contains an extensive online tutorial and context-sensitive help to assist you in understanding its many features and functions. The FrontPage graphical interface is a big plus for Windows users; see Figure 21-2 for a look.

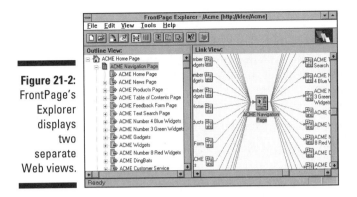

Figure 21-2:
FrontPage's
Explorer
displays
two
separate
Web views.

The FrontPage client/server architecture allows you to develop Web content locally, across a LAN, or over the Internet on a Windows PC or a Macintosh. At the same time, your Web server can reside on Windows NT, Windows 95, or UNIX platforms. In addition, you can copy Web sites between platforms and Web servers while preserving all programming, access controls, and clickable image maps. FrontPage integrates all the functions typically required to develop and administer a Web site into a seamless environment. FrontPage features include the following capabilities:

- ✔ WYSIWYG editing of HTML pages, including text, headings, inline images, and most HTML extensions (background images, custom text colors, font point sizes, and so on)

- ✔ WYSIWYG HTML form editing, including text input fields, scrolling text boxes, check boxes, radio buttons, pick lists, and push buttons

- ✔ Link, Outline, and Summary views of all the hyperlinks, documents, and multimedia files comprising the Web site as a whole

- ✔ Drag-and-drop adding of hyperlinks between pages or from pages to any other file type (sound, video, PDF, and so on)

- ✔ WebBots, which quickly add sophisticated interactive functions (such as threaded discussion groups, full-text search, Web registration, and form-driven surveys) to a Web site without programming

- ✔ Wizards and templates to create complete Webs and individual pages

- ✔ Using the mouse to indicate hotspot boundaries to create clickable image maps

- ✔ Remote, collaborative authoring support so multiple, geographically dispersed authors can develop against the same pages simultaneously

- ✔ Multiuser To Do List, which tracks tasks needed to complete a site

Also, with FrontPage you can:

- ✔ Set site-level permissions for end-users, authors, and administrators.

- ✔ Copy an entire Web site from one server to another including documents, clickable image maps, programming (via WebBots), and permissions. FrontPage can copy between Web servers from different vendors that run on different hardware and software platforms.

- ✔ Verify that all hyperlinks to external Webs are still valid.

- ✔ Automatically convert Rich Text Format (RTF) and plain text files to HTML.

- ✔ Automatically convert most popular image formats into GIF or JPEG, the native formats of the Web.

- ✔ Automatically create transparent GIF images.

- ✔ Browse (and, potentially, import) any page on the global Web from directly within the FrontPage Editor by specifying a URL or by pressing Ctrl and clicking on any hyperlink.

Find out more about FrontPage from Microsoft at:

```
http://www.microsoft.com/frontpage/
```

Let someone else manage your Web

Cookware runs the ClubWeb site to help you with your Web needs for just a little bit every month . . . that is, for just a few dollars, Son, dollars. Check out this site's offerings if you need to put up your Web page in a hurry and if you want to conserve up-front costs. Cookware offers numerous options for Web authors and administrators:

- ✔ **IShop:** Virtual shopping carts for commercial sales over the Web.

- ✔ **Forms4U:** The advanced Forms4U form handler enables you (for a fee) to use HTML forms in your WWW documents without a server.

- ✔ **Find4Me:** If you need to do some database searching for your pages, Find4Me lets you search by clicking a hyperlink, submitting a form, or bringing up a page.

- ✔ **MembersOnly:** If you need to provide membership privileges and security for your site, this system supports pages accessible only to users with passwords and membership status.

- ✔ **Sticky Pages:** The fantastic marketing capabilities of Sticky Pages make your logo, buttons, or advertising stay with users as they surf, even after they leave your site.

✔ **RandomLink:** Add fun to your pages! RandomLink changes the graphics and text each time a page is displayed.

✔ **Demographics:** For a small monthly fee, the ClubWeb site demographics service provides an analysis of your Web site's hits and drops the information off in your home directory every night.

Access ClubWeb at the following URL; be sure to check out the other offerings:

```
http://www.cookware.com/
```

Cool Management Tools

You can find really cool, stand-alone management tools directly via the Internet. Certain management tools enable you to check up on your Web site and its pages from your own Web browser. "How does this work?" you ask. You simply supply the management tool's site with the URL of your Web page; the management tool software does the rest. When the stand-alone tool finishes the checkup, it sends a report back to your browser.

Doesn't this beat running a UNIX command-line utility? Yes and no. Using these tools is better if you're not into UNIX and don't run your own Web server. But these management tools do not create a fully automated system, because you must enter the URL for each HTML page individually — and receive reports one page at a time. If you have a small Web site, tools like these may be all you need. If so, give them a try.

Doctor HTML

Doctor HTML retrieves a specified Web page and performs tests to see whether your document conforms to applicable standards. This tool offers a selectable set of tests on its main page. Enter the URL for the page you want examined; then wait while Doctor HTML performs these tests:

✔ Checks document spelling, so you don't look silly.

✔ Performs an analysis of the images, so you know how much bandwidth is consumed when each image is downloaded, as well as estimated download times.

✔ Tests document structure to find unclosed HTML codes that may cause problems on some browsers.

✔ Looks at image command syntax, so you won't suffer from incorrect image commands. Image tags are important for quick image loading and page display, and provide information to nongraphical browsers.

✔ Examines table structure to make sure that you don't have any unclosed TR, TH, and TD tags inside a properly defined table (one with an open and close table tag). It also reports on TR, TH, and TD tags that appear outside of properly defined tables, because these may cause formatting problems on some browsers.

✔ Verifies that all hyperlinks are valid (to avoid frustrating your users).

✔ Examines form structure. This test is handy for checking input types and variable names. Currently, it only looks at INPUT commands and does not test SELECT or TEXTAREA commands.

✔ Shows the command hierarchy. This task presents the HTML commands that are found in the document.

Give Doctor HTML a look at your Web pages through this URL:

```
http://imagiware.com/RxHTML/
```

Weblint

Weblint checks the HTML code in your Web pages to ensure that the code conforms to your chosen HTML specifications. As with Doctor HTML, you simply supply the URL for a page anywhere on the Web. Alternatively, you can paste or type HTML code for checking directly into a window. Weblint currently performs the following rigorous tests:

✔ Checks basic HTML structure for completeness

✔ Lists unknown elements and element attributes

✔ Performs context checks (where tags may appear only within certain elements)

✔ Lists overlapped elements

✔ Expects to see a TITLE in the HEAD element

✔ Lists IMG elements that do not supply ALT text

✔ Shows illegally nested elements

✔ Alerts you to mismatched tags (such as <H1> ... </H2>)

✔ Displays unclosed elements (for example, <H1> ...)

✔ Catches elements that should appear only once

✔ Flags obsolete elements

✔ Checks for an odd number of quotes in a tag

✔ Checks heading order

✔ Lists potentially unclosed tags

✔ Flags markup embedded in comments, which confuses some browsers

✔ Whines when you use `here` as anchor text

✔ Checks tags where attributes are expected (for example, anchors)

✔ Checks the existence of local anchor targets

✔ Flags the case of tags

✔ Alerts you to leading and trailing whitespace in certain container elements

✔ Flags unclosed comments (comments should be `<!-- . . . -->`)

✔ Supports the format formerly known as HTML 3.0, including elements such as `TABLES`, `MATH`, `FIGURES`, and the rest

The output from a Weblint check looks like this:

```
Weblint Results
Please keep in mind that Weblint is a lint and can be
          picky.
Weblint Warning Messages
    line 23: illegal value for WIDTH attribute of IMG (100%)
    line 23: IMG does not have ALT text defined.
    line 41: illegal value for WIDTH attribute of TD (25%)
    line 43: illegal value for WIDTH attribute of TD (25%)
    line 125: IMG does not have ALT text defined.
    line 147: IMG does not have ALT text defined.
    line 169: illegal value for WIDTH attribute of IMG
          (100%)
    line 169: IMG does not have ALT text defined.
    line 175: empty container element <A>.
The HTML Source Listing
    1.<HTML>
    2.<HEAD>....
```

(The rest of the HTML source listing was omitted to protect the guilty.)

Unfortunately, this site is "for profit." So to check your HTML documents with WWWeblint, you need to purchase a subscription to their service. Complete details and payment options are available from its Web site.

Weblint really gives your HTML code a thorough going-over. You may choose to ignore some of its suggestions, but you should run your pages through this or another similar program to help you understand the process. Access the Weblint program at the following URL:

```
http://www.unipress.com/cgi-bin/WWWeblint/
```

The WebTechs HTML Validation Service

The WebTechs HTML Validation Service checks your HTML files to make sure that they comply with your chosen level of HTML (2.0, 3.0, 3.2, Cougar, Netscape, Internet Explorer, or SoftQuad extensions). The WebTechs HTML validation service works the same way as Weblint. The WebTechs site also has some CGI scripting utilities available for UNIX users. Give the service and the utilities a try at:

```
http://www.webtechs.com/html-val-svc/
```

If you run your own Web server, you can use other Web site management tools. When you're ready to acquire a set of these tools, the following sections can assist you in finding the right ones.

Acquiring the Perfect Tool Set

You can find Web site management tools to help you with various aspects of your Web site or to perform certain Web site functions. In the next sections, we discuss just a few of the more useful tools for your perfect tool set. To find the latest versions of available tools, use the following terms in your favorite search engines and follow the links:

automated messengers	CGIs, applets, and scripts	converters
database access	diagnostic tools	firewalls
gateways	image maps	indexing tools
information retrieval tools	network security	RealAudio
robots and Web crawlers	searching tools	sound players
statistics/tracking tools	verifiers	viewers
VRML	Web forms	Web spiders

Web site usage tools and services

If you're running your own Web site, find out who's visiting the site. Web site usage tools and services can give you a better picture of who's visiting your site and for how long, and if used properly, can even tell you something about why. The Webreference.com site has links to numerous Web site usage packages. Use the following URL to access this site:

```
http://webreference.com/usage.html
```

Log file analysis tools

If you're using a UNIX-based Web server that produces NCSA-compatible log files, you can use one of the stand-alone log file analysis programs such as WWWStat, GWStat, or Wusage. You can combine the HTML output from WWWStat with the GWStat program to produce usage charts and graphs, even in color.

Although Wusage may be less complete than other tools, it is easy to use and produces reports and graphs that can be automatically installed on your Web site by simply setting the location. Be aware that these programs aren't designed for use by the UNIX-challenged (nonprogrammer types), because the programs need to be customized for your specific Web site and in some cases, they must be compiled.

You can find WWWStat at the following URL:

```
http://www.ics.uci.edu/WebSoft/wwwstat/
```

You can find GWStat at the following URL:

```
http://dis.cs.umass.edu/stats/gwstat.html
```

You can find Wusage at the following URL:

```
http://www.boutell.com/wusage/
```

You can get at least the following types of information from most good log file analysis tools:

```
Daily Transmission Statistics
%Reqs %Byte  Bytes Sent  Requests   Date
 ___  ___   _____      |_____
 0.35  0.38    695752      161   |  Jan  9 1996
 0.55  0.92   1692956      254   |  Jan  8 1996
 0.48  1.21   2230875      220   |  Jan  7 1996
 0.30  0.33    606164      137   |  Jan  6 1996
```

```
Hourly Transmission Statistics
Total Transfers by Client Domain
Total Transfers by Reversed Subdomain
Total Transfers from each Archive Section
%Reqs %Byte  Bytes Sent  Requests   Archive Section
 ___  ___   _____      |_____
 0.07  0.33    604700       34   |  /coe/87manapc.htm
 0.04  0.07    126641       17   |  /coe/87manapd.htm
 0.03  0.05     94061       16   |  /coe/87manbib.htm
```

Some of the tools produce nice graphic representations of usage. Look for Windows 95 and Windows NT, as well as Macintosh log file analysis tools, through your favorite Web search engine. We expect more and more of these tools to arrive on the scene in the near future.

The details of Web site management techniques change with the availability of new and improved management tools. However, the basics stay the same. No matter what types of tools you use, your primary objective is to provide unique, original, fresh content to your target audience in an engaging, easy-to-navigate, timely manner. To reach this form of Nerd-vana, you must establish a Web management routine.

Your Web Management Routine

Plan for change! After your Web is up and running, your primary concerns are maintenance and improvement. Your Web management routine should be a process that evolves with changes in your personal situation; changes in your site's content, hardware, and software; changes in the Internet; and changes in your users' needs, desires, and expectations.

Make your management routine workable, so that it doesn't drive you screaming from your office just before a deadline. To create a workable routine, you need a plan based on your (and your staff's) available time, the volume, availability, and timing of your site's content, and the following sound principles of Web site maintenance.

The principles of Web site maintenance

The primary principles of Web maintenance are appropriateness, timeliness, and thoroughness. Use feedback from your readers to find good reasons for changing only appropriate portions of your site. Provide timely updates and renovation of your content and Web pages. Be thorough in your search for new content and in your quest to provide your users with a perfect Web site.

Analyze the following areas for your Web site maintenance process:

- **Content:** Are you updating your site frequently and thoroughly enough? Are you adding new content in your niche?

- **Graphics:** Have you given your users a change of eye-catching graphics recently?

- **Links:** Are the URLs all still available? Have you added any new links to enhance your site?

✔ **Web walker:** Is your site in the top 10 listings of the major search engine sites? Why not?

✔ **Usage:** Is your hit counter working? What does your log file analysis tell you?

✔ **Feedback:** Are you reading user feedback and responding to it in a timely fashion?

✔ **Server:** Have you installed the most recent updates or fixes to your Web server software?

✔ **Browser:** Are you keeping abreast of updates in browsers that let you update your Web's look and feel (frames, Java, and so on)? Do you test your pages with new versions of popular browsers to ensure that they're still compatible?

✔ **CGI scripts:** Do your CGI scripts still work? Do they need updating?

To ensure that maintenance is complete, make a checklist of these areas and fill in the date and time whenever you perform any maintenance task. Recording your maintenance activity should be a part of your overall Web management plan.

Creating your Web management plan

The details of your Web management plan vary depending on whether you administer your own personal Web or manage a Web management team for an organization. However, the basic steps to follow remain the same. Use these steps to create and revise your Web management plan:

1. **Determine your Web site's basic management needs on a daily, weekly, and monthly basis.**

2. **Type the determined needs into a file.**

3. **Prioritize the Web site management needs.**

4. **Describe the task and tools necessary to fulfill each need.**

5. **Guestimate the amount of time necessary to accomplish each task; enter your guestimate into the file.**

6. **Determine how often you want to perform each task.**

7. **Determine who should perform each task.**

8. **Create a critical path chart or sketch a timeline on a sheet of paper.**

9. **Revise the management plan until the plan looks feasible.**

10. **Try your plan on a small scale with a mock Web site on your own computer.**

11. **Revise the plan.**

12. **Try your plan again on a small scale and revise until it works smoothly.**

13. **Use the plan on your Web site.**

14. **Record how long each task takes to accomplish.**

15. **Revise the tasks that take too long, or get better tools, or both.**

16. **Continually look for new tools and techniques to improve your management routine.**

Your Web management plan can be as detailed as you or your organization demands. But whatever you decide, formalize the plan into an electronic or hard-copy form. Using a checklist to record the time, date, and the name of whoever performed each task is a good way to ensure that you get all the tasks done. Make this checklist a part of your Web site management log. You'll be pleasantly surprised at the information this log can produce over time. It may save you considerable effort in the future by providing you with information about your site that you can't get any other way.

The virtues of regular attention

All humans appreciate consistency in their daily lives, up to the point of boredom. We all habitualize mundane tasks so that we don't have to pay too much serious attention to them. This fact is the primary reason that Windows and Macintosh user interfaces have become so popular: They've simplified and standardized many tasks into oblivion. Now, we can concentrate on reaching our objectives by *using* software, rather than spending time trying to figure out *how* to use different applications.

The common navigation buttons and layouts used throughout your Web site should work the same way. Follow this path of consistency to its logical conclusion by providing your users with regular updates, feedback replies, and other types of attention to their needs, wants, and desires.

Regular attention to your Web site, and thereby to your users, shows them that you really care. A basic human desire is to be cared for, so use this need to your advantage. But be aware that regularity is a two-edged sword: If you promise users that you'll provide them with daily, weekly, or other regular updates, you'd better produce on time. They'll turn on you faster than a starving Tasmanian devil if you're late with an update.

On a different tack, scheduling time for attention to your Web — whether you perform maintenance, add new content, or update the look of your pages — helps ensure that you actually perform the Web management function that you intend. If you know that you're scheduled to run the link-checking spider every Monday morning at 8:00, you're more likely to get it done. Schedule each task at regular intervals and set aside a specific time in your schedule to accomplish it. You and your users will be happy that you did.

Web administration is a part/full-time job

Web site administration can range from a part-time job a few hours a week to a seven-day-a-week, on-call-at-night, full-time-plus job. As a Web site administrator, you may be called upon to be an artist, a customer service specialist, a director, an editor, an evangelist, a hardware technician, an HTML programmer, a planner, a revisionist, a salesperson, a server engineer, a visionary, a Web guru, a Web layout architect, a Web link finder, and a Web manager. Whew! Now you can see why many larger organizations assign entire teams to share the job of Webmaster. Can you imagine how many people work to administer the Netscape site with several million hits per day?

You probably won't have to concern yourself with the problems of such a large site tomorrow. However, starting out on the right foot and continuing along the path toward a perfectly administered Web site is an admirable goal. When the number of hats you wear each day outnumbers the hours you work, consider finding an assistant, providing your budget permits. Otherwise, your Web site could become an albatross around your neck, instead of the eagle that carries you to your dreams.

Now that you're thoroughly versed in using a Web management plan for a Web site that contains a myriad of documents, and you are using a variety of management tools on a regular basis, you'll be happy to know that more help is on the horizon. (Take a mental breath after that sentence!) You can get the electronic version of an eight-legged arthropod to assist you in your quest for the fully automated Web site. Just check out the spiders, 'bots, and Web walkers in the next chapter!

Chapter 22

Making Your Content Accessible

. . . .

In This Chapter

▶ Understanding spiders, robots, worms, and other agents

▶ Rounding up the best of the 'bots

▶ Using the `<META>` tag

▶ Registering your site with search engines

. . . .

*Y*ou may create great content and have the most dazzling Web site known to humankind, but if users don't know it's there, quietly waiting, none of them will ever have the privilege of seeing your masterpiece. The Web has given hundreds of thousands of people a voice that can be heard by other legions of users. All those voices speaking at once have turned the Web into a giant shouting match, and each voice must struggle to be heard.

In Chapter 19, we tell you how to publicize a Web using traditional print media as well as Usenet newsgroups. But if you spend any time surfing the Web at all, you know that search engines are the tool of choice to sort through those myriad voices to find truly interesting content. This chapter gives an inside look at the creatures that inhabit the Web and how you can make them work to your benefit, shows you how to provide accurate and useful information about your pages to search engines using `<META>` information, and provides the inside scoop on how to register your site with a wide variety of search engines instead of waiting for them to come to you.

Of Spiders, Robots, Worms, and Other Agents

Spiders, robots (aka 'bots), wanderers, agents, and viruses are all loose on the Web. These are all names for programs that automatically travel around the Web. Most are more than merely benign; they're downright useful. But some are malicious. All go about their jobs invisibly, without bothering anyone.

Many Internet users love these critters. Some Web administrators hate them. 'Bots on the Web are similar to bees on the earth that produce honey, but sting us when we try to get some. We accept their good and bad aspects and learn to live with them.

Web 'bots come in all types and sizes. They've been (somewhat artificially) classified by some Web pundits into these four categories: robots, wanderers, and spiders; commerce agents; MUD agents and chatterbots; and worms and viruses.

Robots, wanderers, and *spiders* are programs that follow hyperlinks in HTML documents to see where they lead. They collect the URLs for those links and report them to their owners. Then these URLs are usually indexed into a searchable database for your use, probably in connection with some kind of search engine.

Do the names Lycos, WebCrawler, Excite, and Yahoo! ring a bell? They all use Web spiders to find new Web sites to add to their collections. Some spiders, such as MOMspider (Multi-Owner Maintenance spider) can help you maintain your Web by locating inactive links within your Web pages.

Commerce agents are just emerging onto the Web. They help you find bargains and do your shopping on the Web. Some of these agents have recently begun to act as brokers or traders to assist in completing transactions on the Web. Look for commerce agents to greatly increase their visibility on the Web in the near future.

MUD agents and *chatterbots* are programs from Multi-User Dimensions, better known as Multi-User Dungeons, of the Internet. These programs answer questions, provide directions, and chat with game players. Whereas MUD agents are limited to their MUD environments, chatterbots are frequently found plying their trade on the Web, much to the delight of humans who interact with them.

The last group, *worms* and *viruses*, are malignant inhabitants from the dark side of the Web. These self-replicating programs slime their way around the Internet, infecting unsuspecting and unprotected computers. Some of these are relatively innocuous and even humorous in their effects on your system. But infection from others can produce disastrous consequences. Run the latest version of your antivirus software frequently on your computer to ensure that you won't be the next victim.

Because spiders are the most prevalent type of useful robots on the Web, the rest of this chapter concentrates primarily on hyperlink-finding spiders and how to use them.

The past and future of Web agents

As long ago as 1970, Nicholas Negroponte (director of the Media Lab at MIT) recognized and wrote about the ultimate value of delegating a program to move around within a network and perform tasks on your behalf. In 1984, Alan Kay expanded on this idea in an article in *Scientific American*. Now that the Internet is used by millions around the world to access an uncounted number of Web sites, the idea of agents is no longer just an interesting concept, it's a necessity.

The goal of most agent visionaries is to produce an easily customizable computer program that knows your preferred working patterns and information desires, and operates on your behalf to accomplish whatever you direct it to do. These agents would keep you informed of their progress, and they may even ask for clarification of instructions after finding and assimilating partial information while completing their tasks.

One of the handiest agents is the ComBot. Instead of sending standard, static e-mail and waiting for a reply or playing phone tag with George, you can instruct ComBot to deliver your message to George ASAP (or *stat* if you're into medical terminology) and to confirm its receipt. Your ComBot contacts George's ComBot and the two work together to deliver your message to George. Your ComBot then tells you when George received it. If you wanted to meet with George in person (or via video-conference), your ConfBot can schedule a workable time with George's ConfBot.

ConfBots work with ComBots to communicate and gather appropriate information from yours and George's schedules. Of course, your schedule calendar is private; thus, your ConfBot knows which areas to protect and which are open. It can act as a gatekeeper as well as a schedule manager.

These examples of next-generation agents may seem unrelated to the Web. However, the role of the Web is changing rapidly. Today we tend to think of e-mail, newsgroups, and the Web as three separate areas of the Internet, possibly on separate servers, accessed by separate programs (e-mail reader, newsreader, and Web browser).

But numerous Web browsers, such as Netscape Navigator and Microsoft Internet Explorer, have already integrated these functions into a single program. The idea is to provide one tool and interface through which you access anything on the Internet. This concept blurs the distinction between information sources, and justifies a single agent focus.

Agents in search engines and other WWW environments

The two primary uses for Web robots are to discover existing Web sites and to maintain hyperlinks by finding stale links — that is, links that no longer reach active Web sites. In addition, robots are also used to mirror popular Web and FTP sites on other servers to spread the load. By using robots, such as HTMLGobble, Tarspider, or Webcopy, you can place a complete copy of a Web site on another server, but internal HTML links must still be updated manually to reflect a new site's base address. Undoubtedly, more sophisticated Web-mirroring robots will be developed in the near future.

Perhaps The ForeFront Group will automate WebWhacker for this use. It's not automated, but you can use this program to copy entire Web sites. And it does convert relative hyperlinks to reflect a new server address. For more information about WebWhacker, visit:

```
http://www.ffg.com/whacker.html
```

Robots that follow hyperlinks around the Web and return URLs for each Web document they encounter provide the basis for search engines such as AltaVista, Excite, Lycos, Webcrawler, and Yahoo!, to name just a few. These sites send their robots onto the Internet to search for new or changed Web sites. Their robots keep track of every URL they visit and report information about each one. All of these robots are designed to gather important information from each HTML document they encounter and to transmit that information back to their owners' sites.

Some robots are programmed to capture the first paragraph or a certain number of lines of text from each document. Others index an HTML document's text and create a keyword set to transmit back to their owners for inclusion in the search engine's database. For example, the Lycos search robots extract a document's title, its headings and subheadings, the first 20 lines of text, the 100 most important words, the total number of words, and the size of each document (in bytes).

Most discovery robots contain sophisticated algorithms to determine what they do when they access a Web site. These controls are extremely important, as the next section explains.

Building search boundaries

Web search robots are self-contained programs that are closely related to much-maligned viruses and worms for release onto the Web without restraints. These restraints usually take the form of carefully set boundaries. Although a search robot won't intentionally impact a Web site, it can greatly disrupt site operation if it fails to behave itself.

Martijn Koster's (1994) *Guidelines for Robot Writers* and Dave Eichmann's (1995) *Ethical Web Agents* offer outstanding insights into the proper use of robots on the Web. You can access these documents at the following URLs:

```
http://info.Webcrawler.com/mak/projects/robots ⤴
        /guidelines.html
http://www.ncsa.uiuc.edu/SDG/IT94/Proceedings/Agents⤴
        /eichmann.ethical/eichmann.html
```

What works globally also sometimes works locally

If robots work well on the Web, just think how useful they may be on your own Web site. You think that your site is too small to benefit from a spider's help? Well, just how can you ensure that all your outside links remain valid? How do you know when a Webmaster at your favorite site decides to shuffle its pages or move them to another server? How can you be sure that your internal hyperlinks remain valid when you change your own pages? You can either do this task manually, one link at a time until you go screaming bonkers, or you can get MOMspider (or its lite version, WebWalker) or some other robot to check your links for you.

Here's how this process works: MOMspider and other maintenance robots can be instructed to traverse your Web site to check for dead links. These robots can even prepare a list of dead links for your perusal, and can save hours of pain and suffering if you take the time to get to know them. To find out how to run these robots locally, read their documentation and user information.

The Best of 'bots

Get your spiders and 'bots here! Visit the following URL to access Webreference.com:

```
http://www.webreference.com/agents.html
```

The following URLs are great sites to start your search for Web robots, wanderers, and spiders. This URL contains a comprehensive, annotated list of about 40 different robots and links to their sites:

```
http://info.Webcrawler.com/mak/projects/robots /active.html
```

This URL is the front page for the World Wide Web Robots, Wanderers, and Spiders site:

```
http://info.Webcrawler.com/mak/projects/robots/robots.html
```

Robot exclusion

If you don't want robots wandering around your Web site, you must place a robot exclusion file, named `robots.txt`, in the same directory as your `index.html` file (usually known as the *Web server root* or *Web root* directory). This file can contain several commands to exclude robots from all or parts of your Web. Not all robots conform to the standards for robot exclusion proposed by Martijn Koster, but increasingly they do, because most robot makers and users understand that politeness and common courtesy — especially in robots — is one of the keys to keeping the Web healthy and thriving.

If you don't want any robots roaming your site, your `robots.txt` file should contain the following lines:

```
# No 'bots allowed here.
User-agent: *
Disallow: /
```

All text following the # symbol is ignored. The * symbol denotes anything or everyone, so the second line excludes all User-agents. The slash (/) in the `Disallow:` field means "Disallow everywhere," as in: "Disallow all robots everywhere on this site."

To exclude all robots except a specific model, place the following lines in the `robots.txt` file after the two previous lines that disallow all robots:

```
User-agent: nicebot
Disallow:
```

This step lets the User-agent named nicebot go everywhere, because `Disallow:` is empty, meaning that nicebot is disallowed nowhere. Of course, because some spiders fail to conform to the proposed standards, they ignore `robots.txt`. They go about their merry way, and you can't do much to stop them. However, you're not completely without recourse, as the next section shows.

The complete text of Koster's standards for robot exclusion resides at:

```
http://Web.nexor.co.uk/mak/doc/robots/norobots.html.
```

They're baaaack!!

What do you do when your Web is invaded by an ill-mannered 'bot? Again, our secret agent man, Martijn Koster, has given this problem serious thought. He suggests several possible steps, which you can find at:

```
http://Web.nexor.co.uk/mak/doc/robots/against.html
```

We hit only the highlights from Koster's list of suggestions. The bottom line is that you can't really do anything to stop a robot while it's rummaging around your Web, unless you want to burn down the barn to get rid of the rat (that is, pull the plug on the server or disconnect from the Internet). First of all, remember that the robot is just a dumb program taking up more of your precious resources than you like, for a short while. Don't waste your time by retaliating. Ignore the robot until the invasion happens again.

After two or three times, check your logs to find out as much as you can about the robot and its owner. Contact the owner directly, if you can, and ask that the robot be stopped. If you can't find the owner, post a message about the invasion on `comp.infosystems.www.providers` to see if any other Webs have experienced the same problem. Help others to help you so that you all can stop the problem. As the man said: "You can run, but you can't hide." A person can't operate a robot on the Web indefinitely without someone finding out who's responsible.

Just the Facts Ma'am: Meta-Information

Many robots look at the first sentences or paragraph of a page to determine its content and categorize it for searches. HTML provides a way for you to tell robots what you want them to know about any given site or page, in a clear and concise way that communicates more than any short collection of words.

The `<META>` tag contains content, author, and document information that search engines can read and interpret. The common attributes for the `<META>` tag include:

✔ `NAME="Author" CONTENT="Your Name Here"`

This value defines not only content authorship but ownership as well. Web page content copyright implicitly belongs to the author even if a formal copyright claim isn't filed. Use this tag to identify yourself and claim your work.

✔ NAME="keywords" CONTENT="cats, computers, two-stepping"

As the name implies the keywords value let you define the content of a page in a few relevant words. This approach is more accurate than a full-text reading of your pages because it focuses on the main ideas of the page.

✔ NAME="description" CONTENT="My hobbies"

This value provides a sentence-style description of a page. We suggest that you write the description as if it were the only thing a person could base their decision to visit your page. Short, concise, and too the point — with a touch of style — is the way to go.

The proper syntax for a ⟨META⟩ tag is:

```
<HEAD>
<META NAME="Author" CONTENT="Your Name Here">
</HEAD>
```

You can only list one value per ⟨META⟩ tag, but you can have as many tags as you like within a ⟨HEAD⟩ ... ⟨/HEAD⟩ tag pair. A sample meta-information set from a real page looks like this:

```
<HEAD>
<META NAME="Resource-type" CONTENT="document">
<META NAME="Description" CONTENT="LANWrights, Inc.">
<META NAME="Keywords" CONTENT="internet, vrml, books,
          networking, mac, windows, www, email, electronic
          commerce, intranet, HTM">
<META NAME="Distribution" CONTENT="global">
<META NAME="Copyright" CONTENT="LANWrights, Inc. 1996">
<META HTTP-EQUIV="Reply-to" CONTENT="webmaster@lanw.com">
</HEAD>
```

The ⟨META⟩ tag has other values that aren't related to searching but rather to header creation information, so don't freak out if you see values in other people's tags that you don't have in yours. You're not missing out.

To use ⟨META⟩ tags effectively, include them on each page you create or, at the very least, on the primary title page of a collection of Web documents. Including informative and useful keywords is important, as well as using concise descriptions that get your message across effectively.

Today few people include meta-information in their pages for search purposes, so it's an underutilized communication tool within the Web community. Current and future standards place more emphasis on meta-information as a standard way to provide information about content. Our two cents' worth is that you should be diligent about including meta-information on your pages, so robots can report more accurately on the content of your pages, and users are better able to hear you above the shouting.

To find out more about meta-information in the newest HTML specifications, take a look at the World Wide Web Consortium Hypertext Links in HTML Working Draft at:

```
http://www.w3.org/pub/WWW/TR/WD-htmllink
```

Here I Am: Registering with Search Engines

Meta-information helps you to better communicate with search engines, but first these engines have to visit your site before they can meet your <META> tags. The engines get around to most pages eventually, but as the Web continues to grow, it becomes more difficult for them to work through all this new information. The process is slow and laborious, even for a computer that never sleeps, eats, or takes coffee breaks.

Rather than waiting for Mohammed to come to the mountain, you can bring the mountain to him. Almost every available search engine offers some way to allow you to register your site in its database without the engine actually having to visit your pages. This option is useful because, as with meta-information, you can define what's said about your pages and also speed up the process of inclusion in an engine's database.

Over 30 publicly available search engines are on the Web, and more are soon to follow. Visiting each one and typing the same information repeatedly in slightly different formats takes more time than you have to give to the task. But we suggest a quick and easy solution to the dilemma: Submit It! is a Web-based service that submits page information to 20 different search engines and catalogs. Visit their free site at:

```
http://free.submit-it.com/
```

After you follow links to the submission form and fill out some general information about your site, you can choose the engines where you want your URL submitted. You must click the Submit button for each engine separately, but Submit It! takes the information you include on the first form and formats it to meet each engine's policies. All you do is click the button. The whole process takes 20 minutes, tops!

The most important part of completing a Submit It! form is not to accidentally skip an engine, but to make sure that your 25-word description is well-written and informative. We suggest that you spend some time writing and proofing your paragraph and maybe even ask a friend or coworker to look it over. Remember, this description is what surfers will see first, so it better be good.

You will notice that some search engines — Yahoo! most notably — are not included in the Submit It! list. You must visit the Yahoo! site yourself and fill out their submission form, but because you've already written a good description, adding your pages to the Yahoo! hierarchy won't take more than a few minutes.

You don't need to submit every page in a collection via Submit It! or any individual submission form. One URL is usually enough to spark the fire and soon the engine will be crawling about your page evaluating the rest of your content as well.

Every now and then we get junk e-mail offering a submission service that does this task for you. The cheapest price we've seen is $20 and that amount is still too much. You can save your money for a good movie; spend a little time at Submit It!, and do the job yourself.

Secret Agent Man

Web agents do the dirty work for people. They crawl the Web, collect and archive information, and then make that information easily accessible. Without them, no search engines, link checkers, or hierarchical URL databases would exist. We would all be searching the Web endlessly ourselves, and that's no fun. The agents help to bring a little order to the chaos of the Web, and make our lives easier. By providing meta-information and registering your pages with search engines, you make their jobs easier and their information more correct. Agents are the means by which users can find you, so appreciate them and work with them to make your pages as widely accessible as possible.

Part VI
Shortcuts and Tips Galore

The 5th Wave   By Rich Tennant

"Children- it is not necessary to whisper while
we're visiting the Vatican Library Web site."

In this part . . .

This part provides a traditional *...For Dummies* conclusion to this book, as we review the highlights of the preceding parts in quick, whimsical — and hopefully useful — restatements of key concepts, principles, and approaches. In Chapter 23 we cover the top maintenance do's and don'ts, which you want to follow as you build and maintain a Web site. In Chapter 24, we cover the highlights of using advanced HTML markup and techniques, including some key points on how to serve that part of the audience that may otherwise not be able to appreciate your work. Finally, in Chapter 25, we conclude the book with a refreshing rehash of the key Web extension technologies and their most appropriate uses.

Chapter 23
Maintenance Tips and Tricks

• •

• •

*B*uilding a Web site isn't anywhere near as hard as living with it afterward. Sure, there's a lot to learn about HTML and setting up a Web site, but it's exciting to build something and call it your own. Just don't ever forget that the real work begins as soon as you open your site to the public. Sure enough, your users will find things that you've overlooked. Or they'll ask you questions that force you to recognize that you've left some important things out. You may even begin to understand that your materials need work because not even you can remember some of the points that you were trying to get across!

Don't despair: You've simply entered the Maintenance Zone, where most of the time and dollars spent on computing-related activities and products go (some 70 percent of the overall costs of software and systems occur during maintenance, after implementation is complete, according to the experts). That's why it's no surprise that you'll spend a lot of time in the Zone, along with everybody else in the business. In this chapter, we take you through maintenance-related do's and don'ts that should help you survive — and even enjoy — this process.

Routine Is Everything

The reason that the word *regular* occurs so often in discussions of maintenance is because irregular maintenance is only slightly preferable to none whatsoever. The whole key to running a shipshape Web site is to plan to work on it regularly and then carry out those plans as scheduled.

Even though the contents of a Web site aren't as perishable as what's in your refrigerator, the two environments have a lot in common. Leave either one of them alone long enough and it will contain things that are unappetizing or that resemble science experiments that the government wants kept secret!

That's why setting aside a significant chunk of time— usually half a day or more — at some regular interval to devote exclusively to your Web site is imperative. Even if you use this time only to look for comparable sites on the Web and compare your stuff to the other guys', it will be time well spent. You are more likely to find yourself looking at things and saying, "Boy, does this need to be renovated!" than you are to find yourself mooning about like the Maytag repairman.

Automating whatever parts of the maintenance routine that you can is also a wonderful idea. UNIX includes a built-in scheduling utility called *cron*; most of the other operating systems support one form of scheduling utility or another. If you set up an automated process to assist you with maintenance, here are some of the things that it can do:

- ✔ Send you e-mail to remind you when it's time for maintenance tasks

- ✔ Tell the Web server to run various maintenance utilities, such as a link checker, a validation service, and other tools that can do their thing without human interaction

- ✔ Remind outside reviewers, content authors, or other contributors to revisit the Web and send you their feedback, all via e-mail

In the final analysis, it's not so much what you do, maintenance-wise, that matters; it's the fact that you do it seriously and regularly, just like a real job!

Remembering the content

While you keep your Web site clean and polished, don't ever forget the real reason that people visit: the content. The durability of content varies with the subject matter. For instance, a recipe for quesadillas will be as good next year as it is today, but the directions to your office must be changed every time you move. That's why staying on top of the content and adjusting it as needed are essential.

Force yourself to look at as much of your site as you can during each regularly scheduled maintenance period. If your site is too big to cover completely each time, schedule a regular rotation through its components. You'll be surprised how many times you can look at something before finding all the boo-boos, typos, and other signs of human involvement.

Inviting others to read their way through your site on a regular basis is also a good idea. Make new employees review the site, beg your regular customers to visit and share their feedback, give prizes or rewards for finding bugs or mistakes, and try to get other "interested parties" involved, at least to read things germane to their interests or that reflect a common business focus. The more people who check out the content, the more feedback you'll be able to elicit from them, by hook or by crook!

Keeping track of dates

When you create content for the Web, always include a last revision date marker on each page. Check out this date each time you review the content of a document so that you can tell at a glance how long it has been since a page has been touched. By itself, the date can deliver a powerful wake-up call, as in "Was last *summer* the last time we updated this page?"

On the other hand, if you're feeling especially productive, you can write a short program or *grep* script (grep stands for general regular expression parser and is a powerful UNIX tool that can be used to read and recognize patterns that occur within text files) to find the update line in each HTM or HTML file on your site and append it to the file name. Then you can scan this list to look for especially old dates.

Of course, the success of this technique depends on you having the discipline to update date information each time that you change anything in an HTML document. If the date is wrong, it won't do you any good to look at it.

Updating your HTML

Because not even your humble authors have been able to avoid the allure of proprietary Web extensions, markup, and widgets, we certainly can't demand that you avoid these potential pitfalls either. But if you do use proprietary markup, you'll need to keep a regular eye on how that markup changes over time. You'll also need to be ready to deal with obsolete or deprecated HTML (deprecated HTML is HTML that's fallen out of favor, is seldom used, or that is on the verge of being declared obsolete by the IETF or W3C).

Make this a part of your regular maintenance routine. Keep tabs on the "What's New" pages and specifications documents at your favorite browser's (or browsers') Web site(s). Stay abreast of what's new and changing. Then, when the rug starts slipping out from under your feet, you will be able to stay upright and shift out the old while shifting in the new. If you keep yourself informed, you've already won half the battle.

Of Test and Production Computing Facilities

For Information Systems (IS) and data processing professionals, the distinction between test and production facilities is too well-known to make reading this sidebar worth your while. If you know what this means, skip ahead to the next section. If not, here's what this distinction means:

✔ A test facility is private, restricted to authorized personnel only, and is used when testing and debugging new computing facilities or capabilities. The term *test Web site* refers to a password- or port-controlled Web site that's not publicized and is used only prior to unleashing its contents to the world at-large.

✔ A production facility is public, available to all (authorized) users, and provides day-in, day-out services as part of an organization's overall information systems offerings. The term *production Web site* refers to those URLs that front for any Web sites that are made generally available, whether only within your organization or to the entire Internet.

In general, it's considered a good idea to develop and debug new or changed materials in a test environment before putting them into use in a production environment. Where the Web is concerned, use a test Web site until such materials are ready for prime time and then carefully transfer them to the production version of that Web site once you're convinced that they're accurate, correct, and meet your audience's requirements. Be sure to test your production Web site thoroughly whenever you add materials from your test Web site; whenever things change is also when they're most likely to manifest problems.

The Beauty of a Test Web

Because change is inevitable, you can do more than expect it to happen to your Web site. You can also plan for change and set up your environment to make coping with its effects easier. One of the best things that you can do for yourself is to create a "test Web" that mirrors your production Web site but contains those portions that have been changed.

By exposing this separate Web site, with its own URL, to a select cadre of alpha and beta testers, you can shake out all the bugs and smooth the rough edges before opening a new set of pages to the public. When you decide that the materials are ready, copy them to your production Web site, perform a quick test to make sure that all the graphics and links are working, and declare victory.

This approach goes double for a complete facelift of a Web site; testing your materials becomes increasingly more important as the volume of change increases. Because a complete facelift involves maximum change, it should get maximal testing, too.

As your site changes over time, you may occasionally suffer from the temptation to shuck an old version and replace it completely with something new. Although a radical Web-ectomy is sometimes required, it's not a treatment for ennui. The best course of action is to let your site evolve with changing times and demands. Integrating a series of small changes into your regular maintenance routine is a lot easier than a wholesale replacement. Your users will also find it easier to digest a step-wise set of changes than a complete and sudden makeover.

Make testing part of the maintenance routine. Every time something changes, even if you just go into a file to correct a typo, be sure to check your work. You never know when an accidental keystroke, or a glitch in a file save routine, might introduce more changes than you think should be present.

The only way to be sure that your changes affect neither more nor less of your materials than you want them to is to check them thoroughly and completely. Be sure to check and double-check the impact of change, no matter how trivial and slight. Because the little things are prone to catching us all in the end, don't let them catch you unaware.

Overcoming Inertia Takes Constant Vigilance

Because the roots of the Web lie deep in the physics community, we decided to close this section on maintenance with a physics metaphor. Physicists spend a lot of time dealing with inertia, which they like to define as the tendency of objects to keep heading in the direction that they're going or to remain at rest when they are not going anywhere.

In human terms, inertia is the tendency to leave things alone that haven't been touched for a while. When it comes to a Web site, the tendency is to revel in its completion (or recent update) and to leave it alone after that. Don't let this happen to your site; make sure that you plan your next visit and schedule those activities so essential to keeping your content fresh and interesting. Check those links, revisit that material, and look at revision dates; in short, stay on top of it so that it doesn't wind up on top of you!

Chapter 24

Advanced HTML Tips and Shortcuts

*W*e hope that one of the many things this book demonstrates is that plenty of new HTML markup is worth contending with — and using — in your Web documents. Although the temptation to rush right out and start using the heck out of advanced HTML may be nearly irresistible, we remind you that not everyone benefits from those efforts.

Don't Forget the Other Guys

Even though a large portion of your viewing audience may use Netscape Navigator or some other advanced browser (some 55 to 60 percent, depending on whose statistics you believe), not everybody has access to a browser with advanced capabilities. It's the old problem of the "haves" versus the "have-nots" in a Webified form: If over half of your viewers can see and appreciate advanced HTML, that also means that the other less-than-half can neither see nor appreciate the results. This problem leads to the inevitable question: Which audience should you cater to? The haves or the have-nots?

Unless you're working on an in-house Web site where organizational policy dictates an advanced browser, we think that the answer to this question should be "Both!" In other words, when you build pages that exploit advanced HTML, provide an alternative view.

The quick-and-dirty approach to this dilemma is to create static, text-only alternatives to advanced markup. We cover this idea in detail in many of the sections that follow. For now, consider the needs of your users who can't render — or benefit from — advanced markup. We strongly suggest that you provide an alternative for these users.

In the broadest of terms, here's how you can accomplish such a goal:

- On those pages that use advanced markup, place a hyperlink to a text-only alternative version near the top of the page. Make it read like this:

```
The following page uses HTML &lt;TABLE&gt;s and
associated tags. Unless you're sure your browser can
display this material properly, please view our
<A HREF="ta-page.html">text-only version</A>instead.
```

- If your entire site is liberally sprinkled with advanced markup, you may want to apprise users when they enter your home page.

  Many sites now advertise themselves as "Netscape-friendly" or as requiring Netscape 3.0 or greater. We don't advocate this approach, but it's best to be up front about it for the benefit of those users who may elect to pass on a visit rather than deal with strange onscreen displays.

- Another alternative to warning off those users ill-equipped to appreciate your advanced markup is to provide a more context-sensitive site implementation. Some designers ask users to identify their browsers upon entry, or read a combination of CGI environment variables, to determine what kinds of information a viewer can handle. Then they generate the right kind of Web pages on-the-fly for those viewers. That way, properly equipped visitors see pages that include advanced markup; others see text-only equivalents that don't strain their browser's capabilities.

  This approach is a great deal more work for Webmasters and content authors, but does the best job of accommodating a broad and diverse audience.

We remind you that a portion of the user base may not really view your pages at all. These users are print-handicapped individuals who may use a Braille printer or text-to-speech translation to access your Web site. Although this is a small portion of the overall audience, to be sure, you must anticipate the special needs of this important component in order to serve them. These needs also help to explain why ALT text is so important for graphics, because it provides information for those incapable of otherwise appreciating graphics content.

Multiple Means of Delivery

In the same vein fm our preceding request that you anticipate some of your users' special needs, we remind you that not all users have built-in e-mail access within their browsers, and that, for some, HTTP-based file transfer isn't always practical. The list continues, but the principle remains the same: Give users another way to accomplish what the built-in functionality provides.

For e-mail, this flexibility means including an explicit e-mail address, prefer-ably at the footer on each page, so that users can reach you by e-mail even if they can't use a `mailto:` URL. For file transfer, provide access to download files through an alternate FTP site, and perhaps provide documentation on how to order file delivery from FTP sites via e-mail. An excellent program by Paul Vixie called *ftpmail* can provide this service; for more information, please visit this URL:

```
http://www.acad.bg/beginner/ftpmail.html
```

Whatever your delivery or communications needs, at least one alternative is usually available. If you use a search engine to help you locate information, you can probably point your users at alternative software, explanations (such as the *ftpmail* document referenced in the preceding URL), and other useful information as well.

Let the Users Choose

Throughout this book, we suggest that whenever special content or a large amount of data appears on your site, you should give your users fair warn-ing and a way to steer around potential difficulties or download delays. These alternatives are always a good idea, whether they apply to advanced HTML or to large graphics or multimedia data.

Here's a short list of summarized suggestions for you to ponder:

✔ Warn your readers when you're about to use advanced HTML. Point them to alternative representations (even if it's a TXT file with statically formatted text) and give them a way to jump around this material.

✔ Warn your readers when something big and time-consuming is about to appear; this advice applies equally to long documents, big graphics, and Shockwave or multimedia content. Build thumbnails of the material, and present them as a hyperlink to the real — and big — version.

Those users who want to see the real thing can choose to download it; then they can't complain when it takes half an hour to see an image. If you force them to download something huge, they will blame you instead.

The best approach can be summed up as "Always leave your users a way out." If you don't, they will simply jump out of your site, never to return.

<TABLE> Alternatives

HTML tables are wonderful and convenient tools. Yet anyone who's using less than a state-of-the-art browser can't appreciate them. Worse yet, viewing table information in this type of browser can be completely unintelligible. For an example, compare the text-only version of a table rendered by the character mode browser, Lynx, shown in Figure 24-1 to its nicely laid-out equivalent rendered by Netscape Navigator in Figure 24-2. A reader must be astute to recognize that the paragraph in mid-screen in the first figure is the same information as in the second figure.

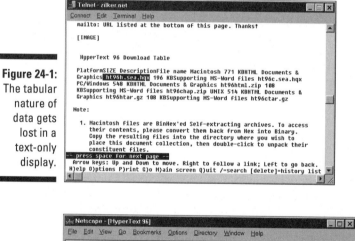

Figure 24-1: The tabular nature of data gets lost in a text-only display.

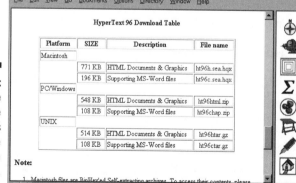

Figure 24-2: Netscape gives the table its true realization onscreen.

This example helps show why text-only alternatives are critical. When you build these alternatives, especially using the <PRE> text tag, you may be able to use the following tips:

- ✔ Enter all text in columnar format first. Use a monospaced font (not a proportional one). Make sure that everything lines up as you want it to.

- ✔ Edit the text within the <PRE>...</PRE> block and insert all HTML markup, without adding extra space. This step maintains a columnar format.

- ✔ Another alternative: Create a simple text file in which no HTML is required. Users can then either download or view this information through their browser, depending on how it's configured.

As an illustration of the first approach, compare the HTML markup in the following code section to its onscreen display, shown in Figure 24-3.

```
<HTML>
<HEAD>
<TITLE>Testing &lt;PRE&gt;</TITLE>
</HEAD>
<BODY>
<PRE>
<B>Column 1    Column2    Column3</B>
Entry1,1    Entry1,2    Entry1,3
Entry2,1    Entry2,2    Entry2,3
<A HREF="#end">Link1</A>            Entry3,2    Entry3,3
</PRE>
</BODY>
</HTML>
```

Figure 24-3:
The inclusion of HTML markup within <PRE> text makes it look unaligned until you see it displayed.

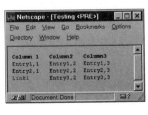

<FRAME> Alternatives

Unfortunately, repetition is the only alternative to the use of frame-related tags. You can either build alternative pages altogether and steer your frame-disadvantaged users (that is, those users whose browsers don't support frame markup) to them explicitly, or use the <NOFRAME>...</NOFRAME> markup to provide an alternative directly within the same pages where you use <FRAME> and <FRAMESET> markup.

Either way, you must set some kind of limit on the number of lines within the unframed materials to display between navigation bars or equivalent static structures within an HTML document. Use this technique to replace elements such as a navigation frame, a company logo, and attribution information. In our own designs, we made a conscious decision that users must never have to scroll more than one screen up or down to get to a navigation bar, and we build our pages accordingly. This strategy seems to work pretty well, but it's a matter of choice, so you can follow your own instincts.

If you construct a side-by-side frame-up (such as the one that Netscape uses for its online documentation, with a table of contents on the left and details on the right), the only reasonable alternative is to make the table of contents a navigation bar item and to make jumping back and forth between the table of contents and related detail documents easy for the user. This arrangement is nowhere near as convenient as jumping between two simultaneously visible frames onscreen, but this approach has the same effect and works acceptably.

Knowing When to Split

By now, you may have the impression that we think that you should build your Web sites in pairs: one for advanced browsers that can handle all the bells and whistles of advanced HTML, and another for the more vanilla capabilities represented by HTML 2.0. This assumption isn't necessarily the case, appearances to the contrary notwithstanding.

We advocate a document-by-document approach in which everyone who visits the site shares at least some common information. Only those documents that incorporate advanced markup need to be available in alternate forms; others can serve both audiences equally well. That's why you should approach the design of each document with a fresh pair of eyes, ready to decide between multiple versions of the same information or a single, vanilla version that will serve everybody.

As you approach this decision, here are some questions to answer:

- ✔ What's your overall design structure? Does it demand advanced markup? (Some sites are built entirely around HTML tables and graphics and must include complete alternatives; others require only selective alternatives.)

- ✔ Why does the document on which you're working need advanced markup? Improved accessibility or intelligibility are valid reasons; advanced markup for the heck of it is not.

- ✔ What benefits does advanced markup confer? Improved navigation, easier access to documents, and quicker selection of relevant materials are the best benefits; the "gee whiz" factor gets lame after a while.

Always try to get a feel for how much of your audience will be unable to appreciate your advanced efforts before you take on the extra work. If you're providing benefits to more than half your user population, go for it; if not, you may want to reconsider.

Managing Miscellany

Some aspects of advanced or proprietary HTML can show up on your pages without affecting the portion of your audience that must remain indifferent to it. We're talking about elements such as background images or colors.

As long as you make your images take on transparent backgrounds, users won't necessarily care that they're missing an embossed 3-D bas-relief of your company's logo as a background. But if you forget and use a colored background, it may look a little funky for some user who has selected her favorite shade of fuchsia only to have her sense of tasteful color completely overwhelmed by your choice of a glaring puce.

Although the many little oddments and markup widgets that you can employ without unduly discommoding your "disadvantaged users" are simply too numerous to mention, we can provide a sure-fire technique to make sure that they don't become too onerous. Make sure to use some older and less-capable browsers when you begin your page testing: With luck, you and your testers can winnow out the less appealing aspects of your documents before the public ever sees them.

Adding Value for Value

As we close this chapter, we want to jump back from markup details and return to the content that gives your Web site its reason to exist. Nothing is wrong with using advanced HTML markup on your Web site as long as it adds to that site's capability to deliver and communicate its content.

When you add functionality or capability to your site, especially by adopting cutting-edge or proprietary markup to your documents, make sure that it enhances the content. You never want anything to detract from the content. As long as you add value for your audience, they will respect and reward you for your efforts. But if you obfuscate the content or alienate your users, you can expect to lose their respect, if not their support (and their continued referrals and visits).

In the next chapter, we move beyond HTML markup to the extensions and plugins that can add visual excitement and dynamism to your Web site. Stay tuned for some tips on how to carry this off with grace and wit!

Chapter 25

Extenuating Extensions

In This Chapter

▶ Warning users about necessary browsers and plugins

▶ Shocking your site with Shockwave

▶ Visualizing VRML worlds

▶ Sampling some Java

▶ Staying focused on content

*T*he proliferation of added capability for advanced browsers has been nothing short of amazing. In the last year, we've seen Netscape, Microsoft, and other leading vendors either deliver or promise support for a list of technologies that range from advanced document presentation (Adobe Acrobat and its Portable Document Format, or PDF) to three-dimensional worldscapes (Virtual Reality Modeling Language, or VRML).

A recent visit to Netscape's plugins page shows more than 60 plugins in commercial release. We're aware of many more in beta test or under development for release sometime in 1997 or 1998. Visit the Netscape page at:

```
http://home.netscape.com/comprod/mirror/↵
          navcomponents_download.html
```

What does all this added capability mean to average users? Well, if those average users are running Netscape Navigator, Internet Explorer, or some other advanced browser, it means that they can add significant functionality to their desktops simply by downloading and installing the appropriate software. On the other hand, if those users don't have an advanced browser, it doesn't amount to a hill of beans!

That's why our most telling point in this chapter is to remind you that you absolutely cannot reach your broadest audience by using content that depends on a plugin. This situation will probably change soon, but for now, we strongly suggest that you refrain from delivering critical content by using plugin-based material unless you have no other choice.

Thus, if your business is multimedia, you are safe to assume that your audience will use a related plugin, such as Shockwave. But if you're simply trying to add spice to conventional text or images, you should provide alternate forms for materials delivered by using a plugin. Avoid withholding important content from anyone who visits your site, even if someone's browser can't handle what you have to offer. We discuss the particulars in the sections that follow.

Warning! Plug In Now!

Be sure to include scaffolding around plugin-based materials on Web pages, whenever they're present. This step includes, but is not limited to, the following:

✔ A warning that certain browsers may be useful (or required) to get the best results from your site. This caution should include pointers to a download site for the correct browser, where appropriate. See Figure 25-1 for an example of this genre.

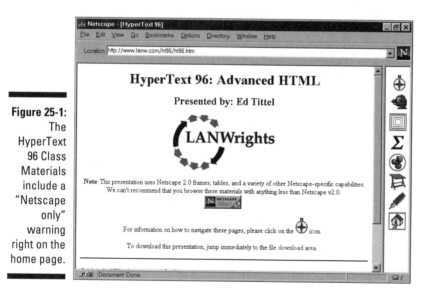

Figure 25-1:
The
HyperText
96 Class
Materials
include a
"Netscape
only"
warning
right on the
home page.

✔ A similar warning before any plugin-specific materials, with a download site for the necessary plugin wherever possible. For some kinds of materials, supplementary materials may also make sense.

For example, Shockwave content can be supplemented by appropriate Macromedia Director Projector files. This alternative lets users download a self-running demonstration, as long as they're using either a Macintosh running Systems 7.*x* or a PC running Windows 3.*x* or higher.

✔ Whenever you can reasonably expect that your audience may be unfamiliar or inexperienced with your plugin(s) of choice, providing pointers to basic introductions and other resources is also a nice touch. This step helps those users who are motivated or curious enough to want to know more about your choice(s) of supplementary technologies.

In short, if you make the process easy for users who may want to try out your plugin-based materials to obtain the building blocks they need, you not only pique their interest but add to their bag of tricks. This effort can help improve your image and your visitation rates.

Shelling into Shockwave

In Chapter 8, we provide a thorough overview of Shockwave technology, its constituent components, and the basics of its use. If you succumb to its allure or are thinking about adding "shocked" materials to your site, follow our advice from the earlier section — namely:

✔ Warn users that your pages contain Shockwave on the home page.

✔ State browser and plugin requirements, and provide pointers to one or both sets of software.

✔ Include a pointer to an "About Shockwave" page, where you give its broad outlines and capabilities; provide pointers to examples and tutorials.

✔ Discuss the Director Projector alternative to "shocked" content; provide alternative downloads for users who aren't Shockwave-enabled.

With that kind of approach, you are sure to alienate as little as possible that portion of your audience that isn't ready to deal with Shockwave. Because you demonstrate ample concern for your users' plight, and show them a path to overcome their lack of Shockwave capability, you also show them that you care.

As for Shockwave content itself, our advice is more pointed:

✔ Given that most users must download via modem, keep content as compact as possible. When files are large, provide ample warning, and give users a choice whether to download (this is another good reason for the Projector alternative).

✔ Make sure that you use the Shockwave `TEXTFOCUS` attribute for the `<EMBED>` tag appropriately. If in doubt, try it on your beta testers and find out what they think.

✔ Use Shockwave content appropriately. Not everything benefits from this type of treatment.

✔ Always test your work on multiple machines, especially the other platform (on a Mac if you've developed your materials on a PC, and vice-versa).

✔ Use the Text tool whenever possible instead of importing bitmapped text; this tool helps keep movies small and manageable.

✔ Always provide instructions if users must interact with Shockwave content. Use icons or consistent signposts so they can find instructions, and tell them what these elements mean in advance. Then, use signposts wherever appropriate so that users can get help when they need it.

If you follow these simple guidelines, you stand a good chance of pleasing your site's visitors. Otherwise, ignore them at your peril!

Visualizing the Virtual with VRML

VRML's introduction to the Web pushes it toward a more realistic appearance. By structuring and organizing information using everyday signs and symbols, VRML promises to extend the Web's capabilities while making virtual worlds familiar.

For developers, the biggest VRML secret lies in the tools. Not accidentally, the most powerful and best-developed VRML toolsets have run on high-end workstations, such as the Silicon Graphics IRIS machines. In this case, the costs of entry are high but the benefits of up-front spending can pay off in increased productivity and in the quality of the resulting final products. This effort requires careful balancing between budget constraints and your natural desires to produce the best possible content.

For users, requirements are similar to those for other plugins — namely, the right browser and the right supplementary software. Here again, point users to those materials and provide explanatory information as well. VRML puts pretty serious demands on bandwidth and on user platforms, as well as on developers, so you also want to warn your users about the size of your materials and about basic processing requirements.

For details on VRML design do's and don'ts, as well as the very best re-sources on VRML online, we suggest that you revisit the final pages of Chapter 9.

Jumping into Java

Java is such a hot topic on the Web right now that we must shrink a little from the task of reducing it to its quintessence (like instant coffee?). Suffice it to say that you can find ample sources of information online — so ample, in fact, that your biggest chore will be separating the good stuff from the dross.

Beyond requiring mastery of the details of an object-oriented programming language and a whole new set of HTML markup, Java also requires a new mindset. The best way to understand is to prowl the Web looking for good (and bad) examples. If you emulate the good stuff and try to avoid the techniques or mistakes that mar the bad, you'll do just fine.

As with other plugin technologies mentioned in this chapter, flag your use of Java on your pages. Provide pointers to appropriate browsers, plugins, and explanatory materials. Build alternate pages, or use the <NOEMBED> tags to provide equivalent information to the less fortunate side of your audience (or at least a blow-by-blow description so that your users know what they're missing).

When you are including Java materials, some of the best tips for effective use of applets in your pages are:

✔ Find out as much as you can about Java or JavaScript before trying to use either one. The more you know, the better you'll do.

✔ Prowl the Web to find out about the latest Java trends, tools, tips, and techniques. Check the list at the end of Chapter 10 for a good set of "getting started" resources.

✔ Start by picking applets that you want to emulate; try to build them yourself by studying sample code and by making your emulation as much like the original as possible. The important thing here is not verisimilitude, though; it's understanding what makes Java tick.

✔ Learn and master the Java toolset: Obtain and use a compiler and a debugger; locate and use other useful tools. Stay tuned to the `comp.lang.java` newsgroup and other Java programmers' hangouts.

> ✔ Test Java classes and commands systematically. Many features and functions in the Java environment are poorly documented, if at all; the only way to be sure how a component behaves is by trying it out.
>
> ✔ Find out how to use the <EMBED> and <APP> tags and how to provide alternate content on your pages.

If you become familiar with the Java development environment and keep track of what others are doing to use it, you can add some super functionality to your Web site. As with CGI programs, don't feel compelled to reinvent the wheel every time you need an applet; be sure to cruise the Web to see what products are already available for your use.

Be sure to revisit the final pages of Chapter 10 for more information about Java do's and don'ts and for a list of online Java-related resources.

Effective Augmentation

Given the plethora of plugins for modern browsers, it's probably just a matter of time before some kind of augmentation appears on your own Web pages. As long as you use this capability wisely and don't neglect the legions of users who may not be able to exploit your plugin(s) immediately, you should do well with whatever extensions you erect around your HTML documents.

The important thing is to stay focused on content. This approach means using plugins where they add to or enhance content, and eschewing them otherwise. Although the temptation to play may be overwhelming, remember that delivering content is the ultimate goal. Among other things, this strategy also means taking the time to provide alternate forms of data that depend on plugins, instead of leaving the less advantaged part of your audience out. The more important the content, the more crucial it is to make the information available to everyone, plugged in or not. If you follow this suggestion, you can grow your user base — and perhaps even persuade those users to upgrade their capabilities to match yours!

Glossary

absolute: When referring to the modification of path names or URLs, absolute means a full and complete specification (as opposed to a relative one).

Acrobat: A viewing program (helper application) from Adobe Systems. Acrobat is used for the portable document format (PDF) text display system. *See* Amber.

ActiveX: Microsoft's third-generation component architecture, which is based on the Component Object Model (COM). ActiveX objects may reside in stand-alone machines, on a LAN or intranet, or on the Internet. Specialized for the Internet, ActiveX objects are automatically downloaded if the object is not in the user's machine.

Afterburner: File compression software, used in conjunction with Shockwave from Macromedia, to compress native Director film strips for delivery over the Internet. Compression is usually by 60 percent or more.

agent: Any of a class of software programs capable of interacting with network or Internet resources on another user's behalf.

alternative selectors: HTML tag attributes that serve a similar function. For example, the functions of the CLASS and STYLE attributes can overlap.

Amber: The Netscape plugin version of Acrobat for viewing PDF files within Netscape.

anchor: A tagged text or graphic element in HTML that acts as a link to another location inside or outside a Web document. An anchor may also be a location in a document that acts as the destination for an incoming link. The latter definition usually applies in this book.

animation: A computerized process of creating moving images by rapidly advancing from one still image to the next.

anonymous ftp: A type of Internet file access that relies on the File Transfer Protocol (FTP) service, by which any user can typically access a file collection by logging in as *anonymous* and supplying his or her e-mail address as a password.

AppleScript: The scripting language for the Macintosh operating system, AppleScript is used to build CGI programs for Macintosh-based Web servers.

applet: A small application that performs a specific task, such as the Calculator in Microsoft Windows. In Internet speak, this term usually refers to a small Java application.

ASCII (American Standard Code for Information Interchange): A coding method that represents standard alphabetic, numeric, and other keyboard characters in computer-readable, binary format.

attribute: A named characteristic of an associated HTML tag. Attributes may be required or optional. Depending on the tag and the attribute, some attributes take values (if so, the syntax is `ATTRIBUTE="value"`).

authoring software: Programs that understand HTML tags and their placement. Some authoring programs can even enforce HTML syntax; others can convert from word-processing or document-formatting programs to HTML formats.

authoring tool: *See* authoring software.

back end: The server-side of client/server structure. This part of the processing is usually handled by programs running in obscurity on the server, out-of-sight (and mind) of most users.

bandwidth: Technically, the range of electrical frequencies that a device can handle. More commonly, bandwidth is a measure of a communications technology's carrying capacity.

Basic (Beginner's All-purpose Symbolic Instruction Code, also called *BASIC*): A programming language that is easy to learn and use. The most popular implementation of the language is QuickBasic from Microsoft Corporation.

beta test: The phase of software testing during which a program or system is turned over to a select group of users outside the development organization for use in more or less real-life situations.

BIOS (Basic Input-Output System): A basic driver software for a PC. The BIOS permits component devices to communicate with one another.

bitmapped: A graphic image that's represented as a matrix of binary on-off values, usually by conversion from some other graphics format.

body: One of the main identifiable structures of any HTML document. The body is usually trapped between the `<HEAD>` information and the footer information.

bookmark: The Netscape Navigator browser facility for building a list of URLs that users wish to keep for future reference.

Boolean: Computer shorthand for logical operations, such as those defined to combine or compare values (AND, OR, NOR, NOT, NAND, and so on).

'bot: *See* robot.

broken graphic icon: A standard icon that appears within a browser when an `<IMG>` or other graphics tag is encountered, but the associated image file cannot be located or displayed.

browser: A Web access program that can request HTML documents from Web servers and render these documents on a user's display device. *See* client.

BSD (Berkeley Software Distribution): A flavor of UNIX that was particularly important in the late '70s and '80s when most of the enhancements and add-ons to UNIX appeared first in the BSD version (such as TCP/IP).

bugs: Small verminous creatures that sometimes show up in software in the form of major or minor errors, mistakes, and gotchas. Bugs got their name from insects that, having been attracted to the glow of the filament in a tube, were found in antiquated tube-based computers of the late '50s and early '60s.

burn: To convert a file from its original uncompressed Macromedia format to a compressed Shockwave format.

bytecode: The intermediate, semicompiled form of Java code created by the Java compiler *javac*.

C: A programming language developed at AT&T Bell Laboratories, C remains the implementation language for UNIX and the UNIX programmer's language of choice.

Cascading Style Sheets (CSS): The latest World Wide Web Consortium-sponsored specification for HTML document style sheets, which describe formatting and layout rules and conventions.

case-sensitive: Indicates that the case of the letters used in computer input is significant. For example, HTML tags can be input in any mixture of upper- and lowercase (HTML tags are not case-sensitive), but because HTML character entities (such as É) are case-sensitive, these entities must be reproduced exactly.

cast: The collection of objects in Macromedia Director. These objects may be graphics, sounds, animations, or other data that appears on the main display area.

CD-ROM (Compact Disc-Read-Only Memory): A computer-readable version of the audio CD; CD-ROMs can contain up to 650M of data, making them the distribution media of choice for many of today's large (some would even say *bloated*) programs and systems.

CERN (Conseil Europeen pour la Recherche Nucleaire): The Center for High-Energy Physics in Geneva, Switzerland, and the birthplace of the World Wide Web.

change log: A record of changes made to elements within a Web site, including files, text entries, graphical objects, and so on. The change log is used to keep track of changes and enhancements during the maintenance process.

character entity: A way of reproducing strange and wonderful characters within HTML. Character entities take the form &string; where the ampersand (&) and semicolon (;) are mandatory metacharacters, and string names the character to be reproduced in the browser. Because character entities are case-sensitive, the string between the ampersand and the semicolon must be reproduced exactly.

character mode (also called text mode): Indicates that a Web browser can reproduce text data only. Character-mode browsers cannot produce graphics directly without the assistance of a helper application.

chatterbots: Software agents that provide help, give advice, and explain local conditions in chat rooms and other interactive environments on the Web.

clickable map: A graphic in an HTML file that has had a pixel coordinate map file created for it. This map file enables regions of the graphic to point to specific URLs for graphically-oriented Web navigation.

client: The end-user side of the client/server arrangement. Client typically refers to a consumer of network services. A Web browser is, therefore, a client program that talks to Web servers.

client/server: A model for computing that divides computing into two separate roles that are usually connected by a network: The client works on the end-user side of the connection and manages user interaction and display (input and output, and related processing), while the server works elsewhere on the network and manages data-intensive or shared processing activities (such as serving up the collections of documents and programs that a Web server typically manages).

comment: In programming, a descriptive statement in a source language program that is used for documentation.

Common Gateway Interface (CGI): The specification governing how Web browsers can communicate with and request services from Web servers. CGI is also the format and syntax for passing infor-mation from browsers to servers via forms or document-based queries in HTML.

Common Ground: A portable document format used to create input to one kind of text display engine available via the Web.

compiler: A special computer program that takes human-readable source code from some programming or scripting language and turns the code into a computer-readable binary equivalent.

computing platform: A way of referring to the kind of computer someone is using. This term encompasses both hardware (the type of machine, processor, and so on) and software (the operating system and applications) in use.

connections per minute: The measurement for the number of user requests that a Web server can simultaneously handle over the course of 60 seconds.

content: The reason users access Web documents and keep coming back for more. This is the information you provide to the public and is your major consideration in Web site development (although form is also important).

content-type: A MIME convention for identifying the type of data being transported over a network for delivery to any of a set of programs, including e-mail readers and Web browsers.

convention: An agreed-upon set of rules and approaches that enables systems to communicate with one another and work together.

conversion program: In general, a program that converts one type of format to another. In the context of the Web, the term refers to a program that reads a native word processor or page layout file format and converts it to a corresponding HTML layout.

CPU (Central Processing Unit): The master circuitry or chip that provides the brains of a typical computer.

cron: A UNIX utility that permits programs to be scheduled to run at specified times or at regular intervals. The *cron* utility is useful for handling automated maintenance tasks.

CSU/DSU (Channel Service Unit/ Data Service Unit): A special translating piece of hardware, found between a network and a digital telephone line, that translates data between the two formats. CSU/DSU is most commonly used to attach a network router to a T1 or other digital telephone line.

daemon: A special type of program (usually in the UNIX world) that runs constantly in the background, ready to handle certain types of network service requests. E-mail, HTTP, and other Internet services depend on daemons to handle user service requests.

DBMS (Database Management System): Software that controls the organization, storage, retrieval, and security of information stored in a database.

DCR: File extension for a Director film strip that has been converted from its original format by using Afterburner. The file is destined for Web delivery.

default: In general computer-speak, a selection that occurs automatically in a program or instruction when the user hasn't made an explicit choice. For HTML, the default is the value assigned to an attribute when none is supplied.

desktop (desktop machine): The computer that a user typically has on his or her desktop. Desktop is a synonym for end-user computer or computer.

dial-up: A connection to the Internet (or some other remote computer or network) that is made by dialing up an access telephone number.

DIR: File extension for an original, editable Macromedia Director file.

Director (Macromedia Director): A large, complex software program used to create animated multimedia presentations on either a Macintosh or a PC. Director provides multimedia content for delivery via Shockwave technology.

directory path: The device and directory names needed to locate a particular file in any given file system. For HTML, UNIX-style directory paths usually apply.

directory structure: The underlying file container structure that describes the hierarchical organization of most computer file systems.

DNS (Domain Name Server): *See* domain names.

document: The basic unit of HTML information. The term refers to the entire contents of any single HTML file. Because this concept doesn't always correspond to normal notions of a document, we refer to what could formally be called *HTML documents* more or less interchangeably with *Web pages,* which is how these documents are rendered by browsers for display.

document headings: The class of HTML tags that we generically refer to as ⟨H*⟩. Document headings enable Web-page authors to insert headings of various sizes and weights (levels 1 through 6) to add structure to their documents' contents. As structural elements, headings identify the beginning of a new concept or idea within a document.

document root: The base directory where HTML files and other components for any particular Web site are located on a Web server, or where the directories containing these components are ultimately attached.

document structure: The methods used to organize and navigate within HTML documents or related collections of documents.

document transfer rate: The speed at which a Web server can deliver pages to users in response to their document requests (usually measured in documents per minute).

document-based queries: One of two methods of passing information from a browser to a Web server. Document-based queries are designed to pass short strings of information to the server by using the METHOD="GET" HTTP method of delivery. This method is typically used for search requests or other short lookup operations.

domain names: The names used on the Internet as part of a distributed database system for translating computer names into physical addresses and vice versa.

DOS (Disk Operating System): The underlying control program used to make most Intel-based PCs run. MS-DOS, from Microsoft Corporation, is the most widely used implementation of DOS and provides the scaffolding atop which the equally widely used Microsoft Windows software runs. *See* OS.

download: To transfer a file from a server to a user across a network or the Internet.

DSSSL (Document Style Semantics and Specification Language): An early contender for HTML standardization. This formal language is used to define SGML style sheets. DSSSL users unanimously agree that this language is too complex and difficult for Web use.

DSSSL-Lite: A svelte subset of DSSSL. This style sheet language was considered for adoption as an HTML standard, but it, too, was judged too complex and difficult for ordinary mortals.

DTD (Document Type Definition): A formal SGML specification for a document. A DTD lays out the structural elements and markup definitions that can then be used to create instances of documents.

dumb terminal: A display device with attached keyboard that relies on the intelligence of another computer to drive its display and interpret its keyboard inputs. These devices were the norm in the heyday of the mainframe and minicomputer and are still widely used for reservation systems, point of sale, and other special-use applications.

Dynamic HTML: A set of special extensions to standard HTML that are interpreted and substituted as a Web page is delivered to a user. Versions have been proposed by both Netscape and Microsoft, and the World Wide Web Consortium is in the process of creating a proposal for a standard version.

electronic commerce: The exchange of money for goods or services via an electronic medium. Many companies expect electronic commerce to take the place of the majority of mail order and telephone order shopping by the end of the century.

e-mail (abbreviation for electronic mail): E-mail is the preferred method for exchanging information between users on the Internet (and other networked systems).

encoded information: A way of wrapping computer data in a special envelope to ship it across a network, encoded information refers to data-manipulation techniques that change data formats and layouts to make them less sensitive to the rigors of electronic transit. Generally, recipients (of encoded information) must decode the encoded information before using it.

Envoy: A portable document format and reader created by Novell for delivery and viewing of formatted documents over the Internet.

EPS (Encapsulated PostScript): A special form of PostScript that includes all external references within the file to make it self-containing and ready to render in any environment.

error message: Information delivered by a program to a user, usually to inform the user that things haven't worked properly, if at all. Error messages are an ill-appreciated art form and contain some of the funniest and most opaque language we've ever seen (also, the most tragic for their unfortunate recipients).

error-checking: A collection of software utilities that systematically checks input or data for errors. An error-checking utility can respond to any condition for which it has a programmed response.

Ethernet: The most common local-area networking technology in use today, Ethernet was developed at about the same time (and by many of the same people and institutions) as the Internet.

event-handling mechanism: A built-in software facility that permits a program to respond to conditions or circumstances as they occur.

external reference: A resource that is stored somewhere other than the location of a Web document or program.

FAQ (Frequently Asked Questions): A list of frequently asked questions that Usenet newsgroups, mailing list groups, and other affiliations of like-minded individuals on the Internet usually designate a more senior member of their band to assemble and publish, in an often futile effort to keep from answering them quite as frequently.

file dependencies: Contents of one file that depend on the contents of some other file (so that the containing file depends on the contained file).

file extension: In DOS, the 3-letter part of a file name after the period. In UNIX, Macintosh, and other file systems, file extension refers to the string after the right-most period in a file name. File extensions are used to label files as to type, origin, and possible use.

flame: A particularly hostile or nasty e-mail message ("That was a real flame."). As a verb, the term means to be a recipient of this type of message ("He got flamed.").

flamewar: The result when two or more individuals start exchanging hostile or nasty e-mail messages. This exchange is viewed by some as an art form and is best observed on Usenet or other newsgroups (where the `alt.flame` newsgroup is a good place to browse for examples).

font manipulation: In the display of a Web document, increasing or decreasing the default font size, typeface, and style based on HTML extensions or style sheet settings.

footer: The concluding part of an HTML document. The footer should contain contact, version, date, and attribution information to help identify a document and its authors.

forms: A mechanism that enables users to interact with servers on the Web. In HTML, forms are built on special markup that lets browsers solicit data from users and then deliver that data to specially designated input-handling programs on a Web server.

frames: An HTML construct that allows a number of documents to be displayed simultaneously within a browser, based on a master document that defines where the individual part displays onscreen. Although HTML can support a theoretically unlimited number of frame areas, most good designs use four or less.

front end: The client side of the client/server model, where the user views and interacts with information from a server. For the Web, browsers provide the front end that communicates with Web servers on the back end.

FTP (sometimes ftp; File Transfer Protocol): An Internet file transfer service based on the TCP/IP protocols. FTP provides a way to copy files to and from FTP servers elsewhere on a network.

full-text indexing: The ability to search on any string that occurs within a text file. Full-text indexing permits a collection of HTML or other documents to be searched by keyword, string, or substring.

fuzzy logic: A way of matching terms or keywords (for search activities) that finds terms or patterns that are somewhat like the terms supplied to drive the search, as well as exact matches.

garbage collection: The ability to reclaim and reuse computer memory that has been allocated within a program, after the variables or data structures that used that memory are no longer needed.

gateway: A type of computer program that knows how to connect two or more different kinds of networks, how to translate information from one network's format to the other's, and vice versa. Common types of gateways include e-mail, database, and communications.

GIF (abbreviation for Graphics Information File): One of a set of commonly used graphics formats within Web documents. GIF is commonly used because of its compressed format and compact nature.

global renaming: The capacity to change a name in one place on a Web site and have a software tool make equivalent changes to any other occurrences (of that same name) throughout the entire site. Global renaming is very useful when moving a site or changing existing content and references.

GNU free software license: A software license promulgated by the Free Software Foundation that permits royalty-free distribution of software, as long as all source code is included with the distribution package, and all changes to the original are clearly marked and attributed to their authors. This is also known as a General Public License (GPL).

gopher: A program/protocol developed at the University of Minnesota. Gopher provides for unified, menu-driven presentation of a variety of Internet services, including WAIS, Telnet, and FTP.

graphics: In HTML documents, files that belong to one of a restricted family of types (usually GIF or JPEG) that are referenced via URLs for inline display on Web pages.

grep (abbreviation for general regular expression parser): A standard UNIX program that looks for patterns found in files and reports on their occurrences. The grep program handles a wide range of patterns, including so-called regular expressions that can use substitutions and wild cards to provide powerful search-and-replace operations within files.

group: A named collection of nodes in VRML that acts as a single object within a virtual world.

GUI (Graphical User Interface, pronounced *gooey*): A visually oriented interface that makes users' interaction with computerized information easier. GUIs make graphical Web browsers possible.

Gzip: A popular file compression technology, used largely among the UNIX community. Gzip is freely available through any of the countless GNU licensees.

HDTV (High Definition TeleVision): An emerging, fully digital, high-resolution form of video data that should become the next prevailing broadcast TV standard.

header files: Files containing information that identifies incoming data by MIME type (and subtype, where applicable).

heading: A markup tag in HTML that adds document structure. The term is sometimes used to refer to the initial portion of an HTML document between the $\langle HEAD \rangle$ . . . $\langle /HEAD \rangle$ tags, where titles and context definitions are commonly supplied.

helper applications: Applications that help the Web browser deliver information to users. Today, browsers can display multiple graphics files (and other kinds of data); sometimes, browsers must pass particular files — for example, motion picture or sound files — over to other applications that know how to render the data they contain.

hierarchical filing system: A typical computer file system, where directories are organized in a hierarchical organization (one directory acts as the root, with a tree of other directories beneath it).

hierarchical structure: A way of organizing Web pages by using links that make some pages subordinate to others. *See* tree structure.

history list: A list of all the URLs a user visits during a session on the Web. This list provides the user with a handy way to jump back to any page that he or she has already visited while online. History lists normally disappear when the user exits the browser program.

host: An Internet-connected computer that supports one or more of the standard services, including Web access, e-mail, file transfer, and more.

hot key: A special keyboard combination that has the same effect as one or more mouse clicks or menu selections in a GUI interface (for example, CTRL+O means "open file" in many applications).

HotJava: The Java-enabled Web browser from Sun Microsystems, which is written in the Java programming language.

hotlist: A Web page that consists of a series of links to other pages, usually annotated with information about what's available on that link. Hotlists act like switchboards to content information and are usually organized around a particular topic or area of interest.

HTML (HyperText Markup Language): The SGML-derived markup language used to create Web pages. Not quite a programming language, HTML nevertheless provides a rich lexicon and syntax for designing and creating useful hypertext documents for the Web.

HTTP or **http** (Hypertext Teleprocessing Protocol, or Hypertext Transfer Protocol): The Internet protocol used to manage communication between Web clients (browsers) and servers.

httpd (http daemon): The name of the collection of programs that runs on a Web server to provide Web services. In UNIX-speak, a daemon is a program that runs all the time and listens for service requests of a particular type; thus, an httpd is a program that runs continually on a Web server, ready to field and handle Web service requests.

hyperlink: A shorthand term for hypertext link. *See* hypertext link.

hypermedia: Any of a variety of computer media — including text, graphics, video, sound, and so on — available through hypertext links on the Web.

hypertext: A method of organizing text, graphics, and other data for computer use that lets individual data elements point to one another. Hypertext is a nonlinear method of organizing information (especially text).

hypertext link: A user-selectable document element (defined by special HTML markup) that, when selected, can change the user's focus from one document (or part of a document) to another.

IETF (Internet Engineering Task Force): The official standards organization (a suborganization of the Internet Architecture Board, or IAB) that governs all TCP/IP and other Internet-related standards.

image map (a synonym for clickable image): An overlaid collection of pixel coordinates for a graphic. An image map can be used to locate the region of a Web page graphic that a user selects by clicking the mouse. The map location, in turn, is used to select a related hypertext link for further Web navigation.

inheritance: Defines a relationship among objects in a hierarchy in object-oriented programming. Objects that are subordinate to other objects acquire attributes and characteristics because of that relationship. By inheritance, subordinate objects automatically include information defined for their parents in the hierarchy.

INIT: On the Macintosh, a program that runs during the computer's initialization phase to augment or modify the basic operating system's behavior or characteristics.

ink effects: Text-based colorization or animation effects in Macromedia Director.

input-handling program: For Web services, a program that runs on a Web server and is designated by the ACTION attribute of an HTML <FORM> tag. The job of the input-handling programs is to field, interpret, and respond to user input from a browser. The program typically custom-builds an HTML document in response to a user request.

interleaved: A graphical image on the Web that displays onscreen in increasing levels of detail instead of from the top down. The levels of detail appear as individual lines of pixels separated by a constant interval during the display. This process gives interleaved images the appearance of being drawn in slices.

intermediate code: A way of representing a computer program in a form that's somewhere between human-readable source code and machine-readable binary executable code. Java bytecode is a form of intermediate code, ready to be converted into a binary executable form at the user's workstation through the agency of the Java runtime system.

internal link: A hyperlink on a Web site that links to a resource on the same site (or in some cases, within the same document).

Internaut: Someone who travels using the Internet (like *astronaut* or *argonaut*).

Internet: A worldwide collection of networks that began with technology and equipment funded by the U.S. Department of Defense in the 1970s that today links users in nearly every known country, who speak nearly every known language.

Internet Relay Chat (IRC): An Internet application and protocol that permits multiple users to communicate with one another by typing comments, all of which appear in the IRC application display, labeled by each user's supplied "handle" (also known as the user name).

Internet Service Provider (ISP): An organization that provides individuals or other organizations with access to the Internet, typically by purchasing large amounts of communications bandwidth and reselling small chunks of that bandwidth to its customers.

Internet Studio: A planned Microsoft software product (formerly code-named *Blackbird*) that will include Web document authoring, management, and maintenance utilities.

InterNIC (Internet Network Information Center): The Internet agency that handles IP address allocation and domain name registration facilities.

intranet: A TCP/IP-based network that uses standard Internet services and applications within the confines of a particular organization, to create a sort of "in-house Internet."

IP (Internet Protocol): The specific networking protocol that ties computers together over the Internet. IP is also used as a synonym for the whole TCP/IP protocol suite. *See* TCP/IP.

IP address: A unique numeric address for a particular machine or physical interface on the Internet (or any other TCP/IP-based network). An IP address consists of four decimal octets separated by periods (such as, 108.28.36.51).

IPnG (IP Next Generation, or IPv6): An emerging replacement standard for TCP/IP that will broaden the address space for IP from its current ceiling of available addresses.

ISAPI (Internet Service Application Programming Interface): An Internet API developed by Microsoft that enables remote server applications.

ISDN (Integrated Services Digital Network): An emerging digital technology for telecommunications that offers higher bandwidth and better signal quality than old-fashioned analog telephone lines. Not yet available in many parts of the United States or in the rest of the world.

ISO (International Standards Organization): The granddaddy of standards organizations worldwide. The ISO is comprised of standards bodies from many countries. The ISO sets most important communications and computing standards, such as the telecommunications and character code standards in this book.

Java: A specialized object-oriented programming language designed for creation of platform-independent, network deliverable, client-side applications. Some Java applications may be invoked within Web documents to add dynamic, ongoing behavior.

JavaScript: A scripting language that draws on underlying Java classes and objects to provide a simplified method to include dynamic behavior within Web documents.

JPEG or **JPG** (Joint Photographic Experts' Group): An industry association that defined a particularly compressible format for image storage that is designed for dealing with complex color still images (such as photographs). Files stored in this format usually take the extension JPEG (except on DOS or Windows machines, which use the three-character JPG equivalent). Today, JPEG is emerging as the graphics format standard of choice for use on the World Wide Web.

Kbps (Kilobits per second): A measure of communications speeds, in units of 2 to the 10th power bits per second (2^{10} = 1024, which is just about 1,000 and explains the quasi-metric K notation).

kerning: The relationships between characters as they appear on a document, including spacing and relative positioning.

KISS (Keep It Simple, Stupid!): A self-descriptive philosophy that's supposed to remind us to eschew obfuscation, except it's easier to understand!

LAN (Local Area Network): Typically, one of a variety of communications technologies that links computers together in a single building, business, or campus environment.

LaTeX: A specialized version of Donald Knuth's TeX typesetting program, LaTeX includes templates and definitions for creating book-length manuscripts.

layout element: In an HTML document, a layout element is a paragraph, list, graphic, horizontal rule, heading, or some other document component whose placement on a page contributes to its overall look and feel.

leading: The amount of space between lines of text (pronounced properly, rhymes with "bedding").

linear text: Shorthand for old-fashioned documents that work like this book does: by placing one page after the other, ad infinitum in a straight line. Even though books have indexes, pointers, cross-references, and other attempts to add linkages, users must apply these linkages manually (instead of clicking a mouse).

Lingo: A scripting language used within Macromedia Director to create and automate animation and other repetitive or time-based behaviors in a multimedia presentation.

link: A pointer in one part of an HTML document that can transport users to another part of the same document or to another document entirely. This capability puts the *hyper* in hypertext. In other words, a link is a one-to-one relationship or association between two concepts or ideas, similar to cognition. (The brain has triggers, such as smell, sight, and sound, that cause a link to be followed to a similar concept or reaction.)

link map: A directed graph in a Web site that shows the links between and among constituent documents.

linked media files: Multimedia content files that include references to other files within themselves. Shockwave for Director does not currently support these files for Internet-based delivery.

list element: An item in an HTML list structure tagged with the `<LI>` (list item) tag.

list tags: HTML tags for a variety of list styles, including ordered lists `<OL>`, unordered lists `<UL>`, menus `<MENU>`, glossary lists `<DL>`, or directory lists `<DIR>`.

`listserv`: An Internet e-mail handling pro-gram, typically UNIX-based, that provides mechanisms to let users manage, contribute and subscribe to, and exit from named mailing lists that distribute messages to all subscribed members daily. A common mechanism for delivering information to interested parties on the Internet, this program enables the HTML working group members to communicate with each other.

LOD (Level of Detail): The name of a specific root node in the VRML environment often acts as the basis for the construction of entire virtual worlds.

log files: Web server files that accumulate data about errors, data access, and user activity that may later be analyzed to determine site behavior, solve problems, and improve document relationships and designs.

logical markup: A number of HTML cha-racter-handling tags that exist to provide emphasis or to indicate the involvement of a particular kind of device or action.

Lynx: A widely used UNIX-based character-mode Web browser.

maintenance: The process of regularly inspecting, testing, and updating the contents of Web pages; also, an attitude that these activities are both inevitable and advisable.

`majordomo`: A set of Perl programs that automate the operation of multiple mailing lists, including moderated and unmoderated mailing lists and routine handling of subscribe/unsubscribe operations.

map file: A set of pixel coordinates on a graphic image that correspond to the boundaries of regions that users may select when using the graphic for Web navigation. This map file must be created by using a graphics program to determine regions and their boundaries, and then stored on the Web server that provides the coordinate translation and URL selection services.

markup: A method of embedding special characters (metacharacters) within a text file to instruct a computer program how to handle the contents of the file itself.

markup language: A formal set of special characters and related capabilities that define a specific method for handling the display of files that include markup; HTML is a markup language that is an application of SGML and is used to design and create Web pages.

Mbps (Megabits per second): A measure of communications speeds, in units of 2^{20} bits per second (2^{20} = 1,048,576, which is just about 1,000,000 and explains the quasi-metric M notation).

metacharacter: A specific character within a text file that signals the need for special handling. In HTML, the angle brackets ($< >$), ampersand (&), pound sign (#), and semicolon (;) can all function as metacharacters.

method: A legal operation or transformation associated with a particular object in object-oriented programming. For HTML, a method refers to one of several types of data delivery associated with communicating `<FORM>` input from a user to a Web server.

MIDI (Musical Instrument Digital Interface): A computer-industry standard for interconnecting musical instruments, synthesizers, and computers. MIDI provides methods to translate music into computer data, and vice versa. Any file with a MIDI contains music or other multivoice signals.

MIME (Multipurpose Internet Mail Extensions): HTTP communications of Web information over the Internet rely on a special variant of MIME formats to convey Web documents and related files between servers and users, and vice versa.

mismatched tags: Opening a marked segment of text with one HTML tag, and attempting to close it with an invalid or incorrect closing tag (for example, `<H1>This is wrong!</H2>`).

modem (acronym for **mo**dulator/**dem**odulator): A piece of hardware that converts between the analog forms for voice and data used in the telephone system and the digital forms for data used in computers. In other words, a modem lets your computer communicate by using the telephone system.

MOO (MUD, Object-Oriented): A particular implementation of a MUD, MOOs are built to be flexible and extensible, rather than bounded and static, like ordinary MUDs. *See* MUD.

Mosaic: A powerful graphical Web brow-ser originally developed at the NCSA, now widely licensed and used for a variety of commercial browser implementations.

MPEG or **MPG** (Motion Picture Experts' Group): A highly compressed format designed for use in moving pictures or other multiframe-per-second media (such as video). MPEG cannot only provide tremendous compression (up to 200 to 1), but it also updates only elements that have changed onscreen from one frame to the next. This feature makes the MPEG format extraordinarily efficient as well. MPEG is the common file extension to denote files using this format and MPG is the three-letter equivalent on DOS and Windows systems (which can't handle four-letter file extensions).

MPPP (Multilink Point-to-Point Protocol): An Internet protocol that allows simultaneous use of multiple physical connections between one computer and another to aggregate their combined bandwidth and create a larger virtual link between the two machines.

MUCK (Multi-User Consensual Knowledgebase): A user-extendable, multiuser adventure game.

MUD (Multi-User Dungeon): A text-based virtual world where multiple users can collaborate and compete within an orchestrated fantasy environment.

multimedia: A method of combining text, sound, graphics, and full-motion or animated video within a single compound computer document.

multiple inheritance: Some object-oriented programming languages, such as C++, support multiple inheritance. In this kind of environment, an object can have multiple parents in the object hierarchy and can inherit characteristics and attributes from all parents.

multithreaded: An operating system concept in which the system or the applications that it supports can divide into logical subtasks, each of which can run independently, but all of which combine to provide a particular application or service.

MVS (Multiple Virtual Storage): A file system used on IBM mainframes and clones.

Native multithreading: A programming language with a built-in thread-handling mechanism (such as Java). Native multithreading enables programs to create and manage multiple execution threads explicitly.

navigate: The process of finding your way around a particular Web site or the Web in general.

navigation: The use of hyperlinks to move within or between HTML documents and other Web-accessible resources.

navigation bar: A way of arranging a series of hypertext links on a single line of a Web page to provide a set of navigation controls for an HTML document or a set of HTML documents.

navigation buttons: Using graphics to provide navigation links; otherwise, a form of navigation bar. *See* navigation bar.

NCSA (National Center for Super-computing Applications): A research unit of the University of Illinois at Urbana, where the original Mosaic implementation was built and where the NCSA httpd Web server code is maintained and distributed.

nesting: In computer terms, one structure that occurs within another structure is said to be nested. In HTML, nesting happens most commonly with list structures, which may be freely nested within one another, regardless of type.

netiquette: The written and unwritten rules of behavior on the Internet (a networking takeoff on the term *etiquette*). When in doubt about whether an activity is permitted, ask first, and then act only if no one objects. (Check the FAQ for a given area, too. The FAQ often explicitly states the local rules of netiquette for a newsgroup, mailing list, or other group.)

network link: The tie that binds a computer to a network. For dial-in Internet users, the network link is usually a telephone link. For directly attached users, this link is whatever kind of technology (Ethernet, token-ring, FDDI, or so on) is in local use.

newsgroup: A named collection of messages collected and distributed via the Network News Transport Protocol (NNTP), through the public Usenet on the Internet, or through any number of private NNTP services (such as the Microsoft msnews.micorosoft.com NNTP server).

node: A basic object within the VRML environment, a node can appear to be an independent graphic within a scene or may be a constituent part of a group node.

numeric entity: A special markup element that reproduces a particular character from the ISO-Latin-1 character set. A numeric entity takes the form &#nnn, where nnn is the one-, two-, or three-digit numeric code that corresponds to a particular character.

object: The basic element within an object-oriented environment. Any single object represents a particular instance of a class of possible objects, where all share a common underlying definition and an associated set of methods.

object type: A named type of data structure in programming languages. An object's type is the specific data type associated with an object.

object-oriented: A programming methodology that concentrates on the definition of constituent parts of a program and the operations that can be performed on the parts (called methods).

obsolete elements: HTML markup codes that are no longer supported within the current HTML specifications.

OCR (Optical Character Recognition): A class of software that can "read" and interpret image data to convert pictures of text into a best-guess translation of actual textual data.

on-demand connection: A dial-up link to a service provider that is available whenever it's needed.

online: A term that indicates that information, activity, or communications are located on, or taking place in, an electronic, networked computing environment (such as the Internet). The opposite of online is offline, which is what your computer is as soon as you disconnect from the Internet.

operator overloading: The ability to use one type of operator (in programming lan-guages, such as C or C++) on data that may not belong to that type (for example, to use the + operator to add two strings together).

orphan file: A file on a Web site that is not referenced by any other file (so you have no way to get to the orphan file, except through its absolute URL).

OS (Operating System): The underlying control program on a computer that makes the hardware run and supports the execution of one or more applications. DOS, UNIX, and OS/2 are all examples of operating systems.

packet: A basic unit (or package) of data that describes individual elements of online com-munications. In other words, data moves across networks like the Internet in packets.

pages: The generic term for the HTML documents that Web users view on their browsers.

paragraphs: The basic elements of text within an HTML document. `<P>` is the markup tag used to indicate a para-graph break in text (the closing `</P>` tag is currently optional in HTML).

parser: A program that reads text input for the purpose of recognizing and interpreting particular strings. A parser is the first part of a compiler, and it reads the source code to recognize language terms and operators, to build a formal representation of the program's contents and structure.

path, path name: *See* directory path.

PC (personal computer): A generic term that refers to just about any kind of desktop computer. Its original definition was as a product name for the IBM 8086-based personal computer, the IBM PC.

PDF (portable document format): The name of the document format for Acrobat from Adobe Systems, Inc. PDF is also used as the file extension for files in this particular format.

Perl: A powerful, compact programming language that draws from the capabilities of languages such as C, Pascal, and BASIC. Perl is emerging as the language of choice for CGI programs. Its emergence is partly owing to its portability and the many platforms that currently support it, and partly owing to its ability to exploit system services in UNIX quickly and easily.

pipe: The bandwidth of the connection in use between a user's workstation and the Internet (or the server on the other end of the connection, actually).

pixel: (abbreviation for picture element) A single group of phosphors on a CRT that creates a dot of color. When it is considered part of an image being displayed, this dot corresponds to a pixel.

plain text: Usually refers to vanilla ASCII text, as created or viewed in a simple text-editing program.

platform: Synonym for computer.

plugin: A Web browser add-in program that operates under the umbrella of the browser itself, thereby extending the program's overall capabilities (for example, Amber and Shockwave are both Netscape plugins).

port address: Lets a TCP/IP application know which program to talk to on the receiving end of a network connection. Because many programs may be running on a computer at one time — including multiple copies of the same program — the port address provides a mechanism to uniquely identify exactly which process the data should be delivered to.

portable document technology: *See* PDF.

PostScript: An Adobe page description language, used as a format for printing and display purposes by many programs and devices.

POTS (Plain Old Telephone System): The normal analog telephone system, just like the one you probably have at home.

PPP (Point-to-Point Protocol): A modern, low-overhead serial communications protocol, typically used to interconnect two computers via modem. Most Web browsers require either a PPP or SLIP connection in order to work.

preprocessor: A special program that parses source code or other text to translate embedded strings into (more verbose or complex) final forms before interpretation or compilation occurs.

property: A particular object attribute or its associated value.

proprietary: A data format, specification, or operation that's defined (and owned) by a company, rather than by a standards organization. Proprietary HTML markup is that markup created and used exclusively within certain browsers (such as the <CENTER> tag in Netscape, for example).

protocol: A formal, rigidly-defined set of rules and formats that computers use to communicate with one another.

provider: *See* service provider.

publication process: The process of gathering, organizing, and delivering to the Web information in the form of HTML documents and supporting materials.

Push: A Web-based information distribution technology that permits a special type of server (called a Push server, naturally) to distribute information to a designated group of users, whenever new or changed content is posted to that server's information base. This technology lets changes and new materials be delivered to users almost as soon as such materials are recognized.

QED (Latin abbreviation for *Quod erod demonstrandum*, or "I have shown it"): A mathematical organization devoted to promoting effective uses of mathematics and computers, this group is advising the World Wide Web Consortium on the final form of HTML mathematics notation.

QuickTime: An Apple-derived multimedia/animation format. QuickTime is used across a broad variety of platforms today.

radio button: A type of interface control that's supported in HTML forms, where a selection of only one option out of a possible collection of options is permitted. Based on the old push-button radios so popular in cars in the '60s and '70s, the key concept is that only one selection at a time is allowed.

RAM (Random Access Memory): The memory used in most computers to store the results of ongoing work and to provide space to store the operating system and applications that are running at any given moment.

RealAudio: The audio helper application, from Progressive Network, that adds audio playback to a variety of Web browsers across multiple platforms.

relational database: A special type of database that organizes individual records into tables, where the columns specify the fields and attributes for all records, and the rows contain individual record instances.

relative: In the absence of the <BASE> tag in a URL, the link is relative to the current page's URL in which the link is defined. This arrangement makes for shorter, more compact URLs and explains why most local URLs are relative, not absolute.

request: In a client/server environment, clients request information to be delivered by a server. When you click a URL, you're implicitly requesting some server to deliver the corresponding HTML document or other resource to your workstation.

rescale: To resize a graphic image while maintaining its original aspect ratio and relative dimensions.

resource: Any HTML document or other item or service available via the Web. Resources are what URLs point to.

response: In a client/server environment, the server's reply to a user's request for information. The server supplies the information or provides some other kind of response that reports on the request itself (for example, invalid request or data not available).

return (short for carriage return): In text files, a return is what causes the words on a line to end and makes the display pick up at the leftmost location on the display.

RFC (Request for Comment): An official IETF standards document.

RGB (Red Green Blue): The name of a computer-based color representation scheme for graphics displays.

RGB code: A specific numeric value that corresponds to particular values for red, green, and blue components, used to designate particular colors and shades.

robot: A special Web-traveling program that wanders all over the place, following and recording URLs and related titles for future reference (for example, in search engines).

ROM (Read-Only Memory): A form of computer memory that allows values to be stored only once. After the data is initially recorded, the computer can only read the contents. ROMs are used to supply constant code elements, such as bootstrap loaders, network addresses, and other more or less unvarying programs or instructions.

root: The base of a directory structure above which no references are legal.

router: A special-purpose piece of Internet working gear that helps to connect networks together. A router is capable of reading the destination address of any network packet. The router can forward the packet to a local recipient if its address resides on any network that the router can reach or on to another router if the packet is destined for delivery to a network that the current router cannot access.

RTF (Rich Text Format): A platform-independent text representation often used as an intermediate format when converting one type of text, word processing, or page layout file into some other form. Also, the file extension for a Rich Text Format file.

sampling rates: The number of bits used to represent audio information over a particular time interval. The higher the sampling rate, the more true-to-life the corresponding sound information.

scene graph: Defines the ordering and precedence among all the VRML nodes in any virtual world. The earlier a node appears in a graph, the higher its precedence and the more impact it has on how the scene is rendered for display.

score: In Macromedia Director, the sequence of events and animation actions that are scheduled to occur as individual frames are played in sequence. The score also describes conditional processing and frame sequence alterations that can occur during playback.

screen: The glowing part on the front of your computer monitor where you see the Web do its thing (and anything else your computer shows you).

SEA (abbreviation for Self-Extracting Archive): File extension for a self-extracting version of the most popular Macintosh file compression format, StuffIt (.SIT).

search engine: A special Web program that can search the contents of a database of available Web pages and other resources to provide information that relates to specific topics or keywords supplied by a user.

search tools: Any of a number of programs that can permit HTML documents to become searchable by using the <ISINDEX> tag. This tag informs the browser of the need for a search window and behind-the-scenes indexing and anchoring schemes to let users locate particular sections of or items within a document.

security: A general term that describes how an operating system or network operating system establishes and manages user access to the resources and objects under that system's control.

server: A computer on a network whose job is to listen for particular service requests and to respond to those that it knows how to satisfy.

server root: Defines the root of a Web server's programs and documents. This concept is used to define the scope for file access permissions for users and administrators alike.

service provider: *See* Internet Service Provider.

setup: The phase at the beginning of the communications process when negotiating a network connection. At this point, protocol details, communication rates, and error-handling approaches are worked out, allowing the connection to proceed correctly and reliably thenceforth.

SGML (Standard Generalized Markup Language): An ISO standard document definition, specification, and creation mechanism that makes platform and display differences across multiple computers irrelevant to the delivery and rendering of documents.

shading: In a graphics environment, shading represents the results of the complex calculations that must occur to depict the effect of light and shadow on three-dimensional graphical objects.

shell: *See* UNIX shell.

Shocked: Often indicates that Web materials have been prepared for use with a Shockwave plugin for display.

Shockwave: The Macromedia technology (and plugin) used to create Internet-deliverable Director presentations and to display them within a Web browser.

single inheritance: The capacity to inherit attributes and characteristics from only one parent object (as is the case with Java) in object-oriented languages.

singleton: An HTML tag that has no corresponding closing tag. For example <P> and <BASE> are both singletons, even though <P> takes no attributes, and <BASE> does.

SIT (abbreviation for StuffIT archive): File extension for the native StuffIt Macintosh compressed-file format.

SLIP (Serial Line Interface Protocol): A relatively old-fashioned TCP/IP protocol used to manage telecommunications between a client and a server that treats the phone line as a slow extension to a network.

SMTP (Simple Mail Transfer Protocol): The underlying protocol and service for Internet-based electronic mail.

spider (Web spider, WebCrawler): A class of Internet software agents that tirelessly investigate Web pages and their links, while storing information about their travels for inclusion in the databases typically used by search engines.

SSL (Secure Sockets Library): A Netscape-designed Web commerce programming library, intended to help programmers easily add secure transactions across the Web.

stage: The display window where a presentation ultimately appears during playback in Multimedia Director.

stdin (UNIX standard input device): The default source for input in the UNIX environment. It is the input source for CGI programs as well.

stdout (UNIX standard output device): The default recipient for output in the UNIX environment. It is the output source for Web browsers and servers as well (including CGI programs).

style sheet: A document that rigorously describes how classes of markup are to be rendered in an HTML document display, including font selections, font styles, leading, kerning, and color schemes.

syntax checker: A program that checks a particular HTML document's markup against the rules that govern HTML's use; a recommended part of the testing regimen for all HTML documents.

syntax: Literally, the formal rules for how to speak. In this book, syntax describes the rules that govern how HTML markup looks and behaves within HTML documents.

T1: A high-speed (1.544 Mbps) digital communications link.

table: An HTML construct that allows data to be represented in onscreen areas called cells. The cells are organized into columns and rows.

tag: The formal name for an element of HTML markup, usually enclosed in angle brackets (< >).

TCP (Transmission Control Protocol): The transport layer protocol for the TCP/IP suite. TCP is a reliable, connection-oriented protocol that usually guarantees delivery across a network. *See* TCP/IP.

TCP/IP (Transmission Control Protocol/Internet Protocol): The name for the suite of protocols and services used to manage network communications and applications over the Internet.

Telnet: A means of running programs and using capabilities on other computers across the Internet. Telnet is the Internet protocol and service that lets you take a computer and make it emulate a dumb terminal over the network.

template: The skeleton of a Web page, including the HTML for its heading and footer and any consistent layout and navigation elements for a page or set of pages.

template-based search: A search that follows a set of values specified within a form.

tenant: A term applied to the Webmasters or administrators who manage a site located on somebody else's Web server (usually an ISP's).

terminal emulation: The process of making a full-fledged, stand-alone computer act like a terminal attached to another computer, terminal emulation is the service that Telnet provides across the Internet.

test plan: The series of steps and elements to be followed in conducting a formal test of software or other computerized systems. We strongly recommend that you write — and use — a test plan as a part of your Web publication process.

TeX: Donald Knuth's powerful typesetting environment, which pioneered the delivery of comprehensive, practical mathematical typesetting that defines the foundation on which HTML <MATH> notation is based.

text controls: Any of a number of HTML tags, including both physical and logical markup, text controls provide a method of managing the way that text appears within an HTML document.

text engine: A browser plugin or helper application that can render highly-formatted text and graphics based on a particular and specific format, either for printing or computer display.

text-mode: A method of browser operation that displays characters only. Text-mode browsers cannot display graphics without the assistance of helper applications.

throughput: The amount of data that can be "put through" a connection in a given period of time. Throughput differs from bandwidth in being a measure of actual performance, instead of a theoretical maximum for the medium involved.

thumbnail: A miniature rendering of a graphical image, used as a link to the full-sized version.

tiling: A technique for filling an entire region with graphics data that relies on taking a small area of graphics within that region and repeating it like a set of tiles to cover the area.

title: The text supplied between <TITLE> . . . </TITLE> defines the text that shows up on that page's title bar when displayed; the title is also used as data in many Web search engines.

transparent background: *See* transparent GIF.

transparent GIF: A specially rendered GIF image that takes on the background color selected in a browser capable of handling these GIFs. This process makes the graphic blend into the existing color scheme and provides a more professional-looking page.

tree structure: Computer scientists like to depict hierarchies in graphical terms, which makes them look like upside-down trees (a single root at the top, multiple branches below). File systems and genealogies are examples of tree-structured organizations that we're all familiar with, but examples abound in the computer world. This type of structure also works well for certain Web document sets, especially larger, more complex ones. *See* hierarchical structure.

unclosed elements: A marked region of HTML text that's missing a required closing tag (for example `<H1>This is wrong`).

UNIX: The operating system of choice for the Internet community at large and the Web community, too, UNIX offers the broadest range of tools, utilities, and programming libraries for Web server use.

UNIX shell: The name of the command-line program used to manage user-computer interaction. The shell can also be used to write CGI scripts and other kinds of useful programs for UNIX.

URI (Uniform Resource Identifier): Any of a class of objects that identify resources available to the Web. Both URLs and URNs are examples of URIs.

URL (Uniform Resource Locator): The primary naming scheme used to identify Web resources. URLs define the protocols to be used, the domain name of the Web server where a resource resides, the port address to be used for communication, and the directory path to access a named Web file or resource.

URL-encoded text: A method for passing information requests and URL specification to Web servers from browsers, URL encoding replaces spaces with plus signs (+) and substitutes special hex codes for a range of otherwise unreproduceable characters. This method is used to pass document queries from browsers to servers.

URN (Uniform Resource Name): A permanent, unchanging name for a Web resource. URNs are seldom used in today's Web environment. They do, however, present a method guaranteed to obtain access to a resource, as soon

as the URN can be fully resolved. (A URN can consist of human or organizational contact information, instead of resource location data.)

Usenet: An Internet protocol and service that provides access to a vast array of named newsgroups, where users congregate to exchange information and materials related to specific topics or concerns.

validator: A special token or password that accompanies a user's request for system resources, used to determine if the request may be satisfied or if it must be denied, based on the user's security profile.

VBScript: A special interpreted object-based scripting language developed as an offshoot of the Visual Basic programming language by Microsoft.

videoconferencing: A type of networked application where sounds and video signals are transmitted across a network, permitting users to communicate simultaneously via sounds and pictures.

ViewMovie: A Netscape plugin for viewing `MOV` animation files.

virtual shopping cart: A Web construct that lets users visit multiple Web pages, gathering a set of items that they've selected along the way, and pay for all items at once.

virus: A type of self-replicating program that seeks to distribute itself around a network, or the Internet, for either benign or malignant purposes.

VRML (Virtual Modeling Reality Language): VRML is a fully-fledged computer programming language designed to facilitate creation of complete, three-dimensional, graphical spaces called *virtual worlds*.

wanderer (a synonym for spider or robot) : A class of software agents that prowl the Web, following links and documenting what they find as they go. These programs provide much of the raw material that's organized by search databases for investigation by search engines.

watermark: A technique for maintaining a fixed background for HTML documents that stays the same, even as foreground materials scroll across the display.

Web: Shorthand for the World Wide Web (or W3). We also use Web in this book to refer to a related, interlinked set of HTML documents.

Web pages (a synonym for HTML documents): Sets of related, interlinked HTML documents, usually produced by a single author or organization.

Web server: A computer, usually on the Internet, that plays host to `httpd` and related Web-service software.

Web server administrator: The individual responsible for the setup, configuration, and maintenance of a Web server.

Web site: An addressed location, usually on the Internet, that provides access to the set of Web pages corresponding to the URL for a given site. Thus, a Web site consists of a Web server and a named collection of Web documents, both accessible through a single URL.

Webify: The process of converting a document of any kind into a Web-viewable format, typically by translation into HTML.

white space: The parts of a document or display that aren't occupied by text or other visual elements — the breathing room on a page. A certain amount of white space is essential to make documents attractive and readable.

Windows (MS-Windows): The astonishingly popular (and sometimes frustrating) GUI environment for PCs from Microsoft Corporation. Windows is the GUI of choice for most desktop computer users.

World Wide Web (WWW or W3): The complete collection of all Web servers available on the Internet, which comes as close to containing the "sum of human knowledge" as anything we've ever seen.

World Wide Web Consortium (W3C): The computer industry-funded technical organization that is jointly responsible for maintaining and managing HTML and related standards (along with the Internet Society's Internet Engineering Task Force, or IETF).

worm: A self-replicating computer program that seeks to visit as many locations on a network as possible. More of a nuisance than viruses, worms consume precious network bandwidth and are abhorred for that reason.

WWWInline: Another basic VRML node. WWWInline is often recommended as the root node when constructing a virtual world for Web display.

WYSIWYG (What You See Is What You Get): A term used to describe text editors or other layout tools (such as HTML authoring tools) that attempt to show their users onscreen what final, finished documents will look like.

X Windows: The GUI of choice for UNIX systems. X Windows offers a graphical window, icon, and mouse metaphor similar to (but much more robust and powerful than) Microsoft Windows.

Xobject: Externally defined data resources, such as sounds, graphics, or animated sequences, for inclusion within a Director film strip. Director support for Xobjects greatly expands the type and quality of materials that can be included within its playback environment.

Index